CAREER CHANGE

EVERYTHING YOU NEED TO KNOW TO MEET NEW CHALLENGES AND TAKE CONTROL OF YOUR CAREER

Second Edition

DR. DAVID P. HELFAND

VGM Career Horizons

NTC/Contemporary Publishing Group

Library of Congress Cataloging-in-Publication Data

Helfand, David P.
    Career change : everything you need to know to meet new challenges
and take control of your career / David P. Helfand. — 2nd ed.
        p.   cm.
    Includes bibliographical references and index.
    ISBN 0-8442-4269-1
    1. Career changes.   2. Vocational guidance.   I. Title.
HF5384.H44   1999   98-41215
650.14—dc21   CIP

*To those of you considering or in the midst of a career change—may you
find a new career you'll enjoy and feel successful at.*

Published by VGM Career Horizons
A division of NTC/Contemporary Publishing Group, Inc.
4255 West Touhy Avenue, Lincolnwood (Chicago), Illinois 60646-1975 U.S.A.
Copyright © 1999, 1995 by David P. Helfand
Printed in the United States of America
International Standard Book Number: 0-8442-4269-1
99 00 01 02 03 04 cu 13 12 11 10 9 8 7 6 5 4 3

CONTENTS

✫

PART I

*Self- and Career Awareness: The Basis
of a Successful Career Change*   *1*

CHAPTER 1
ADULT DEVELOPMENT AND HOW
IT AFFECTS YOUR LIFE CHANGES   2

CHAPTER 2
NOT YOUR CHOICE: LAYOFFS, FIRINGS,
VOLUNTARY SEPARATIONS, AND RELATED DILEMMAS   24

CHAPTER 3
YOUR CHOICE: A QUESTION OF VALUES   37

PART III

---

*Strategies for Groups with Special Challenges
in the Workplace   269*

PREFACE

★

If you are considering, have just decided to make, or are in the midst of a career change, this book is for you. It is designed to help you better understand the challenges of changing careers and offers strategies for dealing with them. Much of the contents will also benefit job seekers within the same field.

You might be wondering how this book differs from other career-related publications. *Career Change* pulls together in one volume strategies for facing all of the major challenges of changing one's career.

This approach includes the following features:

- A Work Values Satisfaction Self-Assessment to help you decide whether it's time to consider a career change

- An Entrepreneurial Personal Characteristics Self-Assessment to help you judge your potential success in starting a business

- Strategies for overcoming your fears of change, failure, and success, as well as perfectionism and procrastination

- Practical steps to help you increase your self-esteem and thus expand your opportunities

- An in-depth case study reviewing the assessment and testing process to help you identify relevant career options

- Guidance in interpreting your Strong Interest Inventory and Myers-Briggs Type Indicator tests if you're among the millions who have taken them or will take them in the near future

- Ideas for dealing with the practical challenges of career change: the need for education, training, experience, time, and money

- Strategies for dealing with the competitive job market of the new millennium

- Suggestions for groups with special challenges in the workplace, including women, minorities, people over 50, people with disabilities, dual-career couples and single parents, ex-military personnel, and mid-level managers

- Steps to take if you're considering pursuing professional career counseling

- Internet sites related to a wide variety of career planning topics

In addition to discussing the major challenges of and strategies for the career change, we profile ten career changers. We will refer to their real-life experiences periodically throughout the book. We asked the ten career changers if they had any advice to pass along to potential career changers. Here's what they had to say:

- **Larry:** "Don't stop developing yourself; look for opportunities to grow; have a plan in place."

- **Victoria:** "Just go ahead and try it. If you don't find out, you are always going to wonder—should I have done that?"

- **Mac:** "You may not be able to control your age in *years,* but you can control your *attitude,* one of thinking and feeling younger. If so, you'll have the energy, know-how, and intelligence to make that change, just like anyone else. It's just one more life adjustment. You've made many previously."

- **Martha:** "Look forward; be determined; do your best."

- **Allen:** "Never let age be a factor. It's a figment of one's imagination. You could make it a benefit or a hindrance—it's up to you. You have a direction, a purpose, you know exactly what you want, and you're mature."

- **Patricia:** "Go for it—believe that everything will be okay (with careful planning, of course). You're expanding, moving, going on to new things."

- **Ed:** "Don't give up on your dream—life is too short. If you're confident and feel good about yourself, give it a try. Give it your best shot."

- **Zephree:** "Pursue your goals; don't be afraid; be true to yourself."

- **Vincent:** "There's a lot of pressure that comes with a career change. Having self-confidence and doing your research is important, so consult with others who are already doing what your intended career goal encompasses. Develop a well-thought-out plan (the entire change process may take a year, or more, to complete), and welcome the support of family and friends."

- **Sandra:** "Don't underestimate the positive influences that changing to a satisfying career can have on the overall quality of your life."

Remember that what all these people had in common is not being afraid of facing the possibility of failing. They felt secure enough with themselves to allow themselves to take the risk. In their minds, if things did not work out, they would just pick themselves up and try again. We hope you'll find the information in this book to be practical and helpful in your quest for a satisfying career.

ACKNOWLEDGMENTS

★

To my family and friends, thank you for your patience, understanding, and support throughout the years and especially during the period of writing this book.

To my colleagues at Northeastern Illinois University and throughout the career counseling field, thank you for sharing your knowledge, feedback, and insights during the course of this project.

To my clients, from whom I've learned much, thank you for the opportunity of working with you in your quest to find a satisfying career.

Thanks to the staff at NTC Publishing Group: Sarah Kennedy, former VGM Editor, for providing overall guidance to the development of the first edition of this book through her sense of professionalism, talent, and skill; Betsy Lancefield, VGM Editor, whose assistance since the publication of the first edition has been greatly appreciated; Amy Ng, Designer, for adding her creative touch to the final "look" of the book; Scott Rattray, for an attractive and colorful book cover; and Anne Knudsen, Executive Editor, for her overall support from the beginning to the end of this project. And thanks to Paula Dempsey and Regina Wells, Copyeditors, and Michelle Davidson, Project Editor, for transforming my many pages of transcript into a finely tuned finished product.

And finally, thanks to the Committee on Organized Research at Northeastern Illinois University, whose grant helped to make this project possible.

INTRODUCTION

Meet Our Ten Career Changers

★

We experience change all our lives, yet we deal with it with varying degrees of success. Whether we're changing careers, getting a divorce, remarrying, mourning the death of a loved one, buying a home, getting that long-awaited promotion, moving to another city, watching our children leave home, being assigned to a new supervisor, returning to school to earn a degree, or experiencing any of the other possible life transitions, our ability to deal with change will have a profound impact on the course of our lives. Some of us will adjust well, and others will find changes traumatic.

To set the stage for understanding the career change process, we will suggest a framework within which to view transitions in general and career transitions specifically. Researchers of adult transitions have shown that our lives follows a sequence of stages. As our life cycles progress, we move through developmental and transitional periods, and each presents tasks to be mastered and problems to be solved. These developmental tasks pose a challenge that must be met and overcome if we are to move ahead to the next period of development and cope successfully with its demands.

Now let's meet the ten career changers whose real-life experiences will be used throughout the book to illustrate key concepts. They show the wide range of career change situations and strategies for tackling them. Perhaps one of them has a background similar to your own.

Larry

Larry, a 45-year-old Caucasian, had spent 20 years working as an environmental technician in a variety of related positions that involved monitoring and overseeing heating, ventilation, and air-conditioning equipment. At age 37, Larry had become a senior training specialist for a major manufacturer of heating and cooling building controls. Thus, Larry had gone from a blue-collar to a white-collar job.

Larry's interest in the training field began as a result of his enrollment in a university career planning course. He saw it as an excellent way to take his mechanical skills and move them into a more people-oriented position with greater salary potential.

Larry's B.A., with an emphasis in training, was part of a nontraditional academic program in which he designed his own major. Larry and his wife have two sons and a daughter (ages 4, 8, and 6 at the time of Larry's career change).

Larry reported in a follow-up interview that he had moved up in his company to several service operation management positions. After he and his wife decided to divorce, Larry requested a transfer to a branch office in another city, which was granted. Within a year he found himself in constant turmoil. A new vice president, with whom Larry had conflict regarding management style, was put in charge and expected 80-hour workweeks. Then a reorganization eliminated Larry's position. Rather than be relocated with the same company to yet another city, Larry chose to resign.

Larry has decided to move out of technical management and pursue a more people-oriented management position. He has a strong desire to work with people and make a difference. He thinks he'd like to be a business coach for others and perhaps one day have his own business.

Read more about Larry's experiences on pages 38, 40, 111, 187, 204, 208, 238, 247, and 261.

Victoria

Victoria, a 47-year-old Caucasian, had earned a B.A. in sociology with a minor in journalism. During high school, Victoria was the editor of the student newspaper. She combined these two areas of interest by working as a diagnostic social worker for 15 years, which involved significant report writing.

After experiencing a layoff, Victoria returned to school for a certificate program in technical writing. She was spurred on by a TV commercial. Seven years ago, she became a technical editor for an auto parts franchise corporation.

Thus, Victoria's career change had represented moving from the nonprofit area to a for-profit corporation. She believes that about 20 percent of corporations have a positive work environment.

When her supervisor (with whom she aligned herself) was pushed out of his job and the company wanted to move her to an undesirable location, she decided to resign from her position. These events left an impression with Victoria of just how fast changing and unpredictable the business world is.

She has decided to take her technical writing, desktop publishing, and print purchasing skills from a struggling industry (auto parts franchise) and conduct her job search in a field with more promise—print buying. Her longer-range goal, with some additional education, is to return to the social work profession.

Victoria predicts that those recovering from the unsettling effect of having their careers at the mercy of others, like herself, will need some help. She also sees her long-range goal of social work as a good bet to survive the current unpredictable business climate. As she points out, it can't be computerized, it's portable, and you can do it part-time.

Read more about Victoria's experiences on pages 26, 40, 81, 187, 233, and 236.

Mac

Mac, a 62-year-old African-American, had earned a B.A. in sociology and then had worked for ten years in the recreation departments of two major midwestern cities. He had earned two master's degrees, in counseling and educational administration and supervision, by the age of 34. Mac had completed his Ph.D. in educational administration at the age of 36.

While completing his Ph.D., Mac began working in the field of market research, specifically related to the consumer needs of African-Americans. After working for someone else for about two years, Mac set out on his own to develop a market research business, which he owned and ran for 18 years.

Four years ago, because business was slow and Mac had some health problems, he decided to become a high school guidance counselor, something for which he had trained some 25 years earlier. Mac and his wife have two grown children.

Mac reported, in our interview a year later, having just completed his third year as a high school counselor in a lower-income area of a major midwestern city. Mac added that his greatest challenge, one that has brought much satisfaction, has been helping his senior students gain college scholarships. In addition, much of his time is spent just trying to keep other teens in school. Mac has come to really value the impact he's been able to have on the lives of many students.

Read more about Mac's experiences on pages 7, 38, 49, 52, 81, 172, and 204.

Martha

Martha was born in Cuba and came to the United States at the age of 10. She stayed with foster parents until her real parents followed four years later. At the age of 28, after seven years of teaching elementary school, Martha and her husband became the owners of a liquor store.

Soon thereafter, they added groceries and a small restaurant. Their business eventually became one of the most popular Hispanic restaurants and lounges in a major U.S. city. In addition, three years ago they opened a second restaurant, specializing in Mexican food.

Martha has a B.A. in foreign language secondary education, with a minor in psychology. She and her husband have a 20-year-old daughter and a 18-year-old son.

During her interview Martha reported that she and her husband sold the second restaurant after having it for just over a year. She felt somewhat overwhelmed trying to be at both restaurants and was used to working with her husband, which then was not always possible.

Martha is about to set out on still another path. It involves an idea that she has considered for years and that was rekindled recently by her mother's open-heart surgery: that of becoming a nutritionist. The vocation uniquely captures skills from her first two careers—teaching and owing a restaurant. She feels that initially it will help her to prepare meals for restaurant customers who maintain special diets (diabetic, low sodium, low cholesterol, etc.). Later, she sees herself filling a need in the community by becoming a bilingual nutritionist.

If Martha does return to college for training in nutrition, she will be attending at the same time that both her children are.

Read more about Martha's experiences on pages 38, 81, 187, and 247.

Allen

After earning a business degree with a minor in education, Allen, a 48-year-old African-American, taught elementary and secondary school for two years. He then switched back to a job more related to his business degree, becoming a budget analyst at a university, where he remained for seven years.

At age 30, Allen returned to school for training to become a dentist, something he had been thinking about since he was 25. He explained that his own family dentist from his childhood had had a big influence on him.

After four years of dental school, Allen became a dentist at the age of 34. He joined two established dentists in their practice. Four years later, at the age of 38, Allen opened his own dental practice, which he has now operated for 10 years.

Allen reports that, three years after our first interview, his dentistry practice is doing fine. A recent challenge has been adapting to a new accounting and data processing system. Allen has also continued his education in order to expand his practice, particularly in the area of implants.

In addition, Allen has come full circle in a way: he's teaching dentistry residents in a hospital setting on a part-time basis, thus returning to his earlier career in education, which he did enjoy and value.

In looking back, Allen says that making this career change at the age of 34 has turned out to be an advantage. He feels more and more confident about his decision and believes his age and maturity helped him to be more serious. He believes he's more accepting now of the ups and downs of having a dentistry practice than he would have been at a younger age.

Read more about Allen's experiences on pages 38, 49, 187, 190, 204, and 239.

Patricia

With master's degrees in both music history and library science, Patricia, a 48-year-old Caucasian, had spent eight years as a music librarian in the libraries of two major cities, as well as at a prestigious university. At the age of 35, she had become a law librarian, which rekindled an earlier interest from her teenage years (discouraged by her parents at the time) in becoming a lawyer.

With one year left in law school, Patricia gained a summer clerkship position pertaining to copyrights, trademarks, and patents for music and art professionals. Upon completing law school at age 40, she accepted a law firm position with a similar emphasis on the creative arts. Five years later, at the age of 45, Patricia set out on her own, opening a practice with a specialty in serving professionals in the creative arts.

Patricia is currently single, with no dependents, after being married twice.

When interviewed again recently, Patricia stated she had discovered that her administrative secretary was not completing her necessary work and was forced to fire her. Patricia felt that her trust had been violated. After the firing, she found herself suffering with the administrative duties, especially billing, which really bogged her down and kept her from completing the legal work she needed to do.

Patricia fears hiring someone new after this recent episode. She's considering looking for a general counsel position with a smaller corporation, preferably arts related. This move would allow her to do more of what she enjoys the most—the practice of law.

Read more about Patricia's experiences on pages 26, 40, 46, 49, 52, 187, 190, 197, and 266.

Ed

Ed was born in Puerto Rico and came to the United States at the age of 5. Since the age of 12, Ed had wanted to become a police officer. This desire had been influenced by his friendship with the police officer stationed at his school, whom he had admired.

Ed earned his B.A. in criminal justice (with minors in sociology and foreign language). He also became involved in local politics as a college student. After experiencing some discrimination with regard to becoming a police officer, Ed took a job as a criminal law clerk at the age of 20 and began law school via a special program for minority students.

At the age of 26, Ed passed the police examination. After just two months in police training, Ed learned that he had finally passed the bar exam. Ed worked for five years as a police officer. Because of further discrimination and department politics, he decided, at age 31, to focus on a career in law with his own practice. Ed and his wife have no children.

In a recent follow-up interview, Ed reports that during the past one and a half years, he had been back on his own after working in a partnership with others for a few years. His practice, which provides living trusts, is targeted toward the Hispanic community. Similar to Martha's plans for becoming a nutritionist, Ed is taking advantage of his Hispanic background and is providing community members with a needed service.

Looking ahead, Ed is thinking of yet another career move. He'd like to take advantage of his persuasive/sales skills, which became finely tuned through the practice of law, by working in sales for a major company doing business in Mexico. He's anticipating moving from his current midwestern city to one in the southwestern United States.

Read more about Ed's experiences on pages 6, 26, 114, 187, 197, and 213.

Zephree

Zephree, a 45-year-old African-American, had had an interest in law enforcement that dated back to high school. However, she was uncomfortable dealing with death and thus began to focus more on a career as a juvenile probation officer. In the years that followed high school graduation, she used her secretarial skills to gain employment in hospital and university settings, as well as a secretarial position in a county pre-adult probation program. This allowed her to test out her career interest in probation work, and it confirmed her interest.

After completing a paralegal training course, Zephree applied for another secretarial position, this time at a social service agency, only to be told she was overqualified. She was then offered the position of research assistant instead, which involved working on a project investigating child abuse. So at age 39, she changed careers.

Zephree is currently working toward finishing her B.A., via a credit-for-life-experience program, with an emphasis in criminal justice, continuing toward her goal of becoming a juvenile probation officer. She has one son from a previous marriage and has since remarried.

At a recent interview, Zephree noted that during her three years in the research assistant position, she underwent a 40-hour training program and became a volunteer, helping sexual assault and violence victims in hospital emergency rooms through a federally funded program. Because of her paralegal training and this volunteer experience, when a paid position opened up, Zephree was hired as a legal advocate.

Zephree has one year left to complete her undergraduate degree. She's planning a thesis paper on developing a court advocate manual to be used to train future volunteers working with sexual assault/violence victims. She is also contemplating one day going to law school.

Read more about Zephree's experiences on pages 38, 114, 187, 192, 194, 237, and 267.

Vincent

Vincent, a 47-year-old Caucasian, changed careers at age 39. After nine years in investment banking (he was a victim of a reorganization), he opened his own bookstore specializing in history and mystery.

Vincent has a B.A. in political science (with a minor in history) and an M.A. in history, as well as an M.B.A. in finance. History is a favorite subject dating back to Vincent's childhood, and he became interested in mystery during his undergraduate college years. He appreciated being able to combine these two favorite interests into a specialty bookstore, as well as the chance to use the skills he acquired through his M.B.A. program. Vincent is married and has a 12-year-old son.

Vincent has been successfully operating his specialty independent bookstore and claims that staying competitive, especially with the mega-bookstores, is an ongoing project.

Vincent has differentiated his bookstore through its in-depth focus on the two areas of history and mystery, and in-store presentations by noted authors (which have included those from the world of entertainment and politics), as well as the overall atmosphere of the store.

In fact, Vincent reports that the megastores actually refer customers to him when they're unable to fill a particular order in a certain amount of time.

Read more about Vincent's experiences on pages 26, 48, 114, 238, 239, and 247.

Sandra

Sandra, a 37-year-old Asian-American, had become a lawyer after earning a B.A. in political science and history and a law degree from a prestigious private university. Her interest in law had begun in high school, where she'd been active in student organizations.

After eight years as a practicing attorney, Sandra felt dissatisfied and became a full-time writer/publisher of multicultural books for children. This career choice was much more in line with what Sandra saw as her mission, or purpose. Having attained what her friends and family members would consider a position of great status for a female Asian-American, Sandra felt some pressure *not* to follow through with her career change, which made letting go even more difficult. Sandra is married with no children.

Three years later, Sandra's business of writing and publishing multicultural books for children is doing well. This year (her third full-time, following three years part-time), Sandra's publishing company will publish its tenth book (she authored the first two). Sandra reports that the real "payoff" is when a parent tells her that his or her child loves her book and wants to read all the time, or when a teacher writes her and says that he or she reads her book in class and describes how much the children enjoy it.

Sandra's feeling satisfied with her career change. She reports that her work fulfills her desire for a sense of purpose, and she's having fun as well. A new aspect for Sandra is that recently she has been speaking to student, community, and professional groups and organizations about the experience of growing up as a minority child in this country.

Read more about Sandra's experiences on pages 38, 41, 45, 49, 114, and 190.

STAYING POSITIVE

As the updates to Victoria's and Larry's experiences illustrate, managing a successful career or career change isn't easy. Even when we take all the right steps, success is not guaranteed. There may be situations that are beyond our control and for which no amount of careful planning could have made a difference.

Yet, these two unemployed career changers, like our other eight, have shown courage and determination; they are on track and staying positive. You'll find excerpts throughout these pages describing their experiences and what worked for them. Whether they succeed or not in reaching their goals, they've proven themselves unafraid of change and possible failure. They all agree that they would not want to go back to their former careers if they had the chance. They're glad they made the change, even though the road was a bit bumpy at times.

After all, our careers could be viewed as a microcosm of life itself—full of ups and downs. Even more reason, then, to be as prepared as possible. Hopefully, ideas and suggestions in this second edition will help to lead you to many more career ups than downs.

PART I

*Self- and Career Awareness: The Basis of
a Successful Career Change*

★

CHAPTER I
ADULT DEVELOPMENT AND HOW IT AFFECTS YOUR LIFE CHANGES

★

This chapter discusses three ways of viewing life transitions: age related, life stage related, and life events/transitions related. This will give us a context from which to view adult life transitions, including changing careers, and a better understanding of the role they play in our overall personal development. We'll also look at a definition of career change and a description of the various reasons why one might undertake a change of careers. This theoretical background will prepare us for the all-important groundwork of self-assessment.

AGE-FOCUSED APPROACHES

Studies of Men

In 1978, Dan Levinson set out to create a developmental perspective of adulthood in men, presenting the male life course as consisting of alternating stable and transition periods. With its career emphasis, much of Levinson's work also applies to women now.

Levinson identified developmental periods occurring at approximately the same ages for the men he studied. Of course, individuals' ages vary for the onset and ending of these stable and transition periods, but by no more than five to six years from the age span indicated. The pattern of developmental periods Levinson identified is shown in Figure 1.1.

FIGURE 1.1

Levinson's Research on Men's Life Patterns

Early Adult Transition (17–22):	Moving from pre- to early adulthood
Entering the Adult World (22–28):	First adult life structure
Age 30 Transition (28–33):	Changing the first life structure
Settling Down (33–40):	Second adult life structure
Mid-Life Transition (40–45):	Moving from early to middle adulthood
Entering Middle Adulthood (45–50):	Building a new life structure

---

According to Levinson, a central component in individuals' lives is their work. Through our work we are plugged into an occupational structure that will exert a heavy influence on the cultural, class, and social aspects of our lives. Occupation is the primary factor in determining income, prestige, and place in society. It places us in a particular socioeconomic level and strongly influences the options available to us, the choices we make, and our possibilities for advancement and satisfaction. Occupation becomes the medium for fulfilling our dreams and achieving our goals—or possibly the opposite, which can lead toward a growing alienation from self, work, and society.

Studies of Women

With a variety of possible combinations of how to pursue education, career, and family, women today face many choices. In fact, because of the many alternative ways to approach these major life issues, women may experience more confusion and stress at these points in their lives than do men. Gail Sheehy described patterns in the lives of women (see Figure 1.2).

FIGURE 1.2

Sheehy's Research on Women's Life Patterns

Caregiver: Marries during early 20s, no intention of going beyond domestic role

Either/Or: Feels, in 20s, required to choose between love and children or work and accomplishment and thus can be one of two types:

- **Nurturer Who Defers Achievement:** Postpones career efforts to marry and start a family; will pursue a career later

- **Achiever Who Defers Nurturing:** Postpones motherhood and often marriage, spends 6–7 years in career

Integrator: Combines marriage, career, and motherhood

Never Married: Pursues work on a permanent, full-time basis

Transient: Wanders sexually, occupationally, and geographically

---

Age 30 Transition

For both men and women, the Age 30 Transition is a period of self-evaluation and assessment of career and marriage. It's an opportunity to work on flaws and create the basis for a better future. Men and women view this stage in their lives as one of growth and expansion. However, it's not necessarily a smooth transition. Both men and women experience difficulty at this time if things have not progressed as planned and hoped for.

Sheehy points out that some people experience an inside stirring during the Age 30 Transition and seek greater independence. Likewise, those who chose not to marry or not to have children might have second thoughts at this time. Possibilities at the Age 30 Transition follow:

- Has already entered career, still single; wants change (career or getting married)

- Has already entered career, married, no children; wants children or career change

- Married, has children in school; wants to enter or reenter career

For some, the Age 30 Transition represents a time to move toward new choices or recommit to existing ones. People may question themselves about how well they're meeting goals and whether they're progressing toward their dream. If things are going well with job, family, and friends, then the transition will most likely be smooth. However, for most it is stressful. Self-evaluation can be painful if things haven't gone according to plan. Possible life adjustments during this period could be career related (getting/not getting a promotion, losing a job, or making a career change), family related (birth of children, children starting school, divorce, or caring for aging parents), or friends related (job change, move to another city, or just growing apart). Issues at the Age 30 Transition are summarized by the following questions:

- What have I done with my life so far in my career and with my family and friends?
- Have I progressed toward my dream (hopes and wishes in life)?
- How do I feel about it?
- What new directions might I choose?

Mid-Life Transition

During the period between the Age 30 and Mid-Life Transitions (Settling Down, ages 33 to 40), what becomes central for many men is the symbol of the "ladder," which represents advancement. This is hoped to lead to desired affirmation, independence, or seniority. However, the reality of today's job market reveals that many positions the "ladder" once led to are gone. In fact, some are worried about still having a job, much less climbing the corporate ladder. Desired goals may not be obtainable, and thus, people experience frustration and dissatisfaction with their career situation.

In addition, with the onset of the Mid-Life Transition (40–45) comes another self-evaluation process. Questions people might ask themselves include the following:

- What have I done with my life?
- How are my significant relationships (spouse/partner, children, friends) going? What am I getting from and what am I giving to these relationships?
- How is my career going?

- What is my role in the community?
- What do I really want for myself and those close to me?

At this point in life, men want to be able to express their true desires, interests, values, skills, and goals. However, the degree of success in the prior period could predict how well this transition goes. For some, this period is one of moderate to severe crisis. The focus shifts to the future. The Mid-Life Transition is a bridge between early adulthood and middle adulthood. (See Figure 1.3.)

Possible external changes at this time include getting divorced, remarrying, sending children away to college, changing job/career, changing functioning level, losing or supporting a parent, and increasing social mobility. Internally, it is common to feel a shift in values, a desire to give something back to society, and a need to express more emotion.

Some men encounter obstacles to pursuing the goal of having a stronger sense of who they are and what they want. Anxiety, guilt, dependence, and animosities from earlier years keep them from examining the real issues at mid-life. This can result in emotional turmoil, despair, and a feeling of not knowing where to turn.

CAREER CHANGER UPDATE

★

At the age of 46, Ed is in the midst of reevaluating his current career situation. As he thinks ahead toward retirement, he's not so sure he wants to stay with a law career up to that point. Nor is he sure he wants to continue living in the same area.

He's contemplating a move to a major southwestern U.S. city where he thinks his sales and bilingual skills, as well as legal knowledge, can gain him a position with a company wanting to set up business in Mexico. He anticipates greater satisfaction working in this capacity at this stage of his personal and career development.

FIGURE 1.3

Issues and Needs for Men at Mid-Life Transition

- Experience a time shift, realizing their own mortality
- Reassess the dream (recognizing that some aspects are illusory), marriage, and relations with others
- Choose to change jobs for greater challenge and satisfaction or decide to emphasize other areas of their lives to a greater extent, such as family or leisure
- Feel a need to give something back to society, to make some type of contribution, to help others in some way
- Desire to express more emotion

Sheehy viewed the mid-life passage for women as a crossroads, with many opportunities presenting themselves. Her research revealed women arriving at this point earlier, at about 35, than when men experienced it (age 40 to 45) as reported by Levinson. During the early 1970s, when Sheehy's research took place, age 35 represented the average age when a mother sent her last child off to school, a divorced woman remarried, biological limitations came into sight, and a married woman reentered the workforce. Even though 35 represented the age that many married women reentered the workforce, very few homemakers were prepared to do so at the time Sheehy completed her research. However, even today, many women considering reentering the workforce are confused about which path to take and how their family will fare as a result.

CAREER CHANGER UPDATE

★

Mac chose to change careers and became a high school counselor, where an opportunity exists to give something back, to make a contribution through helping others. He says that running a profitable business for 18 years was very satisfying. However, he has found that the satisfaction of helping his high school students is both deeper and greater.

In addition, reentry after a long absence often presents another problem. The field that a woman originally entered (if she is still interested) might have advanced to the point where she now needs additional education to catch up and be competitive for jobs. If a career change is desired, further education or experience might be necessary as well.

Along with the increased possibilities for women at mid-life (see Figure 1.4) comes a feeling of last-chance urgency, similar to that for men at mid-life. The choices made at this time will depend, largely, on what path was followed earlier. Though initially hesitant, many women at their mid-life passage gather the necessary courage, perhaps with the help of personal or career counseling, and respond in an energized way.

"The Switch": Age 40

Sheehy asserts that at around the age of 40, the changes identified in Figure 1.5 occur. This can result in an interesting situation, sometimes causing a crisis for married couples.

As the wife expands into new pursuits, the husband often feels less needed. As a result, the wife sometimes feels guilty. The fact remains, however, that today more than ever, the wife needs to return to work out of financial necessity. So even if this is somewhat threatening for the husband, overall he's probably glad to see it happening.

If the couple is going to survive this difficult period intact, the partners will need to renegotiate their relationship, readjust over a period of several years, and eventually reach a point where the relationship can continue in a healthy manner.

FIGURE 1.4

Possibilities for Women at Mid-Life Transition

- The **Caregiver** could resume education or take a job.
- The **Deferred Achiever** could enter a career.
- The **Deferred Nurturer** could have children.
- The **Integrator** could decide to own a business.

FIGURE 1.5

"The Switch": Age 40

WOMEN	MEN
• Increasing strength of opinion	• Increasing emotional vulnerability
• Increasing assertiveness	• Increasing emotional response
• Increasing independence, setting out to pursue education, career, or community involvement	• Reacting with envy to wife's new pursuits, which occur at an awkward time in his personal development

LIFE STAGE–FOCUSED APPROACHES

Life Stages and Related Developmental Tasks

Some theorists state that adults pass through developmentally sequenced stages. Erik Erikson studied the progression in ego (self) development. Each stage consists of a developmental problem/task. The resolution of that primary task determines future personal development, good or bad. Some of us move through these stages faster than others, and some become stuck at certain points and never move forward.

Let's look at an example. At mid-life, the central developmental task is a choice between generativity and stagnation. If you are dealing effectively with this task, you are able to shift focus from your own interests and concerns to the development and achievement of others, especially the next generation.

You may have chosen to be a mentor to a younger employee on the job, gaining satisfaction from helping someone by sharing your career knowledge and experience. As a healthy individual, at this stage you would accept responsibility for the generation to come. Those who do not often find life to be missing something.

Stage Theory and Women

Erikson's research on life stages was based on men. Some stages might be applicable to women, but Carol Gilligan believed that for women the stage theory overemphasized education, occupation, and achievement as one progressed through the various stages. She found that women have different central issues: attachment, caring, and interdependency. Her approach stated that renegotiating interdependence in important relationships is a critical issue for women's adult development. These relationships include a woman and her husband (partner, significant other), children, or friends, and the process is continuous. A woman at the Age 30 or Mid-Life Transition often experiences increasing aspirations for personal achievement and accomplishment and seeks greater independence and autonomy.

You may be feeling a need to renegotiate your interdependence in your important relationships. You may be desiring to reduce dependence on your husband, or significant other, as you shift away from a role that centered on providing nurturance and support. However, if you're married, this can be complicated by the fact that your husband, if also at mid-life, could be seeking greater intimacy and increased emotional contact. It's important that couples communicate effectively so that as they pass through these different stages, which are listed in Figure 1.6, they understand what the other is experiencing and can adjust their relationship appropriately.

Current Trends and an Additional Perspective

The age- and life stage–focused approaches to adult development are important for helping us to better understand our own personal development and the forces operating in our lives. Perhaps they became popular because we like predictability and may feel a need, at times, for a definition of "normality" to make sure we're within the range.

Yet it is also important to consider current trends, which make it difficult to plug people into particular stages. These trends include the following:

- More men and women are delaying marriage while pursuing further education and careers.

- When people do marry (delayed or not), they more frequently choose to delay having children or to not have children.

FIGURE 1.6

Additional Research on Transitions

ERIKSON'S ADULT STAGES	GILLIGAN'S CENTRAL ISSUES FOR WOMEN
Identity: Who am I?	**Attachment**
Intimacy: Can I be committed and close to others?	**Caring**
Generativity: Can I nurture others?	**Interdependency**
Ego Integrity: Am I satisfied with my life?	
Critical Issue: Resolving each stage's primary developmental tasks	**Critical Issue:** Renegotiating interdependency in important relationships

---

- The high divorce rate leaves many women as single parents who need to enter or reenter the workforce, resulting in an increase of women working full-time, perhaps when they didn't expect to.

- Because of different circumstances (such as losing jobs and getting divorced), many adults are returning to college to begin, complete, or extend their education.

To further emphasize how life events in today's society are difficult to tie to chronological ages and life stages, Nancy Schlossberg points out that one could be a grandparent at 40 or 80, newly divorced at 20 or 60, and a first-time parent at 20 or 40.

Rather than looking at someone as being 45 years old, it's more important to note that this person has college-age children, is recently divorced, and needs to find full-time work. The actual life experience, or event, is more significant than the person's age. We need to view life flexibly to incorporate this variety of individual experiences. The life event– or transition-focused approach attempts to accomplish this goal.

LIFE EVENT– OR TRANSITION-FOCUSED APPROACHES

What Constitutes a Life Transition?

Changes in your roles, relationships, routines, and assumptions about yourself or the world constitute a major life transition. Descriptions of these aspects of significant life events/transitions, as defined by Schlossberg, follow:

Change in role:	New set of responsibilities (job promotion, career change, new baby, etc.)
Change in relationship:	Getting a new job means new coworkers; being a new parent puts one in contact with new people
Change of routine:	A new job requires some overtime, which affects one's routine; a new baby alters one's sleeping hours
Assumptions about one's self or the world:	Changed career; took on challenge and succeeded; recognized one's own strengths

A major transition involves all four changes identified here. One of less magnitude could involve one or two of these changes.

Similar transitions can affect people differently. How you handle your transition will depend on your self-esteem, confidence, attitude/outlook, coping ability, and preparedness as well as the degree of your ability to deal with change. For example, retirement is a major trauma for someone who is unprepared for and not good with change, but it is a minor adjustment for someone who is better prepared and more adept at dealing with change.

Most important, however, is to recognize that whether a transition is major or minor, it will still take time for a person to adjust. Major transitions for some people can take anywhere from six months to one year, and even up to two years, before they can pass through and move on with their lives. A good example is divorce. For some, depending on the circumstances and the individuals involved, no more than six months might be required. For others, this is a major trauma requiring a few years to adjust to it. Even a positive, less disruptive transition (e.g., a promotion) requires a period of adjustment.

Phases of Life Transitions

No matter what transition you experience, William Bridges states in *Transitions: Making Sense of Life's Changes* that each begins with an ending. We have to let go of the old before beginning the new, no matter what the nature of the transition is. The second phase of a transition is the neutral zone. This is described as a time of confusion and emptiness, a period of needing to be alone, a time of inner reorientation, leading to greater self-understanding, renewal, confidence, and courage to move forward to the third phase: a new beginning. The new beginning involves adjusting to the change that has just occurred in one's life and thus successfully passing through the transition.

Types of Life Transitions

Researchers on the subject of transitions agree that events that change our lives come in a variety of shapes, sizes, and combinations. There are three basic types: elected, unelected, and nonevents. **Elected transitions** are transitions that we expect and that are up to us, that we have time to think and plan for. These could include graduating from college, moving away from home, the first "real" job, getting married, having children, some career changes, and retiring.

Unelected transitions are unexpected and therefore test our coping skills. Examples could include a spouse of 30 years leaving, losing a job after a long tenure, or the unexpected death of a child. These terrible events shock us, leave us numb, and challenge our ability to adjust.

However, not all unelected transitions are negative. We can still be surprised by positive transitions, such as an unexpected job promotion or proposal of marriage. These transitions can also require adjustment of our roles, relationships, routines, and assumptions about ourselves or the world.

Nonevents, the third type of transition, are changes we thought would occur but do not, such as unsuccessful attempts to have children, a love relationship not developing as expected, or not getting a much-desired job promotion. Even though these do not occur, our expectation that they would occur leaves us in a potentially difficult position, possibly just as difficult as an unelected transition. We did not elect for the change to not occur.

Coping with Endings

It's very difficult for many of us to move on, to let go of aspects of our past. Bridges suggests that we can accept transitions better by recognizing that letting go can be at best confusing; trying to understand the phases related to transitions; and developing skills to better negotiate our way through these phases. To accomplish this, we need to understand how one copes with endings. When we are breaking our connections with the familiar and approaching the unfamiliar, fear is a common response. Four key aspects of the ending experience are described in Figure 1.7, with related suggestions, using the example of losing one's job.

For example, a person who gets fired needs to pass through disengagement, disidentification, disenchantment, and disorientation in order to complete the ending phase of the transition. The problem is not necessarily that the person does not want to give up the job or can't let go of that piece of his or her identity. The real problem is that before people can identify a new something, they need to deal with a period of nothing.

People in the midst of a transition seem to find a way to be alone and away from the many familiar distractions. Some people lack the initiative to find another job, because they don't want to take the chance of getting fired again. Bridges suggests that the neutral zone provides a way of viewing life that isn't always available otherwise.

For fired workers, this could be a good time to try to identify what they really want in terms of life goals in general and career goals specifically. They can view this as an opportunity to begin a new chapter in life. (Here's where self-esteem and a positive attitude pay off.) Perhaps they will even get a chance to regain old dreams, ideas, and interests.

The empty time (neutral zone) is important because we simply can't always leave one thing and go right into another. We need to take time out and give some thought to what we want for ourselves and the important people in our lives. As new ideas for the future emerge during the neutral

FIGURE 1.7

Phases of the Ending Experience: Suggestions for Coping

1. **Disengagement:** To break away from the context (activity/job, relation-ship/coworkers, setting/workplace, or role/job title) in which we have known ourselves.

   Suggestion: The process of change can begin when you recognize and accept that this change must be made, either by your choice (career change) or not by your choice (being fired). Therefore, move toward what you fear, rather than away from it. If you need help in doing so, get it.

2. **Disidentification:** By breaking old connections (with the job itself or with coworkers), we lose self-definition, or a role that determined our behavior and made us more identifiable. The impact here is usually greater than we expect.

   Suggestion: At this time, it becomes important to attempt to be more open and flexible in how we think of ourselves so that we can move on through a transition toward a new self-identification.

3. **Disenchantment:** Once separated from the old situation, we seem to be floating between two worlds (former job and next job). We learn that the world is no longer the way we believed it to be.

   Disenchantment related to your career occurs when an organization or individual betrays your trust, when the perfect job turns out not to be so perfect, or when you lose a job and recognize your false sense of security.

   Suggestion: To really change, you need to ascertain whether an important part of your old reality was only imagined (e.g., the "noble" boss or the "perfect" job). Recognize the disenchantment as a minor or major signal of your need to look below the surface of what was thought to be true in order to bring your perception and reality together.

4. **Disorientation:** As a result of your leaving the old reality (former job) behind, your sense of orientation is gone, resulting in the following:

   • Feelings of being lost, confusion, and not quite knowing where you are

   • Feeling that life is breaking down and no longer going anywhere

   • Plans for the future being disrupted

   The disorientation aspect of the ending is meaningful but not enjoyable.

   Suggestion: The confusion and disruption are inevitable. Perhaps recogniz-ing its part in the process can help you cope better as you enter the neutral zone, or "time-out" period. This will lead to adjustment to the transition, with increased self-understanding, on your way to a new beginning.

zone phase, people begin to enter the third and final phase of the transition: making a new beginning. This phase involves an inner realignment and renewal of energy. This inner realignment is more important than only an external shift (e.g., obtaining a new job). If the new beginning is consistent with a person's purpose and mission in life, it will help him or her overcome many obstacles. The shift may not be easy. For example, a change to a more desirable area of work might involve a cut in salary. This could affect one's affluence, requiring adjustments in lifestyle.

ADULT DEVELOPMENT INFLUENCES ON CAREER TRANSITION

Now that we have discussed adult transitions in general, it is worthwhile to discuss career transitions more specifically. Most principles presented for transitions in general are also applicable to career transitions. By understanding the different types of career transitions, you will be able to form a framework from which to create a plan for mastering career change and profiting from it.

The Twenties

Levinson's age-focused approach states that people in their twenties are busy making and testing tentative career choices. However, they're feeling pressure from two opposing needs: to experiment and explore and to begin settling down. This could be considered the entry stage of one's career. We make a first commitment to a job and become involved in developing the skills and the personal meaning that make up our career identity.

The Thirties

The thirties are a time for evaluating the validity of the choices we've made, including our career choices. This questioning of past decisions might reveal that we have actually ignored important needs, interests, and desires. At this time some people decide to make changes and new commitments, in their careers as well as in other areas of life.

If our experiences are similar to those of the men Levinson studied, then we will probably place more value on the quality of our lives at this time. What's becoming important is leading a more balanced life, becoming more family oriented, and developing our relationships. All or some of these goals might take priority over our careers.

Toward the end of the thirties, job satisfaction starts to become more important than climbing the corporate ladder or earning a higher salary. Feeling self-fulfilled, deriving challenge and independence from a career, and using valued skills become most important. This shift in values often leads to a career change if the job presents too great an obstacle to attaining new levels of job satisfaction. Even if we take no action during our thirties, there is often an imperceptible shift in the way we feel about our lives that could, very likely, lead to later changes.

The Forties

The forties are the years when career change becomes even more likely. Some experts believe that mid-life career change (particularly voluntary change) cannot be separated from the developmental issues of mid-life. Career change can be a strategy for coping with developmental issues. It can be either growth-oriented or a step backward. If it offers us an opportunity to integrate more of our total personality into our lifestyle, then it stimulates growth and even helps us to better manage other mid-life developmental tasks. Yet, career change can also represent a retreat, in the sense that we may not be true to ourselves in finding what we would identify as meaningful work involving our strongest interests, skills, values, and personality preferences.

Mid-life career change involves an attempt to find a better fit between our mid-life self-identity and a work environment that provides an opportunity to integrate our dreams and goals. Around the age of 40, we must deal with the disparity between what we are and what we dreamed of becoming. If our dreams have not been realized, then it could be a time to begin to come to terms with failure (including the accompanying feelings of loss and grief) and to decide on a new group of choices from which to rebuild our lives. For those who have experienced success in attaining their dreams and goals, mid-life becomes a time to consider the meaning and value of success and generally to sort things out in life.

CAREER CHANGING IS NOT JUST A MID-LIFE SITUATION

Of the three approaches to describing adult development and related career transitions, perhaps the events-focused approach applies to most of us. Further support for viewing adult career changing from an events-focused approach comes from Richard Bolles, who analyzed a 1986 survey of 10 million job/career changers. He found only one of ten to be at mid-life. This strongly suggests that career changing is not just a mid-life situation. When it becomes necessary, it must be dealt with, regardless of one's age or related life stage.

CAREER CHANGE DEFINED

Sometimes the terms *career, occupation,* and *job* are used interchangeably, which can be confusing. In *Taking Charge of Your Career Direction,* Robert Lock clarifies these terms as follows:

Career: One's entire work history

Occupation: One's vocation, business, profession, or trade

Job: A position of employment within an organization (One can have a succession of jobs in the same occupation.)

The term *career* covers a working life that might include one occupation or several occupations in which one job or several jobs were held.

Therefore, in keeping with these definitions, this book should be titled *Occupation Change.* However, in common usage, the terms *career* and *occupation* are equivalent. Perhaps *career* is a more modern reference than is *occupation.* Therefore, most people who change occupations think of it as being a "career change."

Paula Robbins claimed that a true career change involves **a marked shift in jobs requiring new (primary) skills or knowledge or a totally different work environment or both.** Therefore, one could experience a job change that is not a career change (consisting of similar skills and work environment) or a job change that can be classified as a career change (involving a change in skills/knowledge applied or environment or both). Thus, the term *job change* alone can be confusing. In one situation it could be a job change, and in another it could be a career change as well. (Not to mention that some might use the term *occupation*.)

Because career change can occur in varying degrees, how and if one gets classified as such should depend more on the purpose of the endeavor. The major focus of this book is to help readers learn about overcoming the challenges of changing careers. Therefore, I will adopt Robbins's career change definition.

Reasons for Job or Career Change

Reasons for career changes/transitions can be classified as being internal (motivation to change comes from within oneself, and the individual has some degree of control over the situation) or external (the change has primarily to do with trends in society and other factors outside the person, and the individual has little control).

Internal Reasons

Career transitions for internal reasons are related to developmental issues in one's life. As a result of dealing with these issues, one decides on new goals, desires to satisfy higher-level needs, or seeks new purposes and aspirations. A shift in personal values is often related to wanting more time with family, seeking activities involving different interests or skills, experiencing a changed financial situation, or deciding to no longer put up with excessive stress.

Other reasons for a career change are more directly tied to the work environment itself.

Following are seven areas of potential job satisfaction or dissatisfaction, with examples of job/career involvement:

1. **Company/organization:** Is the company highly regarded in its field? Is it growing? Are its policies satisfactory overall?

2. **Work environment:** Is it a safe, pleasant work setting? Are the hours, dress code, distance to work, and coworkers satisfactory?

3. **Supervisor relations:** Are you treated fairly and given deserved recognition and some degree of freedom? Are supervisors open to your suggestions?

4. **The job itself:** Is the work enjoyable, interesting? Are you using your preferred skills? Do you find your work to be challenging? Do you have an opportunity to be creative?

5. **Rewards/benefits:** Are you receiving an appropriate salary and related benefits (e.g., health insurance, vacation time)? Do you have a reasonable amount of job security?

6. **Professional growth opportunities:** Is there potential to increase your autonomy? Are there possibilities for a leadership role, chances for advancement (in position and/or salary), or opportunities to be more creative in your work?

7. **Personal development:** Do you identify with a sense of purpose in your work? Are you fulfilling, to some degree, your mission in life?

If you are currently dissatisfied with your career and contemplating change, one or more of these categories could be the source of dissatisfaction.

External Reasons

We have little or no control over external reasons for career change. External reasons can be categorized into four areas: societal trends, economic conditions, demographics, and technology. Any of these could have a negative impact on your current job, thus leading to the need for change. They are important factors to consider when seeking your next job or change in career.

Some current trends that impact the job market are listed here. As you read the list, consider which trends have impacted your career, and how.

1. **Societal trends:**
   The women's movement and growth of women's representation in the workforce

Hiring of older workers and changing retirement policies

Emphasis on environmental awareness and action

Health and fitness consciousness

Use of leisure time (increased travel, cultural events, and related entertainment)

Young adults staying single longer

Those who do marry waiting longer to have children

2. **Economic conditions:**

Growth of a global economy

Government spending cutbacks

Corporate restructuring

Increased opportunities for small business

3. **Demographics:**

Increased representation of minorities in the workplace

Aging of the population

Baby boomers having to care for both young children and older parents as they themselves are at mid-life

Increased divorce rate

4. **Technology:**

Rapid advancement in high-tech machinery and computers

Many of us are well aware of the tremendous negative impact that internal and external reasons, especially economic trends and technological advancements, can have on our job/career changing. Most of us have been touched in one way or another by these forces of change, and they have spurred some of us to pursue a job/career change.

If you have any doubt about the number of workers affected by these changes, consider the statistics that Bolles reports from a 1991 survey. They indicate that 39 million U.S. workers (one-third of the total) thought seriously about changing their jobs during the previous year. Sixteen million (14 percent of the total) actually did change jobs over a two-year period. That leaves 23 million workers who are probably still considering a job/career change. When you add the estimated 9 to 17 million unemployed people who are seriously looking for work, you have well over 30 million workers who are job seekers or career changers. The goal of this book is to help career changers overcome the challenges that face them, whether they want to change or have been forced to change their job/career.

TYPES OF JOB OR CAREER CHANGES

Whether one's career change is by choice (voluntary) or not by choice (involuntary), it can also be anticipated or unanticipated. When we know it's coming (anticipated), we have time to think about it and plan for it. However, when we're unaware that it's coming (unanticipated), it can leave us shocked, feeling helpless, and having far less time to think it over or plan. Figure 1.8 depicts the intersection of four possible types of job/career changes within the framework of Voluntary/Involuntary and Anticipated/Unanticipated.

The goal would be to move the situations in boxes 2, 3, and 4 toward the more favorable situation in box 1, the Voluntary/Anticipated box, where you have the most control over your job/career situation. This means that in order to be prepared for outcomes like plant closings, mergers, and large layoffs, you need to stay abreast of general conditions in society mentioned earlier and their relationship to your particular industry. These include societal trends, economic conditions, demographics, and technology. In addition, you need to stay on top of the sit-

---

FIGURE 1.8

Types of Job or Career Changes

	VOLUNTARY	INVOLUNTARY
ANTICIPATED	#1 Offered expected promotion (accepted)	#3 Plant closing (laid off)
UNANTICIPATED	#2 Change in management; offered voluntary separation (accepted)	#4 Merger; middle managers fired (lose job)

uation at your specific organization. What is its financial condition? Is it focused on keeping pace with the latest advancements in the field? Do you or other experts in the field see it as being susceptible to reorganization, merger, or buyout? Keep abreast of changes inside and outside of your organization by networking, which is discussed in Chapter 10.

Your research in these areas could generate information that would allow you to at least move the decision from Unanticipated to Anticipated, even if it's still Involuntary. You could then be in a position to better prepare and to consider changing sooner rather than later, when, most likely, there would be greater stress and pressure to be dealt with. In closing, when a career change is up to you (voluntary) it tends to not be too stressful, though it wouldn't be unusual for you to seek some counseling for help in understanding and managing fear.

CHAPTER 2

NOT YOUR CHOICE: LAYOFFS, FIRINGS, VOLUNTARY SEPARATIONS, AND RELATED DILEMMAS

★

Three major possible ways of losing your job are being laid off, being fired, and being requested to take voluntary separation. This chapter addresses each of these situations in context. It's helpful for you to learn to recognize the warning signs of being laid off or fired, so that you will be in a position to take action, if you decide to, before others do it for you (or to you). You will then need to be prepared to cope with the emotional turmoil of losing your job, if that becomes a reality. This involves taking care of yourself (coping with the emotions of job loss, diet, exercise, creating a routine, and self-esteem). In addition, this chapter outlines beginning steps you can take related to losing your job, searching for a new job, and financial concerns.

WARNING SIGNS OF LAYOFFS

There are numerous warning signs that can help clue you in to a possible layoff. Kathleen Riehle identifies the following:

- Economic conditions worsen; news of falling revenues or rising losses for your division, company, or industry

- Mergers produce redundant positions in the new, merged company

- Best employees leave with concern over financial trouble

- Long closed-door meetings; department manager or director called into a series of meetings

- Managed attrition, retaining current personnel for other tasks, or requests for new positions canceled

- Pay cuts or revisions of vacation policy (either canceling, deferring, or giving short-term vacation without pay)

- Widespread early retirement, especially those with the highest salaries; layoffs may still follow

- A large contract/project is fulfilled, especially for smaller companies; additional ones are not forthcoming

If you're able to read the signs of a layoff ahead of time, you can help put yourself in a position to take action. Keep your network current, both in-house and on the outside. In-house information can be gained via the office grapevine and by communicating with the right people, those who are at the level where decisions are made.

WARNING SIGNS OF BEING FIRED

Times have changed: being fired is not viewed as harshly as it once was. The impact of a changing economy has contributed to the fact that job loss is much more common today. At the same time, reasons for being fired could be personal, related to your job performance, or just a management decision, and these are more difficult to deal with. Consider your being fired a possibility if you

- Are having difficulty with your supervisor (relationship deteriorating, possible angry encounters/confrontations)

- Are assigned less important duties or projects, or if some of your current responsibilities are delegated to others

- Are past due for a raise or promotion and someone else gets it, or you are the only one at your level not to get a bonus

- Are being avoided by your supervisor, coworkers, and subordinates

- Are not receiving information and resources needed to get the job done

- Are not being personally productive

- Are always being criticized by someone at a higher level

- Have had three consecutive poor job performance ratings

- Are unable to set up a meeting to discuss your job dissatisfaction or future possibilities

If you decide to leave, follow the steps outlined in Chapter 3. If you decide to stay, and you end up losing your job, you will need to contend with the inevitable flood of emotions stemming from losing one's job.

Four of our ten profiled career changers had left prior positions not entirely by their choice. Both Ed and Patricia were more or less pushed out as a result of negative politics on the job.

Ed had experienced this as a police officer and decided to pursue a law career. Patricia also decided to pursue a law degree after negative politics in a music librarian position pushed her toward becoming a law librarian and eventually on to law school.

Both Victoria and Vincent were victims of downsizing. Victoria went from a social-work position in a nonprofit organization to a corporate position in technical writing. Vincent went from investment banking to opening his own specialty bookstore.

THE EMOTIONS OF LOSING YOUR JOB

We have specified four types of career transitions:

- Anticipated, voluntary

- Unanticipated, voluntary

- Anticipated, involuntary

- Unanticipated, involuntary

The first two changes, which are more in our control, will be addressed in Chapter 3. These are the types of situations where we can decide to change or not.

However, being laid off or fired is not up to us or within our control and therefore stirs up strong emotions. Loretta Bradley identifies five stages of reaction you might experience as a result of losing your job:

Denial:	Many respond with shock when told they're going to lose their job (especially if it was unanticipated). They think that it can't be true—it can't really be happening to them.
Anger:	After the realization of losing one's job does set in, many people become hostile and angry. After all, they're losing something valuable.
Bargaining:	Some people try to bargain for more time on the job or to be given another chance. They promise to do better and make a last effort to work something out.
Depression:	When one realizes the job is lost and faces the fact that it is happening, there could be a desire to be alone. Feeling sad is not unusual.
Acceptance:	Although unhappy about what's happening, eventually one begins to accept it and starts to look for a new job. (This is easier when you're laid off than when you're fired.)

These stages are not applicable to everyone, but generally speaking, you might identify with a number of these stages, if not all of them. In fact, two stages (or emotional states) that could be added are *fear* and *shame*. Fear may occur between denial and anger and include concerns such as needs of family, paying bills, and the question of "Will I ever work again?" You might also fear losing some of your identity and telling others about what has occurred. Shame may come after anger and prior to depression, which is largely due to the importance and authority we give to the opinions of others.

If one doesn't experience these stages of job loss as presented, it's more than likely that, in addition to shock, anger, depression, fear, and shame, a variety of other emotional responses may be experienced, including disbelief, disappointment, despair, hurt, sadness, betrayal, confusion, self-pity, and possibly even relief.

However, some people who lose their jobs do not necessarily respond as outlined here. Some people are able to let go of anger and unhappiness about having been fired and are often the ones who conduct the best job search. They generally end up with a better job than the one they left.

Taking Care of Yourself

Coping with the Emotions of Job Loss

The emotional impact of job loss can become a huge psychological burden, not to mention a financial one. As indicated earlier, the initial shock is usually followed by anger. Sometimes depression can follow anger. In response, one might tend to withdraw more and more, wanting to be alone. Counseling professionals suggest recognizing and accepting one's feelings and explaining to family or significant others what has happened, as soon as possible.

Talking it out with people can include, in addition to one's family or significant others, friends or personal confidants as well. In fact, joining a support group can be beneficial. To find groups of people dealing with the same problems, contact places of worship (churches/synagogues), social service agencies, and local colleges. Check the phone book under headings such as Career Counseling or Vocational Guidance (or Counseling).

Seeking help is not a weakness; it is a sign of strength and an indication that you intend to improve your situation and are not wallowing in it. The purpose of this "talking it out" phase is to finish dealing with the past in order to prepare yourself to deal with the future. Letting go of anger is an important step in the process, and personal counseling can help achieve that. One's thoughts will shift from what has happened to what to do next.

Still Finding Yourself Thinking Negatively?

Try to take positive action through the steady, ongoing completion of small, meaningful goals. You'll be able to gain a new attitude and perspective, increase your self-satisfaction and self-esteem, and realize the power and control you do have in your life. Don't underestimate the importance of diet, exercise, a routine, and self-esteem in turning around negative thoughts.

Diet   During periods of unemployment, people can get depressed and neglect themselves. This may lead to skipping meals and possibly just taking anything from the refrigerator without considering its impact on your health. Many try to eat or starve away their problems. They also fail to exercise enough, which, in combination with a haphazard diet, could lead to health problems such as high blood pressure, heart attacks, arteriosclerosis, and even cancer. In addition, these bad habits can feed the depression and anxiety already happening and even help make a person look and feel older.

If health reasons alone weren't enough to encourage someone to stay in shape, there's always the fact that there is a prejudice against overweight job seekers and workers. They could be viewed as lazy, less productive, and even a health risk, as unjustified as such an opinion might be.

A proper diet can truly help you be more mentally alert, increase your stamina, and thus deal most effectively with stress. Your diet should include vitamin-rich and high-fiber foods such as raw fruits and vegetables, bran, wheat, and other cereals. In addition, reduce your intake of foods that are high in saturated fats, salt, or refined sugar, and stay away from alcohol and caffeine.

If you have difficulty properly adjusting your eating habits, be sure to add multiple vitamin and mineral supplements daily. The B-complex and C vitamins, especially, have an effect on your energy level, which gets depleted with excess stress and pressure. These dietary suggestions can help ward off the health risks mentioned above and promote the possibility of having a successful job search as well.

Exercise   It's a simple fact—people who exercise regularly have more energy. Try to maintain at least an every-other-day exercise program of about 30 minutes in length. The goal would be to engage in an aerobic exercise that raises the heartbeat and oxygenates the body: jogging, walking, in-line skating, biking, swimming, cross-country skiing, jumping rope, dancing, or playing racquetball. If you have followed this type of program in the past, you already know the benefits as far as looking and feeling better.

Results of an effective exercise program, when done on a regular basis, include improved physical appearance, increased mental sharpness, less anxiety and depression, a better ability to fall and stay asleep, and simply feeling better as a result of the brain's releasing certain biochemicals that help to ward off depression and anxiety. All of this leads to an improved mental attitude and thereby enhances job search outcomes.

Create a Routine Provide the necessary structure for yourself to accomplish what needs to get done in the areas of job searching (calls, correspondence, interviews, library research, etc.), family, and self. Through effective time management, you will experience greater control in your life as well as increased self-satisfaction as a result of accomplishing your goals.

Get organized about your job search and life. Create daily schedules of things to do. Keep a record of all contacts made and when follow-up correspondence or calls need to be done. Organization can go a long way in helping your job search be successful.

Be sure to schedule quality family time also. Your unemployment takes a toll on them as well, as they try to be helpful to you and make sacrifices related to necessary cutting back of spending. In addition, you'll want to schedule relaxation (or quiet time) for yourself, probably on a daily basis, if possible. This can take on many forms: reading, listening to music, gardening, biking, watching television or a video, sewing, or any number of hobbies.

Self-Esteem How you feel about yourself is important, especially during challenging times such as losing your job. In difficult times, it's important to do the things that help you, whatever they might be. Some could be part of the relaxation time just mentioned. Self-help books and tapes can also be useful. In addition, exercise has all-around positive results: mentally, emotionally, and physically. All of this leads to feeling better about life in general and yourself, specifically. Suggestions for improving self-esteem are presented in Chapter 5.

One could view a period of unemployment as a time of reevaluation and regeneration. Of course, that's easier said than done. However, numerous books take an upbeat, positive view of unemployment. Collectively, they advocate viewing this time, after losing one's job, as an opportunity—an opportunity to take a look at yourself, evaluate who you are and where you want to go, and then proceed to pursue that goal. These are definitely positive perspectives and worth consideration.

Losing Your Current Job: Next Steps

Severance Negotiations

One good reason for handling your emotions well after losing your job is that very soon thereafter you may find yourself discussing and negotiating a severance package. Severance can be seen as a financial bridge to your next job. Take care of it as soon as possible because, as time passes, your employer might not care as much about being fair.

Because offering severance is optional for an employer, whatever they offer can be considered acceptable in that regard. However, with large corporate reductions of employees, the offering of severance has become a regular practice at many companies, whether or not it is part of an official policy.

Severance policies are commonly hidden from view. Many companies prefer to deal with each employee individually. There are several reasons why it's in the best interests of companies to deal fairly when it comes to severance:

- Impact on their reputation in the business field (i.e., information regarding poor treatment of employees can spread)

- Effect on their ability to attract high-quality employees in the future

- Morale of employees still working there

- Avoiding possible lawsuits and bad publicity
- The opportunity to relieve guilt they may feel for potentially messing up the employee's life

Many employees who have lost their jobs enter severance negotiations wondering what would be fair. Some companies use a formula based on a number of possible factors: age, position (title), current salary, and length of service. Of course, different companies give different weights to each, while others use additional, more standardized approaches.

However, certain averages do seem to exist. Usually, one year or less of employment will generate two weeks of severance pay. For longer-term employees, a standard could be one week, two weeks, or at best one month's pay for every year of service. Yet, for larger companies the maximum severance will usually be six months' pay regardless of how long an employee has served. Severance might be offered for a specific time period or until you find a job, whichever comes first.

If you're not satisfied with the length of your severance period, try negotiating for something better. Good reasons to point out could be a long tenure and your contributions to the company (new business, saving money, etc.). Additional possible severance benefits include the following:

- Flexibility in the nature and timing of payments (e.g., lump sum or in installments)
- Supportive counseling
- Medical coverage
- Outplacement counseling
- Office space and/or secretarial assistance
- Unused vacation time

You can now see the importance of maintaining your calm upon losing your job, for much is at stake as you negotiate your way out (assuming you're fortunate enough to have had a position where this was possible in the first place). By being professional, you enhance the possibility of achieving a fair severance package. Keep in mind, if you feel you've been unfairly treated, that federal law entitles you to a reasonably fair treatment. If necessary, contact an employment lawyer (not a generalist). Listings of specialists are available from the National Employment Lawyer Association in San Francisco.

Separation Statement/Letter of Reference

Developing a separation statement is important for presenting yourself to prospective future employers. The separation statement describes the truth as you see it and casts you in as much of a positive manner as possible and one with which your former employer can agree.

If you were laid off due to reasons related to organizational restructuring, this statement will be easier to prepare and probably easier for former managers to agree with. However, even if you've been fired for a personal reason, there may be a way to frame the reason so that it doesn't endanger your future employment and at the same time is one that management is willing to go along with. For example, perhaps some reorganization was going on when you were fired and can be worked into the statement as having an effect. There may be a payoff for management if you do succeed at gaining a new job, and that is a reduction of guilt, if it's there to begin with. Therefore, they may be willing to work with you on this. In fact, you may be able to include a separation statement as part of your severance negotiations.

A separation statement should begin with a positive statement and overview of contributions made on your previous job and follow with an explanation of reasons for leaving that is as honest and positive as possible. Discuss the statement with your former supervisor. Help him or her to remember all of your accomplishments, and then explain your new career objective, in an attempt to build a longer-term perspective rather than focusing on recent problems. It's to your advantage to reach a point of agreement on the separation statement. Then when you do use it, it will be with the knowledge that the former supervisor agrees, in case the person is contacted about you by a potential employer.

Most reference requests are now channeled through human resources departments for legal reasons. This creates an even stronger reason to prepare a separation statement. Otherwise, potential future employers can have inadequate information. If the human resources department offers only limited information, your separation statement can fill in the holes.

VOLUNTARY SEPARATION

Voluntary separation is an outgrowth of the early retirement programs. Companies found themselves with an excess of middle managers who, most likely, would not move any farther up the corporate ladder because of a lack of room or the person's lack of skills, experience, or motivation. At the same time, newer employees were arriving with stronger educational backgrounds and better skills. However, the companies knew that releasing older workers could lead to lawsuits and public relations problems. Early retirement programs were typically offered to workers 55 and over, with ten or more years of service. Incentives in the form of benefit packages were offered to employees who elected to leave voluntarily.

Around the early 1980s, voluntary separation was introduced against a backdrop of corporate reorganization, in which companies redefined the focus and nature of their business. More than an issue of too many middle managers, now it was a matter of whether an entire division remained in a company's plans for the future. Voluntary separation involves the company's identifying an eligible group of employees, creating a package of severance benefits (usually not negotiable when presented to a group, as compared with an individual's losing his or her job), and offering those eligible a time period in which to accept the offer. Therefore, the company decides who is eligible, and those individuals decide how to respond.

If you are offered a voluntary separation, it's important to learn as much as possible about the company's future plans and needs. Insight could be gained by talking with your supervisor. Do you have the skills and experience that could plug into its future plans? The implication is that initially the company didn't think so, or you wouldn't be among the group offered voluntary separation. However, that doesn't mean it's not possible for you to persuade them otherwise. In order to do that, you need good information on which to base your argument. You might even simply ask your supervisor whether you should take the voluntary separation offer. Both verbal and nonverbal responses can be important clues for you. If you feel you have a realistic chance, then pursue it. If not, then it might be best to take the offer of voluntary separation and begin a job search campaign.

FINANCIAL CONCERNS

Unemployment Compensation

When you are laid off or fired, you may be eligible for unemployment compensation. If you are laid off because your former company has financial problems, you are eligible for benefits. If you're fired, whether you are eligible depends on the reason. Your former employer would have to prove you were guilty of some form of misconduct to make you ineligible. This would include being caught stealing, sabotaging employer property, or assaulting coworkers, not necessarily personality conflicts or disagreements.

Unemployment compensation is sometimes difficult for hardworking individuals to accept: they don't want handouts. Remember, however, that rather than charity, this is a program administered by the U.S. Department of Labor to which employers have contributed. Keep in mind that its purpose is to help job seekers survive the period between jobs. This period could stretch from six months to a year, depending on such factors as your career objective, related skills and experience, how effectively you market yourself, and the state of the economy.

Find out what amount of unemployment compensation you're entitled to. In most states, it's $200/week for someone with no dependents and up to $300/week with one or more dependents. You can continue to receive benefits in most states even if you obtain a part-time job, as long as it pays less than your total benefit amount. You may still be able to receive the difference between your part-time pay and your benefit amount. The number of weeks you're allowed benefits may be limited. Most states limit the number to around 26 weeks. However, there is the possibility of legislation extending this, so check with your local unemployment office for the most up-to-date information.

Develop an Accurate Budget

Identify your and your family's needs and list all expenses.

- What do you need to keep without interruption?
- What can be delayed? Talk with your creditors; you may be able to arrange some type of payment plan.

- What can be cut back (e.g., housing, food, utilities, or entertainment expenses)?

- If you were covered by a group medical insurance policy with your former employer, you can maintain coverage for a period by paying your and your employer's share under the Consolidated Omnibus Budget Reconciliation Act (COBRA).

If, after figuring all this out, you realize you can't survive 9 to 12 months on your current savings and/or unemployment benefits, you may want to consider a home equity loan or other low-interest loans (e.g., from insurance policies) to help get you by.

This chapter covered involuntary and unanticipated job loss. The next chapter examines the career changes you choose to initiate.

CHAPTER 3
YOUR CHOICE:
A QUESTION OF VALUES

★

This chapter presents a method for assessing your current level of job satisfaction in order to guide you in deciding whether to change or not to change. If you decide to make a change, it will be only the first of many important decisions. This chapter also guides you in the choices of finding a new position with the same employer, working for another employer, or starting your own business.

DEFINING "GOOD" WORK

What is "good" work? C. Wright Mills considered this question almost 50 years ago. According to Mills, good work is

1. Concerned with the quality of a product and the skill that product requires. Rewards such as money, fame, status, and prestige come second to being able to do work one loves and can do well.

2. Owned by the workers. The relationship between the part and the whole is visible.

3. Challenging. It stretches workers as individuals and professionals.

4. Controllable. When workers can decide when to start and stop work, it influences not only work, but leisure time as well.

5. A source of self-development for workers, including techniques (skill).

6. Integrated with play. There should be some pleasures in our work.

7. Companionable. It provides company for the many hours away from friends and family.

This is but one definition of good work. What else might you include? Mills developed this definition in 1951, but it still covers what most people would consider key elements of good work.

Half of our ten profiled career changers changed careers by choice: Larry, Martha, Allen, Zephree, and Sandra. Larry left his environmental technician position to become a trainer for a related manufacturer. Martha left teaching to start a business with her husband that grew to be a popular Hispanic nightclub and restaurant. Allen left his budget analyst position to go to dental school and eventually own his own practice. Zephree left secretarial work to become a research assistant in a social service field. Sandra left the law profession to write and publish books for children.

Mac left his business to become a high school counselor for two reasons: a health problem and a business slowdown. So, even though in one sense it was his choice, there were factors operating that brought him to that choice.

However, many other factors affect how satisfied we are with a particular job. Individuals identify different types of factors as important, both in life in general and on the job. The factors an individual considers important are referred to as *values*.

Defining a Value

A value is anything to which one attributes worth, merit, or usefulness. More specifically, job or work values are the rewards, satisfactions, and desirable qualities one seeks in a career. You might ask, "How do I know if something I attach importance to is really a value?" If you can answer yes to the following seven criteria, then you can be certain that the importance you've attached to something is significant. According to Sidney Simon, Leland Howe, and Howard Kirschenbaum, you can consider something a value if you

1. Chose it freely
2. Chose it from a set of desirable alternatives
3. Chose it after thoughtful consideration of the consequences of each possible alternative
4. Prize, cherish, and feel proud of it
5. Are able to discuss it freely and openly with others
6. Invest your time, money, or other resources in it
7. Act on it consistently for a considerable period of time and across a variety of situations

The Importance of Values

A value is formed by continuously considering and deliberately choosing from alternatives, after careful consideration of the consequences of each. Once it's chosen, you will prize a value, noting its importance with respect and pride. After you've chosen a value, you will affirm it consistently over time by giving it your time, money, or energy.

Thinking about your values helps in your search to find purpose and meaning in your life and work. Setting priorities requires you to think more deeply about what is important in your life. Through identifying and evaluating your values, you can get to know yourself better. With every decision you make, no matter how small or large, you are making a statement about what matters to you.

CAREER CHANGER UPDATE

✶

In the three years since our first interviews, three of our career changers made major career decisions based on a personal value: desired quality of life. Two of them, Victoria and Larry, decided to leave their positions after company reorganizations left them with new supervisors and excessive demands that would interfere with the quality of life they'd come to enjoy and wished to maintain.

In Victoria's case a reorganization was done ruthlessly (to those she cared for), and the results were puzzling to her. The nature of her role changed, and she was being relocated from a desirable location (downtown area of a major city) to an undesirable one (in a surrounding suburban area). She resigned from her position.

Larry's company's reorganization left him with a new supervisor who expected those under him to work an 80-hour workweek. Larry had just moved to a new city where he had come to value the many outdoor recreational outlets, as well as having a new wife and friends. Thus, he decided to resign.

Patricia also found her lifestyle values, including independence (she'll never return to a large law firm), playing a strong role in how she viewed her future opportunities: either remaining with her own law practice or becoming a general counsel for a smaller law firm, preferably an arts-related one.

How Values Develop

Many factors enter into the process of developing values, beginning in early childhood. Relationships play a key role, especially those with parents, siblings, relatives, neighbors, friends, teachers, institutions, and other aspects of your community. Your cultural surroundings also influence your values. This includes newspapers, magazines, radio, television, film, music, art, and books. Values are related to needs. Your needs will usually determine what motivates you. In turn, what motivates you will influence what is important to you.

Figure 3.1 (pages 54–66) gives you a chance to assess your degree of satisfaction by ranking 80 work values on your current job, or the degree of importance you attach to these values if you are currently unemployed.

Very few people ever have a job that satisfies all aspects covered in this self-assessment to a high degree. However, a balance among the seven categories is desirable. Pay particular attention to the categories of work satisfaction values to which you give the highest importance ratings. These are the key values for you.

In addition, pay serious attention to the work value categories with percentage scores of 60 and below. Suggestions for what can be done to improve your situation at your current job are provided in the next section. Consider these carefully before deciding whether to change your career.

Sandra was dissatisfied in her legal work. She felt her work could have a greater purpose, more of a sense of mission. Growing up as an Asian-American was difficult for her, an experience similar to that of other people of color. The books that Sandra writes and publishes feature minority children and describe their experiences growing up. Sandra hopes that minority children who read these books will feel a greater sense of pride in and enjoyment of their own experiences.

If you are currently unemployed and completed your importance ratings for the 80 work values, this can now serve as a source for assessing possible upcoming career opportunities. Zero in on those values that you rated 4 or above (above-average to high importantce). Your goal is to try to find a job that satisfies the values that you identify as most important to you. If you don't achieve some level of satisfaction for a fair number of these work values, then you're more likely to be dissatisfied with your next position.

SEEKING A CHANGE WITH YOUR PRESENT EMPLOYER

Even if you are dissatisfied with your present job and are thinking about seeking a new position with a different organization, the best opportunities might be with your present employer. Three advantages of seeking a change with your present employer are:

- You'll have access to people in the organization who can help you determine the needs of your present campaign.

- By knowing the needs of your company, you could possibly position yourself to help contribute in the most important areas.

- Organizations often prefer to promote from within. There is no need to train someone new, you are a known quantity, and it helps to build morale.

If you decide to stay with your current employer, your choices are to pursue no on-the-job change (perhaps exploring new ideas through part-time work or volunteering) or to attempt to make a change. Possible changes within your current organization include:

Move vertically: Up to a promotion; less possible these days with many career ladders collapsed within flatter organizations

Reshape job: Add or drop tasks/responsibilities

Move laterally: Gain more experience, further develop skills; looked at as a promotion, more and more, in today's job market

Change careers: Change industries and role, inside the organization—if it's large enough to have such a position

Finding a new position with your current employer will favorably affect your salary, pension plan, and other benefits. Negatives of seeking a position with a new employer include starting over somewhere new, having to prove yourself, and a possible drop in salary or benefits. You'll find more information on internal career change on pages 224–228.

Some problems with resigning without having found a new job are

- Financial support while job searching

- Loss of health insurance

- The perception that smart people don't leave their jobs until they have new ones lined up

However, a benefit is that you can give your job search full-time attention, which can pay off in the end.

If you can stay on your job at least until you have a chance to do some research, it might help to reduce stress. It also puts you in a better decision-making position. On the other hand, there may be good reasons not to stay, such as the following:

- You can no longer tolerate the situation.

- Your dissatisfaction is causing significant performance problems, which could hurt you in the future by possibly getting you fired or leading to a poor reference while job searching.

- Your unhappiness is ruining the rest of your life.

SEEKING WORK ELSEWHERE

If you decide to leave your current employer, your choices are:

Similar job/ same field:	Using similar skills in the same field, such as an accountant changing from a large, urban firm to a smaller, suburban firm
Similar job/ different field:	Using similar skills in a new field, such as a college professor changing to become a corporate trainer
Different job/ same field:	Using new skills in the same field, such as a lawyer who specializes in real estate law changing to a specialty in mediation practice
Different job/ different field:	A total career change, to one in which you're using new skills in a new field

Starting your
own business:
- New business
- Existing business
- Franchise
- Consultant/independent contractor

(See the next section, "Starting Your Own Business.")

STARTING YOUR OWN BUSINESS: WHAT ARE YOUR CHANCES OF SUCCESS?

Many baby boomers who sought to climb the corporate ladder didn't like what they encountered as they attempted to build their careers. Competition is fierce at the middle tier of most companies, and workers wanting to advance were frustrated. They learned from their employers what it takes to create and manage their own businesses and had the confidence to try it.

Why Start a Business?

People start their own businesses to have something to call their own, to have greater control over their careers, and to create something from their own ideas. Here are some additional reasons:

- You can live and work where you choose.
- You experience greater independence.
- You can avoid potential difficulties of working for others: difficult or incompetent supervisors, office politics, and so on.
- You can control your own time. In the beginning you will work long hours, but at least you (rather than someone else) are the direct beneficiary of those efforts.
- You have a greater likelihood of remaining vitally interested in your work.
- There is a better chance to make money as an entrepreneur than working for someone else.

- It is a source of self-satisfaction and pride to take your own ideas and establish a business.

How to Succeed in Starting Your Own Business

You need to be aware of the motivations underlying your decision to start a new business. Otherwise, you may be increasing the odds of failing. Reasons such as wanting to make a lot of money soon, being bored with your present job, wanting more free time, having a strong desire to escape from a difficult supervisor, or an unhappy social situation with fellow employees are *not* good reasons to start a business of your own. Entrepreneurship is a risky business with many emotional, mental, and physical demands.

To achieve greater independence, Sandra, in addition to writing multicultural children's books, decided to publish them as well. This was the only way she knew to maintain editorial control. Her mission of writing culturally aware books for children was so central to who she was that she was willing to add to an already difficult transition the role of publisher in order to maintain control over the content of her books.

Some valid reasons for starting a business include lifestyle choices. For example, you might want to choose the hours that you work, rather than being stuck with a 9:00-to-5:00 routine. You will probably work more hours with a new business, but at least it's up to you and for you. It allows you greater freedom and control in your career. However, it's nothing to rush into. There are no salary, benefits, office, or support system, unless you work on providing them yourself.

Figure 3.2 (pages 67–74) is an exercise designed to help you assess your potential to be a successful business owner. By completing the exercise, you will identify to what degree you have attained each of 50 entrepreneurial personal characteristics.

What to Do About Weaknesses

It's unusual for anyone to score 90 percent or better in all eight categories in the self-assessment, but there should be a balance among the eight. Pay particular attention to any category with an attainment percentage score of average (70 to 79 percent) or less, as well as any individual item rated 3 (average) or less. These are areas in which you need to improve, to help enhance the possibility of success, if you plan to open your own business.

Patricia found upon starting her legal practice that she was weak on the administrative, day-to-day aspects of running an office. She hired someone part-time to help with client billing and related matters.

Some of your lower-scoring characteristics will be easier to improve than others. It's important to ask yourself, and others who would know, how much having only an average (or lower) amount of a certain characteristic will affect your chances of success. If the responses are "somewhat to a lot," then you have four choices:

1. Try to acquire more of that characteristic through coursework, workshops, seminars, personal counseling, personal goal setting, and so forth.
2. Find a partner who possesses the qualities you do not have.
3. Use consultants as needed to shore up weak spots.
4. Decide that owning a business isn't the best choice for you and that working for someone else will fit you better.

The Sacrifices Required to Be Successful

Even if you are encouraged by your results on the Entrepreneurial Personal Characteristics Self-Assessment, you must also know that following such a path involves much personal sacrifice in the form of time, energy, money, family, and friends. It's not unusual for new business owners to work 12 to 14 hours a day, seven days a week, taking little or no time off for vacation, as they attempt to get the business off the ground. This takes not only tremendous energy and vigor, but also the cooperation of those close to you. Quality family time will be cut down dramatically, as will social time with friends. Here's where good communication helps out.

The biggest single reason for business failure is undercapitalization. As a beginning entrepreneur, you could go heavily into debt, experience cash-flow problems, and have creditors knocking at your door. Thus, it makes more sense to wait to start your business until you're at least moderately sure that you have enough funds to avoid setting yourself up for major financial distress.

Typically, in the first year, and perhaps in the second, you will be doing well if you break even. Even if you do make some profit with your new business, it would be advisable to reinvest those earnings back into your business.

GENERATING NEW BUSINESS IDEAS

By taking a snapshot of current demographics, economic conditions, and technological information, you can generate some potential small business ideas. Of course, market research is needed to verify the viability of these ideas in your geographic area of interest. It all boils down to creating a specific idea, gathering evidence that it will succeed (based on market research), and knowing whether economic conditions favor your proposed idea.

As a potential business owner, you need to ask yourself the following questions:

- Do I have the interest, expertise, and relevant skills to enable me to succeed in this market?

- Can I identify a related business, service, or product need that no one else is providing or create a new need?

- Can I improve an existing product or service, as far as looking for ways to produce and sell it better and less expensively?

Testing Out Your Business Idea

Once you have a business idea and have done some research, you're ready to test that idea out. Emily Koltnow and Lynne Dumas suggest checking out the competition, talking with potential customers, developing promotional ideas, and conducting formal or informal market research.

Vincent exercised two interesting strategies for researching his target market and testing out his idea. He sent a 3,000-piece mailing to the community where he hoped to locate his bookstore. He included a quarter in each one (hoping to increase the response rate) and asked people to comment on how many paperbacks/hardbacks they bought recently and in which subject areas.

He got a 17 percent response rate (considered strong) and was surprised at how many people not only sent back the quarter (thinking he might need it), but also included personal suggestions to help him get started in his business venture.

Vincent also benefited from his M.B.A. program, where he learned to use government census reports to determine who was buying what and when. He reviewed circulation records at the local library, which revealed that history and mystery (the focus of his intended specialty bookstore) together beat out all other categories. This certainly was encouraging to Vincent as he moved closer to making his business idea a reality.

Should You Start a New Business, Buy an Existing Business, Invest in a Franchise, or Become a Consultant?

When considering your business options, be sure to get feedback from a team of advisors including an accountant, a lawyer, and a financial advisor.

Starting a New Business   The pros and cons of starting a new business are listed here:

Pros: • For true entrepreneurs, the real goal and major appeal is in the creation of something new, not necessarily in the management aspect, so starting a new business is appealing.

Cons: • You need a good idea, potential customers, and knowledge of marketing, finance, and management to succeed.

• There is a high failure rate. (The Small Business Administration reports that 75 percent fail in a year, and 25 percent of first-year survivors fail in the second year.)

• Most new businesses are privately financed with the owner's money and often are undercapitalized.

- It is not unusual for a new business owner to work at least 60 hours, and possibly as many as 80, seven days a week, for the first year or so, which can create stress for yourself and your family.

- It is not as appealing if you are sales oriented and are not as interested in creating as in selling.

To decide whether to open their own businesses, Mac, Patricia, and Allen all worked for related businesses owned by others.

Mac worked for two years with a leader in the market research area of interest to him: the African-American consumer. It was his first exposure to the business world, and he was excited by it— enough so, that he went on to establish his own business.

Patricia, originally a music librarian, switched to being a law librarian and then went on to become a lawyer herself. She worked for five years in a law firm in her area of interest, the creative arts. She found the experience to be good training in preparing to move out on her own.

Allen, a dentist, worked for four years in someone else's practice and gained a good amount of knowledge about running a dental practice, which he was able to apply when he began his own practice.

In addition, Sandra spent her first year in her writing/publishing company on a part-time basis before leaving her job as a lawyer.

Buying an Existing Business   Perhaps after reviewing the pros and cons of owning a business, you're thinking that you want to be self-employed but don't have an innovative idea or are not comfortable taking such a big risk. Then you could consider buying an already existing business or investing in a franchise. Both choices involve less risk, and there's less to learn the hard way, when compared with starting a new business. The pros and cons of buying an existing business follow:

Pros: • There is reduced risk and a better chance of getting financial backing. Banks take a more favorable view because of the existing track record: the existence of customers, staff, supplies, facility, cash flow, and so on.

- It is more attractive to a person with more interest in selling products than in setting up an operation or a marketing system or designing products.

Cons:
- The current owner might have liabilities he or she wishes to foist off on an unsuspecting buyer. Be sure to find out why the person is selling the business before making any commitment.
- It is not as appealing to an entrepreneur who likes to be original, creative, and innovative. This sort of business venture might not reflect enough personal vision.

Investing in a Franchise   The pros and cons of investing in a franchise follow:

Pros:
- The failure rate for a franchise business is less than 5 percent, according to the National Franchise Association.
- Operating costs are lower (franchisors buy in large quantities and can pass the savings on to individual franchises).
- Franchises receive plenty of business support, including advertising, accounting, hiring, and training. Franchisors with better-quality franchises help with financing, legal assistance, site selection, and even management of construction.
- It is a relatively low-cost way to learn how to run a business and a good training ground for learning to operate your own business later.

Cons:
- You're bound by the franchise agreement. Thus, there is a loss of freedom and flexibility in operating the business.
- In exchange for the business support, the franchise must pay a fee, a royalty, or a percentage of the gross.
- The success of each franchise is dependent, to a large extent, on the franchisor's business skills, determination, financial standing, and honesty.

For further information, consult the *Franchise Opportunities Handbook,* published by the U.S. Department of Commerce. The handbook lists most franchises registered in the United States and includes information such as number of franchises, product/service offered, costs, and what training is available. Additional information can also be obtained from the International Franchise Association, 1350 New York Avenue, Suite 900, Washington, DC 20005.

FRANCHISE INFORMATION

Related Internet Sites

- *Entrepreneur* Magazine's Bizsquare: http://www.entrepreneurmag.com/
- Franchise Handbook On-Line: http://www.franchise1.com/
- FranInfo: http://www.franinfo.com/
- Yahoo!:   http://www.yahoo.com/
  Go to Business & Economy, Companies, Franchises.

Becoming a Consultant   You probably have heard the term *consultant* many times and might have wondered what exactly they do. Consultants are expert advisors who are contracted from outside an organization to help solve problems for a fee. Those who hire consultants include large, medium, and small companies; nonprofit organizations, such as associations; government agencies; elementary, junior, and senior high schools; colleges and universities; health care institutions; advertising agencies; public relations firms; and entertainment companies. The types of work consultants are hired to do include identifying and solving problems; providing expert knowledge; generating new ideas; convincing others to accept new ideas; helping identify growth areas; teaching new methods; and exploring ways and means of keeping up with the competition.

Consultants could be expert in a particular type of business or in a cluster of professional skills. For example, a consultant might be knowledgeable in accounting, human resource management, training and development, or data processing or have particular talent in the area of communication and writing. Whatever your chosen area of expertise, in order to succeed you need to be a proven expert with at least five years of experience and a solid network of contacts who trust you and would contract for your services when they have a project to be completed.

As a consultant, you must be comfortable with yourself and able to continuously market or sell yourself and your skills. This requires fortitude, perseverance, and good interpersonal, negotiating, presentational, and written communication skills. Sound technical knowledge in the field of interest is also a must.

Patricia combated her fear of feeling alone (and cut expenses as well) in her legal practice by renting office space within a large law firm. Mac rented space in a friend's company and even got his phone line specially answered (sounding as if it were his company alone) by the secretary already in place.

Following are the pros and cons of working as a consultant:

Pros:
- You can enhance the development of your network.
- Such work provides you with the opportunity to get familiar with companies and vice versa, which could lead to obtaining a full-time job.

Cons:
- You really have to hustle. You are the salesperson as well as the product and service. If you stop hustling, you'll be out of business.
- You have to learn to cope with the rejection that can come from selling both yourself and your knowledge.
- You're only as good as your last job.
- You personally will have to get the work out on time, keep the books, pay the bills, bill customers, and hassle with delinquent accounts.
- Unless you have a clerical worker on hand, you will not enjoy the support that you once knew as a member of a larger organization. For example, if the fax breaks down, you have to get it fixed yourself.
- You might feel a sense of loss from no longer being part of a team effort.
- You might be less secure because you are no longer backed by the prestige and title of your former corporation.

- There is a lack of formalized structure, which is good for some and bad for others. You'll have to learn to adjust to a need for greater personal drive and motivation to get going and stay active in business.

- Because of the need to stay constantly active in order to generate business, your freedom is limited. Thus, you have to limit sick days and structure leisure time into your schedule after finishing an assignment and before prospecting for more work.

STARTING/MANAGING YOUR OWN BUSINESS
Related Internet Sites

- Business of Women: http://www.web-search.com/women.html/

- Business Resource Center: http://www.greatinfo.com/business_cntr/bus_res.html/

- Career Resource Center (small/home office: 475 links):   http://www.careers.org/ Go to Home Office.

- National Association for the Self-Employed (NASE):   http://selfemployed.nase.org/nase/

- Small Business Administration Home Page: http://www.sbaonline.sba.gov/

- Small Business Administration Women's Business Ownership Homepage: http://www.sbaonline.sba.gov/womeninbusiness/ Check Outside Resources (Hotlist) at the bottom.

- Small Business Resource Center: http://www.webcom.com/seaquest/sbrc/welcome/html/

- Smart Business Supersite (information for starting a business):   http://www.smartbiz.com/

- U.S. Department of Labor (labor-related data and small business information):   http://www.dol.gov/

- Working Solo (1,200 self-employment resources):   http://www.workingsolo.com/

- Yahoo!: http://www.yahoo.com/
  Go to Business & Economy, Small
  Business Information.

After reviewing the pros and cons of starting a new business, buying an existing business, investing in a franchise, and becoming a consultant, you are in a better position to judge which option better suits you. If you need more information to help you explore these options, you can contact the Small Business Administration (SBA), 409 Third Street SW, Washington, DC 20416, or call the SBA Answer Desk at (800) U-ASK-SBA (827-5722).

FIGURE 3.1

Work Values Satisfaction Self-Assessment Directions

5 High satisfaction/importance

4 Above-average satisfaction/importance

3 Average satisfaction/importance

2 Below-average satisfaction/importance

1 Low satisfaction/importance

Follow these steps to complete the self-assessment. An example for category D, "The Job Itself," is included for illustration.

1. Focusing on one value at a time, use the 1–5 scale presented to rate your current level of satisfaction on the job by circling the appropriate number. Next, rate its importance to you.

   If you are currently unemployed, complete only the importance ratings. If you're self-employed, complete categories B, D, and G only, and then complete the Entrepreneurial Personal Characteristics Self-Assessment that follows.

   If you're thinking about becoming self-employed in the future, you can still complete this exercise with regard to your current position (if there is one) or potential next position (if there might be one prior to self-employment) and then complete the Entrepreneurial Personal Characteristics Self-Assessment.

2. When you have rated all 80 values, eliminate all work values that you rated as 1 or 2 (below-average to low) in **importance** by drawing a line through them. You will calculate your average level of satisfaction for each category,

continued

and including these would throw off the accuracy of your scores for values that aren't important to you in the first place.

3. For the remaining work values, multiply the satisfaction number by the importance number, and write the result on the line in Column 1.

4. Now complete the Satisfaction Total calculations: Within one category (A–G) at a time, total the work value **satisfaction** ratings only, and divide by the number of work values being calculated (those rated 3 or above in importance). In our example, the satisfaction scores for values rated 3 or above in importance totaled 53. We divided 53 by the number of values included (12), for an average satisfaction rating of 4.4. Record your average in the space provided after the category heading, in the parentheses and to the left of the slash (/).

5. Use the descriptors, low satisfaction through high satisfaction, to judge your average satisfaction rating for each category (A–G).

In our example, 4.4 is a rather high rating, about halfway between 4 (above-average satisfaction) and 5 (high satisfaction). This would indicate that the person represented in our example has an above-average to high level of work value satisfaction in the category "The Job Itself," perhaps the most important category of the seven.

Note in which categories you score the highest and the lowest. You might gain insight from the intensity of satisfaction for the seven categories of values. We'll return to discuss your results after completing the next steps in the scoring process.

6. For a more accurate category total score, compute the following:

   a. Add the scores listed in Column 1, for work values rated 3 or above in importance only. This becomes your Total Score (a). Each category (A–G) has its own separate Total Score (a).

   In our example, the Total Score (a) for "The Job Itself" equals 206.

   b. To calculate each category's Highest Possible Score (b), multiply your importance rating for each work value rated 3 or above in importance by 5 (the highest possible satisfaction score). Write the result on the line in Column 2. Add the scores in Column 2 and write the total at the bottom of Column 2.

   c. To complete the Satisfaction Percentage Score (a/b), divide each category's Total Score (a) by that category's Highest Possible Score (b). Write the percentage at the end of each category in the space provided, as well as to the right of the category heading, in the parentheses and to the right of the slash.

   In our example, 206 divided by 230 equals .895, which can be rounded up to 90 percent. *continued*

The Work Values Satisfaction Self-Assessment might appear a bit over-whelming at first. The best approach is to break it down into "bite-size" pieces. Consider doing one or two work value categories at a time. After just a few sittings, you'll have it completed. I think you'll be glad you did, for your values should play a key role in your career decision making.

EXAMPLE

	LEVEL OF SATISFACTION	x	LEVEL OF IMPORTANCE	= COL. 1	COL. 2
	Low Average High		Low Average High		

D. The Job Itself (4.4/ 90%)

1. The work is enjoyable and interesting.

    1 2 3 4 ⑤ x 1 2 3 4 ⑤ = $\underline{25}$ $\underline{25}$

2. I'm using my preferred skills and knowledge.

    1 2 3 4 ⑤ x 1 2 3 4 ⑤ = $\underline{25}$ $\underline{25}$

3. My job offers me appropriate growth in desired skills and knowledge.

    1 2 3 ④ 5 x 1 2 ③ 4 5 = $\underline{12}$ $\underline{15}$

4. I experience a sense of achievement on the job.

    1 2 3 ④ 5 x 1 2 3 ④ 5 = $\underline{16}$ $\underline{20}$

5. The work is intellectually challenging.

    1 2 3 ④ 5 x 1 2 3 ④ 5 = $\underline{16}$ $\underline{20}$

6. I have an opportunity to be creative in my work.

    1 2 3 4 ⑤ x 1 2 3 4 ⑤ = $\underline{25}$ $\underline{25}$

7. There is a variety of duties, a nice mix of responsibilities.

    1 2 3 4 ⑤ x 1 2 3 ④ 5 = $\underline{20}$ $\underline{20}$

8. The job entails a reasonable level of stress.

    1 ② 3 4 5 x 1 2 ③ 4 5 = $\underline{6}$ $\underline{15}$

9. The work has an element of adventure; I perform new, different, and exciting tasks.

    ~~1 2 3 ④ 5 x 1 ② 3 4 5 =~~ $\underline{\quad}$ $\underline{\quad}$

10. The job provides the desired amount of social contact.

    1 2 3 4 ⑤ x 1 2 ③ 4 5 = $\underline{15}$ $\underline{15}$

11. I'm able to influence job duties to my liking.

    1 2 3 4 ⑤ x 1 2 ③ 4 5 = $\underline{15}$ $\underline{15}$

continued

12. The job involves
    opportunities to travel.   1 (2) 3 4 5 x (1) 2 3 4 5 = _____ _____

13. The work is physically
    challenging.   1 (2) 3 4 5 x (1) 2 3 4 5 = _____ _____

14. I enjoy a familiar
    routine of daily tasks.   1 2 (3) 4 5 x 1 (2) 3 4 5 = _____ _____

15. There's some action/
    activity; I can move
    about on the job.   1 2 3 4 (5) x 1 2 (3) 4 5 = 15   15

16. The work allows me to
    be persuasive,
    convincing others to take
    certain actions.   1 2 3 (4) 5 x 1 (2) 3 4 5 = _____ _____

17. Overall, the job is secure;
    there is little chance of
    becoming obsolete.   1 2 3 (4) 5 x 1 2 3 (4) 5 = 16   20

Satisfaction Total = 53 ÷ 12 = 4.4

Total Score (a) = 206

Highest Possible Score (b) = 230

The Job Itself Work Values Satisfaction
Percentage Score (a/b) = 90 %

Work Values Satisfaction Self-Assessment

	LEVEL OF SATISFACTION	x	LEVEL OF IMPORTANCE	=	COL. 1	COL. 2
	Low Average High		Low Average High			

A. Company/Organization (/ %)

1. The company is highly regarded in its field.

1 2 3 4 5 x 1 2 3 4 5 = _____ _____

2. The company is secure in its field; it belongs to a growth industry.

1 2 3 4 5 x 1 2 3 4 5 = _____ _____

3. The company is experiencing growth.

1 2 3 4 5 x 1 2 3 4 5 = _____ _____

4. The branch or division I work in is valued.

1 2 3 4 5 x 1 2 3 4 5 = _____ _____

5. To a large extent, I agree with the setting and carrying out of company personnel policies.

1 2 3 4 5 x 1 2 3 4 5 = _____ _____

6. The company does not discriminate based on gender, age, race, or sexual orientation.

1 2 3 4 5 x 1 2 3 4 5 = _____ _____

7. Employees are able to observe important religious holidays and are allowed time off as appropriate.

1 2 3 4 5 x 1 2 3 4 5 = _____ _____

8. The company adheres to a solid sense of ethics.

1 2 3 4 5 x 1 2 3 4 5 = _____ _____

9. The geographic location of the company is desirable.

1 2 3 4 5 x 1 2 3 4 5 = _____ _____

10. The company is loyal to long-term employees, whom they treat with respect and look to when promoting.

1 2 3 4 5 x 1 2 3 4 5 = _____ _____

Satisfaction Total = _____ ÷ _____ = _____

continued

Total Score (a) = _____

Highest Possible Score (b) = _____

Company/Organization Work Values Satisfaction
Percentage Score (a/b) = _____%

	LEVEL OF SATISFACTION Low Average High	x	LEVEL OF IMPORTANCE Low Average High	=	COL. 1	COL. 2

B. Work Environment (/   %)

1. The work setting is
   safe and healthy.   1 2 3 4 5 x 1 2 3 4 5 = _____ _____

2. The work setting is
   comfortable and pleasant.   1 2 3 4 5 x 1 2 3 4 5 = _____ _____

3. Resources needed to get
   the job done are provided.   1 2 3 4 5 x 1 2 3 4 5 = _____ _____

4. The office space provided
   is suitable for meeting job
   requirements.   1 2 3 4 5 x 1 2 3 4 5 = _____ _____

5. The work hours are
   decent; they allow for
   some leisure time.   1 2 3 4 5 x 1 2 3 4 5 = _____ _____

6. The company dress code
   is comfortable for me.   1 2 3 4 5 x 1 2 3 4 5 = _____ _____

7. The distance to travel to
   work is reasonable.   1 2 3 4 5 x 1 2 3 4 5 = _____ _____

8. My coworkers are
   pleasant; there is a good
   work team feeling.   1 2 3 4 5 x 1 2 3 4 5 = _____ _____

9. Employee morale is upbeat. 1 2 3 4 5 x 1 2 3 4 5 = _____ _____

10. Back stabbing and other
    ruthless encounters are
    kept to a minimum.   1 2 3 4 5 x 1 2 3 4 5 = _____ _____

11. A healthy competitiveness
    exists among coworkers.   1 2 3 4 5 x 1 2 3 4 5 = _____ _____

12. There's a sense of belonging
    among employees; I can be
    recognized as a member
    of a group as a result
    of the work I perform.   1 2 3 4 5 x 1 2 3 4 5 = _____ _____

continued

13. In general, I am respected and looked up to on the job.

   1 2 3 4 5 x 1 2 3 4 5 = _____ _____

   Satisfaction Total = _____ ÷ _____ = _____

   Total Score (a) = _____

   Highest Possible Score (b) = _____

   Work Environment Work Values Satisfaction
   Percentage Score (a/b) = _____%

	LEVEL OF SATISFACTION	x	LEVEL OF IMPORTANCE	=	COL. 1	COL. 2
	Low Average High		Low Average High			

C. Supervisor Relations (/ %)

1. My supervisor treats me with respect.

   1 2 3 4 5 x 1 2 3 4 5 = _____ _____

2. My supervisor thinks of me as a human being, not just someone to get the work done.

   1 2 3 4 5 x 1 2 3 4 5 = _____ _____

3. I am given appropriate recognition.

   1 2 3 4 5 x 1 2 3 4 5 = _____ _____

4. My supervisor is open to my suggestions.

   1 2 3 4 5 x 1 2 3 4 5 = _____ _____

5. My supervisor is accessible and approachable when needed.

   1 2 3 4 5 x 1 2 3 4 5 = _____ _____

6. I am dealt with honestly.

   1 2 3 4 5 x 1 2 3 4 5 = _____ _____

7. I am motivated with praise, not criticism.

   1 2 3 4 5 x 1 2 3 4 5 = _____ _____

8. I am allowed some degree of freedom in performing my work.

   1 2 3 4 5 x 1 2 3 4 5 = _____ _____

9. My supervisor is knowledgeable and skilled in my area of expertise.

   1 2 3 4 5 x 1 2 3 4 5 = _____ _____

10. My supervisor is able to give me meaningful feedback about my work.

   1 2 3 4 5 x 1 2 3 4 5 = _____ _____

continued

11. My supervisor possesses and upholds solid ethical practices.　1 2 3 4 5 x 1 2 3 4 5 = ＿＿＿　＿＿＿

12. Overall, my supervisor is a competent manager.　1 2 3 4 5 x 1 2 3 4 5 = ＿＿＿　＿＿＿

Satisfaction Total = ＿＿＿ ÷ ＿＿＿ = ＿＿＿

Total Score (a) = ＿＿＿

Highest Possible Score (b) = ＿＿＿

Supervisor Relations Work Values Satisfaction Percentage Score (a/b) = ＿＿＿%

LEVEL OF SATISFACTION Low Average High	x	LEVEL OF IMPORTANCE Low Average High	= COL. 1　COL. 2

D. The Job Itself (/ %)

1. The work is enjoyable and interesting.　1 2 3 4 5 x 1 2 3 4 5 = ＿＿＿　＿＿＿

2. I'm using my preferred skills and knowledge.　1 2 3 4 5 x 1 2 3 4 5 = ＿＿＿　＿＿＿

3. My job offers me appropriate growth in desired skills and knowledge.　1 2 3 4 5 x 1 2 3 4 5 = ＿＿＿　＿＿＿

4. I experience a sense of achievement on the job.　1 2 3 4 5 x 1 2 3 4 5 = ＿＿＿　＿＿＿

5. The work is intellectually challenging.　1 2 3 4 5 x 1 2 3 4 5 = ＿＿＿　＿＿＿

6. I have an opportunity to be creative in my work.　1 2 3 4 5 x 1 2 3 4 5 = ＿＿＿　＿＿＿

7. There is a variety of duties, a nice mix of responsibilities.　1 2 3 4 5 x 1 2 3 4 5 = ＿＿＿　＿＿＿

8. The job entails a reasonable level of stress.　1 2 3 4 5 x 1 2 3 4 5 = ＿＿＿　＿＿＿

9. The work has an element of adventure; I perform new, different, and exciting tasks.　1 2 3 4 5 x 1 2 3 4 5 = ＿＿＿　＿＿＿

continued

10. The job provides the desired amount of social contact.

1 2 3 4 5 x 1 2 3 4 5 = _____ _____

11. I'm able to influence job duties to my liking.

1 2 3 4 5 x 1 2 3 4 5 = _____ _____

12. The job involves opportunities to travel.

1 2 3 4 5 x 1 2 3 4 5 = _____ _____

13. The work is physically challenging.

1 2 3 4 5 x 1 2 3 4 5 = _____ _____

14. I enjoy a familiar routine of daily tasks.

1 2 3 4 5 x 1 2 3 4 5 = _____ _____

15. There's some action/ activity; I can move about on the job.

1 2 3 4 5 x 1 2 3 4 5 = _____ _____

16. The work allows me to be persuasive, convincing others to take certain actions.

1 2 3 4 5 x 1 2 3 4 5 = _____ _____

17. Overall, the job is secure; there is little chance of becoming obsolete.

1 2 3 4 5 x 1 2 3 4 5 = _____ _____

Satisfaction Total = _____ ÷ _____ = _____

Total Score (a) = _____

Highest Possible Score (b) = _____

The Job Itself Work Values Satisfaction Percentage Score (a/b) = _____%

	LEVEL OF SATISFACTION	x	LEVEL OF IMPORTANCE	= COL. 1	COL. 2
	Low Average High		Low Average High		

E. Rewards/Benefits (/   %)

1. My salary is fair and competitive for the level of responsibility.

1 2 3 4 5 x 1 2 3 4 5 = _____ _____

2. Appropriate promotions have been awarded in a timely manner.

1 2 3 4 5 x 1 2 3 4 5 = _____ _____

continued

3. A decent medical
   insurance plan is provided.   1 2 3 4 5 x 1 2 3 4 5 = _____   _____

4. A pension plan/retirement
   fund is provided.   1 2 3 4 5 x 1 2 3 4 5 = _____   _____

5. Profit sharing is available.   1 2 3 4 5 x 1 2 3 4 5 = _____   _____

6. An appropriate amount of
   vacation time is available.   1 2 3 4 5 x 1 2 3 4 5 = _____   _____

7. An appropriate amount of
   sick leave is available.   1 2 3 4 5 x 1 2 3 4 5 = _____   _____

8. Tuition reimbursement for
   continuing education or
   training is available.   1 2 3 4 5 x 1 2 3 4 5 = _____   _____

9. The job includes the use
   of a company car.   1 2 3 4 5 x 1 2 3 4 5 = _____   _____

10. An athletic club
    membership or discount
    is offered.   1 2 3 4 5 x 1 2 3 4 5 = _____   _____

11. Child care provisions are
    available.   1 2 3 4 5 x 1 2 3 4 5 = _____   _____

12. There's good job security
    (considering the current
    status of the job market).   1 2 3 4 5 x 1 2 3 4 5 = _____   _____

Satisfaction Total = _____ ÷ _____ = _____

Total Score (a) = _____

Highest Possible Score (b) = _____

Rewards/Benefits Work Values Satisfaction
Percentage Score (a/b) = _____%

	LEVEL OF SATISFACTION	x	LEVEL OF IMPORTANCE	=	COL. 1	COL. 2
	Low Average High		Low Average High			

F. Professional Growth Opportunities (/ %)

1. There is potential for
   increasing autonomy
   and freedom in decision
   making (how to carry
   out job).   1 2 3 4 5 x 1 2 3 4 5 = _____   _____

continued

2. There is potential for increasing levels of responsibility (freedom to act and solve problems without close monitoring).   1 2 3 4 5 x 1 2 3 4 5 = _____   _____

3. There is potential for an increasing leadership role (directing, managing, or supervising activities of others).   1 2 3 4 5 x 1 2 3 4 5 = _____   _____

4. There is potential for promotion from within (job title or salary).   1 2 3 4 5 x 1 2 3 4 5 = _____   _____

5. There is potential for increasing opportunities to have creative input in my work.   1 2 3 4 5 x 1 2 3 4 5 = _____   _____

6. There is potential to achieve desired levels of status and prestige.   1 2 3 4 5 x 1 2 3 4 5 = _____   _____

7. Continuing education is encouraged, and in-house people move laterally to enhance on-the-job growth.   1 2 3 4 5 x 1 2 3 4 5 = _____   _____

8. Professional development, through participation in outside organizations/ activities, is encouraged.   1 2 3 4 5 x 1 2 3 4 5 = _____   _____

Satisfaction Total = _____ ÷ _____ = _____

Total Score (a) =   _____

Highest Possible Score (b) =   _____

Professional Growth Opportunities
Work Values Satisfaction
Percentage Score (a/b) =   _____%

continued

	LEVEL OF SATISFACTION	x	LEVEL OF IMPORTANCE	=	COL. 1	COL. 2
	Low Average High		Low Average High			

G. Personal Development Goals (/   %)

1. There's a sense of purpose in my work, helping me in fulfilling my life mission.   1 2 3 4 5 x 1 2 3 4 5 = _____   _____

2. I gain a sense of identity from my work.   1 2 3 4 5 x 1 2 3 4 5 = _____   _____

3. There's an opportunity for personal growth; I'm able to gain new knowledge.   1 2 3 4 5 x 1 2 3 4 5 = _____   _____

4. I'm able to help others in some way through my work.   1 2 3 4 5 x 1 2 3 4 5 = _____   _____

5. My work has a positive impact on my personal life. (It doesn't create excessive stress that carries over.)   1 2 3 4 5 x 1 2 3 4 5 = _____   _____

6. My work offers me a chance to influence others' opinions or decisions in positive ways.   1 2 3 4 5 x 1 2 3 4 5 = _____   _____

7. There's an opportunity to serve as a mentor to newer professionals in my field.   1 2 3 4 5 x 1 2 3 4 5 = _____   _____

8. My work helps me attain inner harmony and peace of mind.   1 2 3 4 5 x 1 2 3 4 5 = _____   _____

Satisfaction Total = _____ ÷ _____ = _____

Total Score (a) =   _____

Highest Possible Score (b) =   _____

Personal Development Work Values Satisfaction Percentage Score (a/b) = _____%

continued

CATEGORY SCORING RESULTS

Work Value Categories	Work Values Average Satisfaction Rating/Satisfaction Percentage Score
A. Company/Organization	____/____%
B. Work Environment	____/____%
C. Supervisor Relations	____/____%
D. The Job Itself	____/____%
E. Rewards/Benefits	____/____%
F. Professional Growth Opportunities	____/____%
G. Personal Development Goals	____/____%

Following are interpretations of the Satisfaction Percentage Scores in each category:

90–100%	Congratulations! You are **highly satisfied** with this aspect of your job.
80–89%	You are experiencing **above-average satisfaction** with this aspect of your job.
70–79%	You are feeling **average satisfaction** with this aspect of your job.
60–69%	You are experiencing **below-average satisfaction** with this aspect of your job. This should serve as a warning signal for a problem area.
Below 60%	You have **low satisfaction** with this aspect of the job.

FIGURE 3.2

Entrepreneurial Personal Characteristics Self-Assessment

Directions

In this self-assessment you will rate the degree to which you believe you possess each of the 50 entrepreneurial personal characteristics. The response choices are as follows:

5 High

4 Above average

3 Average

2 Below average

1 Low

1. Read through the entire list to get familiar with the characteristics.

   Try to be accurate in rating yourself. However, if you tend to be a perfectionist, pay close attention to how high (or low) you rate yourself. You don't have to be perfect to give yourself a 5, just a bit higher than "above average." On the other hand, if you tend to rate yourself too high, make an extra effort to be realistic in your self-ratings.

2. Circle the appropriate rating for each characteristic. Write the score in the space provided.

3. Within each category (A–H), add up the ratings and write the total in Total Score (a).

4. Divide Total Score (a) by the number of characteristics in that category to calculate the Average Attainment Level. Record this number next to the category heading, in the parentheses and to the left of the slash (/).

   In the example, the Average Attainment Level is 4.3, which falls between the above-average (4) and high (5) rating levels.

   In addition to the Average Attainment Level, pay particular attention to any individual characteristics that you rated 3 or below. In the example, the person represented rated energy level with a degree attained of 3. This person would need to take a serious look at how only an average attainment level for energy (mental, emotional, and physical), a major demand of having your own business, could impact his or her possible success.

5. Compute your Total Score (a) as a percentage of the Highest Possible Score (b). Multiply the number of characteristics in each category by 5 (the highest rating) to identify the Highest Possible Score (b), then divide the Total Score (a) by the Highest Possible Score (b). Record the percentage next to the category heading, in the parentheses and to the right of the slash.

continued

In our example, 30 divided by 35 equals .857, which can be rounded up to 86 percent.

A word of caution. A high score in any one category is no guarantee of success at running your own business. You may have only one low score in a category, such as confidence, and still have a high overall category score. Yet unless you work on your confidence level, you could have a difficult time attempting to build a business of your own.

In the same vein, a low score is no guarantee of failure. You might grow and learn in weak areas or find a partner who is strong where you are weak.

EXAMPLE

DEGREE ATTAINED
LOW AVERAGE HIGH

E. Motivation/Attitude (4.3/ 86%)

1. I am a self-starter. I take initiative in completing tasks.

   1 2 3 4 ⑤ = 5

2. I have a high energy level to meet the tremendous mental, emotional, and physical demands of establishing and running a business.

   1 2 ③ 4 5 = 3

3. I have a strong drive. I am compelled to move forward and accomplish goals.

   1 2 3 4 ⑤ = 5

4. I am determined and inner-directed. I don't let setbacks or others' opinions (e.g., family) deter me from accomplishing goals.

   1 2 3 ④ 5 = 4

5. I am enthusiastic by nature.

   1 2 3 ④ 5 = 4

6. I am persistent at achieving goals.

   1 2 3 4 ⑤ = 5

7. I am optimistic. I have a basic belief in myself.

   1 2 3 ④ 5 = 4

Average Attainment Level = _30_ ÷ _7_ = _4.3_

Total Score (a) = _30_

Highest Possible Score (b) = _35_

Motivation/Attitude Attainment Percentage Score (a/b) = _86_%

continued

Entrepreneurial Personal Characteristics Self-Assessment

A. Idea Person (/   %)

1. I am creative; I can generate ideas.   1 2 3 4 5   =   _____

2. I always look for a better way to   1 2 3 4 5   =   _____
   do things in an effort to improve.

3. I can develop an idea and make it work, based   1 2 3 4 5   =   _____
   on market research, realistic goals, and constant
   feedback from the marketplace.

4. I am resourceful. When required information   1 2 3 4 5   =   _____
   is not readily available, I am able to find out
   how and where to get it.

   Average Attainment Level = _____ ÷ __4__ = _____

   Total Score (a) =   _____

   Highest Possible Score (b) =   __20__

   **Idea Person Attainment
   Percentage Score (a/b) =** _____%

B. Technical Knowledge (/   %)

1. I have talent and expertise in an area of value   1 2 3 4 5   =   _____
   to the marketplace.

2. I have solid business sense; I can spot   1 2 3 4 5   =   _____
   opportunity readily and act on it appropriately.

3. I am always ready to learn more.   1 2 3 4 5   =   _____

   Average Attainment Level = _____ ÷ __3__ = _____

   Total Score (a) =   _____

   Highest Possible Score (b) =   __15__

   **Technical Knowledge Attainment
   Percentage Score (a/b) =** _____%

C. Management (/   %)

1. I am excellent at organizing and planning, not   1 2 3 4 5   =   _____
   only to get started, but also to keep things going.

continued

2. I can effectively manage time to meet the variety
of demands of business, family, and social life.
1 2 3 4 5 = _____

3. I need to control and direct. I want freedom
to initiate action and attain goals.
1 2 3 4 5 = _____

4. I can identify problems in the midst of confused
and complex situations and work on solutions
faster than most.
1 2 3 4 5 = _____

5. I am far-sighted as well as aware of important,
immediate details. I can prioritize activities and
tasks appropriately to achieve my overall goal.
1 2 3 4 5 = _____

6. I am able to weigh the pros and cons, make
decisions, and live with the consequences.
1 2 3 4 5 = _____

7. I have enough financial and organizational ability
to appropriately budget expenses and income.
1 2 3 4 5 = _____

8. I can delegate tasks effectively.
1 2 3 4 5 = _____

9. I am self-disciplined.
1 2 3 4 5 = _____

Average Attainment Level = _____ ÷ **9** = _____

Total Score (a) = _____

Highest Possible Score (b) = **45**

**Management Attainment
Percentage Score (a/b) =** _____%

DEGREE ATTAINED
LOW AVERAGE HIGH

D. Work Ethic (/ %)

1. I have a good reputation in community
and business aspects of life.
1 2 3 4 5 = _____

2. I strive for a level of excellence in work, product,
or services provided.
1 2 3 4 5 = _____

3. I am willing to take responsibility
for all aspects of the business.
1 2 3 4 5 = _____

4. I can maintain my commitment to business
success for countless hours with no guarantee
of payoff, even if family and friends do not
understand my slow progress.
1 2 3 4 5 = _____

5. I establish goals on a daily, weekly, monthly,
and even yearly basis and pursue their
accomplishment in a realistic manner.
1 2 3 4 5 = _____

continued

6. I am attentive to detail.   1 2 3 4 5 = _____

7. I am honest in dealings with others: clients/   1 2 3 4 5 = _____
   customers, employees, and business associates.

8. I am able to make family and social-life   1 2 3 4 5 = _____
   sacrifices in order to put in 60–80 hours
   per week for the first year or so.

Average Attainment Level = _____ ÷ __8__ = _____

Total Score (a) = _____

Highest Possible Score (b) = __40__

**Work Ethic Attainment
Percentage Score (a/b) =** _____%

DEGREE ATTAINED

LOW AVERAGE HIGH

E. Motivation/Attitude (/ %)

1. I am a self-starter. I take initiative in   1 2 3 4 5 = _____
   completing tasks.

2. I have a high energy level to meet the   1 2 3 4 5 = _____
   tremendous mental, emotional, and physical
   demands of establishing and running a business.

3. I have a strong drive. I am compelled to move   1 2 3 4 5 = _____
   forward and accomplish goals.

4. I am determined and inner-directed.   1 2 3 4 5 = _____
   I don't let setbacks or others' opinions
   (e.g., family) deter me from accomplishing goals.

5. I am enthusiastic by nature.   1 2 3 4 5 = _____

6. I am persistent at achieving goals.   1 2 3 4 5 = _____

7. I am optimistic. I have a basic belief in myself.   1 2 3 4 5 = _____

Average Attainment Level = _____ ÷ __7__ = _____

Total Score (a) = _____

Highest Possible Score (b) = __35__

**Motivation/Attitude Attainment
Percentage Score (a/b) =** _____%

continued

DEGREE ATTAINED
LOW AVERAGE HIGH

F. Personality (/   %)

1. I am independent and self-reliant.   1 2 3 4 5   = _____

2. I have faith in myself. I am willing to take   1 2 3 4 5   = _____
   on challenges with no guarantees.

3. I can exhibit considerable self-control under   1 2 3 4 5   = _____
   difficult circumstances and handle business
   anxieties and pressures with relative ease.

4. I realize the uncertainty involved in having my 1 2 3 4 5   = _____
   own business. I accept that and still remain
   confident.

5. I have a strong desire to excel, accomplish   1 2 3 4 5   = _____
   goals, and be better than others.

6. I am persuasive. I can communicate to others   1 2 3 4 5   = _____
   the value of my product or services in a
   convincing manner.

7. I can handle rejection and failure. I am   1 2 3 4 5   = _____
   challenged rather than discouraged by setbacks
   or failures.

8. I am not too proud to seek the advice of others. 1 2 3 4 5   = _____

   Average Attainment Level = _____ ÷ __8__ = _____

                              Total Score (a) = _____

                       Highest Possible Score (b) = __40__

                              **Personality Attainment
                              Percentage Score (a/b) =** _____%

DEGREE ATTAINED
LOW AVERAGE HIGH

G. Interpersonal Relations (/   %)

1. I enjoy and pursue interactions and involvements 1 2 3 4 5   = _____
   with others, especially within the context of
   running a business.

2. I can work well with others in difficult situations. 1 2 3 4 5   = _____

3. I am more concerned with a person's   1 2 3 4 5   = _____
   accomplishments than his or her feelings. I
   choose experts rather than friends as business
   associates.

continued

4. I am able to negotiate, whether with business   1 2 3 4 5 = _____
   associates, customers/clients, or even family
   members. I can compromise in working out
   arrangements in difficult situations.

   Average Attainment Level = _____ ÷ __4__ = _____

                                  Total Score (a) = _____
                    Highest Possible Score (b) = __20__
             Interpersonal Relations Attainment
                  Percentage Score (a/b) = _____%

                                    DEGREE ATTAINED
                                    LOW AVERAGE HIGH

H. Lifestyle (/   %)

1. I enjoy challenges. I am attracted to situations   1 2 3 4 5 = _____
   that test my skills, knowledge, and ability to solve
   problems.
2. I maintain a healthy lifestyle.   1 2 3 4 5 = _____
3. I am flexible enough to adapt to various demands. 1 2 3 4 5 = _____
4. I am willing to take personal and financial risks. 1 2 3 4 5 = _____
5. I am flexible with lifestyle needs.   1 2 3 4 5 = _____
6. I can handle isolation.   1 2 3 4 5 = _____
7. I am comfortable without structure.   1 2 3 4 5 = _____

   Average Attainment Level = _____ ÷ __7__ = _____

                                  Total Score (a) = _____
                    Highest Possible Score (b) = __35__
                        Lifestyle Attainment
                  Percentage Score (a/b) = _____%

CATEGORY SCORING RESULTS

ENTREPRENEURIAL PERSONAL CHARACTERISTIC CATEGORIES	ENTREPRENEURIAL PERSONAL CHARACTERISTIC AVERAGE ATTAINMENT LEVEL/ATTAINMENT PERCENTAGE SCORES
A. Idea Person	_____/_____%
B. Technical Knowledge	_____/_____%
C. Management	_____/_____%
D. Work Ethic	_____/_____%

continued

E. Motivation/Attitude   _____/_____%

F. Personality   _____/_____%

G. Interpersonal Relations   _____/_____%

H. Lifestyle   _____/_____%

Following are interpretations of the Attainment Percentage Scores in each category:

90–100%   Congratulations! You've attained, to a **high degree,** the entrepreneurial characteristics in this category.

80–89%   You've attained, to an **above-average degree,** the entrepreneurial characteristics of this category.

70–79%   You've attained, to an **average degree,** the entrepreneurial characteristics of this category.

60–69%   Your attainment of the entrepreneurial characteristics of this category is **below average.**

Below 60%   You indicate a **low degree** of attainment of the entrepreneurial characteristics of this category.

A Grand Total Attainment Percentage Score for the entire assessment exercise can be computed by completing the following calculation:

Add the Total Scores (a) for categories A–H: = _____

Divide by the sum of Highest Possible Scores (b): = _____250_____

Grand Total Attainment Percentage Score = _____

CHAPTER 4
UNDERSTANDING AND CONQUERING
YOUR CAREER CHANGE FEARS

★

PROCRASTINATION

Procrastination is postponing, delaying, deferring action on, or putting off something. Not all procrastination is bad. It's only a problem when it becomes troublesome to you in some way.

Everybody procrastinates once in a while, but for some people, procrastination is a problem that can ruin relationships, cause emotional pain, and sabotage careers. You may have experienced this state of indecision yourself or with someone you are close to. Procrastination can be tremendously frustrating. Those close to the procrastinator cannot understand why it's taking so long for the person to decide and take some action. Those experiencing procrastination feel frozen in a state of indecision.

Procrastination and Career Decision Making

Following are a few of the general reasons why someone might procrastinate with respect to career decision making and some suggestions on how to deal with the difficulty.

Unclear Career Goal   You may not be very clear about who you are and what you want for yourself. This could be an issue of identifying what is important to you—your interests, skills, values, and personality preferences—and combining them with related career information to generate some ideas for career goals. If that process doesn't work for you, then the issue could be a deeper one related to identity and self-esteem.

Variety of Interests and Abilities   One might not think that people with multiple interests and abilities would have difficulty in career decision making. However, their interests may be of equal importance, with no one option standing out as best. Such a person could decide on any number of directions and probably feels pulled in several. In this case, setting priorities could help maintain focus.

Or it could be a case of not wanting to let go of the other options that's keeping a person from making a decision. If this applies to you, it's important to recognize that having it all is a much different issue from not knowing what career to go into. The challenge here would be to set priorities and to identify a career that includes a number of your top interests, if possible.

In addition, you could pursue other interests away from the job during leisure time as hobbies or avocational pursuits. If this approach does not work, counseling might be needed to deal with this "having it all" mentality. Try to "have as much as possible" instead.

Finding Fault with All Alternatives   Perhaps, somehow, you find something wrong with each possible choice. No alternative looks appealing, so you decide not to act (or not to decide). We all know that every situation, every decision, has its pros and cons. Determine whether the aspects that you value the most regarding a potential career are more in the pros column or more in the cons column.

Once you are clear on your values and understand the various aspects of a particular job, you are in a position to assess whether most of your top values have the potential of being met. You can then proceed accordingly.

Possibilities for dealing with negative factors range from lessening their percentage to possibly removing them from the job description and replacing them with something else. Again, here's where research pays off. You need to be aware of your employer's needs, as well as your talents and skills, to be able to accomplish this challenging bit of negotiation.

Unsure of Self   This whole career decision-making process can leave you in a nervous state, unsure of what to do. As mentioned previously, with change comes risk. It's natural to have some self-doubt. This is another reason to be certain that you have done your homework on yourself and have established a relevant, meaningful career goal. This will help remove some of the doubt.

In the process of establishing your career goal, which includes identifying your skills, you could seek out the opinion of experts in your field as to how they see your level of skill and potential success. This would also put you in a position of either knowing you had the skills necessary (relieving your doubt) or knowing you need further skill development.

Procrastinating in making a career decision could have its roots in fear: the fear of change, failing, or even success. Even perfectionism fits in here, because some of us won't do anything unless we can do it perfectly. Many of these fears are grounded in unrealistic thinking. Let's look at possible fears as well as perfectionism in order to better understand them.

FEAR OF CHANGE

The average American will work for ten different employers, keep each job 3.6 years, and change careers three times before retiring. With career-related and general forecasts of change, people who are flexible and adaptable will be better off. One might think that the only security is having the confidence to cope with the insecurity that accompanies change. In situations like these, real inner security means trusting yourself to be able to handle the unexpected.

Being afraid to change is natural. You're going from the familiar (even if dissatisfying) to the unfamiliar. Many people desire stability and dislike breaks in routine. Your identity and self-esteem might be tied to your surroundings, your security comes from predictable events, and you know what to expect. However, sometimes desire for routine can lead you to miss out on many of the possible satisfactions in life, including an enjoyable and rewarding career.

Even though change can often initially appear threatening, it can serve as a catalyst to go on to new and better possibilities. Although it is easier to just stay put, try to view change as an opportunity to allow new experiences into your life. If you hang in there, the new situation can also become comfortable, and you will have eliminated the dissatisfying aspect of your former position.

Whether you are forced to take action as a result of external factors or are internally motivated to do so, it is certain to involve some degree of change. Of course, if internally motivated you usually have the luxury of being able to plan for it, as opposed to externally motivated situations where you are taken by surprise.

Some other fears of potential career changers are listed here:

1. Disruption of a familiar and comfortable routine
2. Possible unanticipated events as a result of taking action
3. Risking job security in current position (when change is your choice)
4. Financial risks of being unemployed (when change is not your choice)
5. Self-doubt and the unknown
6. Validating whether you have the skills you thought you had by sticking your neck out in a new career
7. Losing status and sense of identity
8. Not getting along with new supervisor and coworkers

These concerns could lead career decision makers to make no decision at all or to choose inaction at a time when they either are losing a job or know it's best (or urgent, depending on their circumstances) to make a change.

To overcome your hesitation about career decision making, you need to face your fears. This implies taking risks. To take that step forward into the unknown, you need to be flexible enough, as well as courageous enough, to leave the familiar routine and try something new. You should improve your chances of success through sound planning, preparation, and research. As a result, you will help to make the unknown more known, which will lessen your fear.

However, if you are unsuccessful, it might mean getting hurt, experiencing rejection in not getting a job interview, feeling nervous while taking a test during the interview process and doing poorly, or finding out that your skills are judged to be not good enough.

As painful as these outcomes may be, try not to be afraid to fail. Failing is a learning experience. If you try your best and take a positive approach and still fail, at least you know you gave it your best shot. Recognize that you are only human, and forgive yourself for not being perfect. Then take the time to figure out what went wrong. Do everything within your power to remedy the situation, and then try again.

Change with regard to work involves important factors such as money, status, power, relationships, self-image, self-confidence, personal satisfaction, and other factors that shape our lives both directly and indirectly. This can result in a fair amount of worry, if not downright anxiety. However, worrying about change tends to cause more anxiety than the change itself.

Usually, change means giving something up, letting go in order to move forward. Letting go can be difficult. It could involve losing some sense of self. Often, letting go is the biggest block for some career changers who want it all.

Fear has a purpose. Once you accept and recognize it, it serves to alert you to take action to protect yourself from possible loss. One approach for coping with your fear of change is to imagine the worst possible result of your decision. What is so frightening about the change? If this happened, what would you do? Can you prevent this? How?

People who are most afraid of taking risks might experience high levels of anxiety that could interfere with their ability to realistically assess their interests and skills, see the various alternatives, and set and accomplish goals. If the fears are severe, there is probably a self-esteem and identity problem to be attended to first in order to benefit from career counseling.

On the other hand, if your fears are more within the norm, you need to recognize the phases involved in making a career change. By breaking down what seems to be an overwhelming problem into smaller, more manageable steps, you can help to eliminate much of the mystery and self-doubt involved in changing your career.

Making a meaningful career decision, one that fits well, takes a combination of understanding your interests, skills, values, and personality preferences as well as career awareness (what's really involved in a particular job). When you accomplish a good match, you'll know it. It will feel right, and you'll be able to proceed with confidence. This will help to alleviate much of your fear about changing careers.

FEAR OF FAILING

The fear of failing is probably the most common fear that keeps people from taking risks of all kinds. If you associate your self-worth with external success to an unrealistic degree, then you might be troubled by this fear. Many people who fear failing are concerned about being judged by others or by themselves. Perhaps they or others feel they're not living up to their own expectations, and their inner voice expresses disappointment. They often fear they'll be found to be deficient in some way and that their best attempts won't be satisfactory.

Often, those who fear failing at tasks view it as failing as a person. Society values success over failing and equates failure with inadequacy. Therefore, one might think, "If I perform well, that means I have a lot of ability, so I like myself and feel good about myself." This person considers his or her performance to be a direct measure of ability and worth. But if performance is the only measure of a person and nothing else is taken into account, self-esteem and confidence can be destroyed by failure. Self-worth cannot be measured by external success alone. You are no less a person if you don't succeed at what you try to do.

What is success anyway? Each of us would define it differently. Success is a subjective perception; it's what any one individual values. Often, those who fear failing measure themselves against an unrealistic standard of perfection of how successful, smart, or talented they think they should be and then fail to measure up. That's assuming they've tried in the first place. Such people often elect not to try. (If they can't attain these high expectations, why bother at all?)

The key to conquering the fear of failing is to ask yourself, "How do I define success?" Determine what measuring stick you're using to decide whether success has been achieved. Is your measuring stick realistic? Are you expecting perfection or close to it? If you can adjust how you judge yourself and attempt to be more realistic in both your expectations and measurement of success, you will be more inclined to take a chance in situations that you previously avoided. You will be on your way to overcoming your fear of failing.

With healthy self-esteem and confidence, you're not as vulnerable to others' opinions at times of failure. You'll be more inclined to pick yourself up, assess the situation, note what needs to be remedied, and try again. It's not to say that you won't feel bad; it's just that it won't feel like the end of the world.

Three of our career changers—Martha, Mac, and Victoria—reported fearing failing. Martha's biggest fear was going from dealing with children (in the classroom) to adults (employees, suppliers, and the customers). Not only did she succeed in her transition, but also her teaching skills came in handy when she was instructing employees.

Mac wasn't sure how well he would relate to high school students as a counselor, after almost 20 years of being in business for himself and dealing only with adults. Mac was glad to find that inner-city high school counselors are well respected by the students. They often have the last word about whether a student in trouble stays or goes. This, in combination with the type of person Mac is (easy to talk with, personable), helped Mac in making a successful transition.

Victoria feared making mistakes. Her career change created a risky situation. For 15 years she had a secure government position with seniority (even though it ended with a layoff). Now she was facing a corporate position with less security. Victoria helped to smooth her transition by doing well at freelance work in technical writing for six months prior to making the complete move into a new position. In addition, she consulted with a friend who had recently made the same career change, and her positive experience also helped calm Victoria's fear.

Sidney Simon offers some possible consequences of fearing failing and how it affects us and our lives. The fear of failing

- Reduces the number of available alternatives or keeps you from pursuing them

- Persuades you to set easier goals and do less than your best

- Leads you to create good reasons not to change (perhaps by painting a rosy picture of the here and now)

- Causes indecisiveness and confusion, which stop you from knowing what you really want
- Keeps you from asking for help when you need it or accepting support from others when offered
- Distorts your perception of your life and what you can do to make it better
- Can keep you from asserting yourself, so you tend to settle for less
- Can lead to the development of unhealthy habits and behavior patterns (e.g., substance abuse)
- Keeps you from taking risks and therefore experiencing possible growth

Two Different Outlooks

Martin Seligman discusses how two different types of people, optimists and pessimists, respond to failure. Optimists see defeat as a temporary setback. They view it as a singular situation and do not generalize it to their whole being. They don't blame themselves. If things don't work out, they realize that at least they've tried and make note of what needs further attention to help improve their chances of success when they try again. When optimists are confronted by a bad situation, they perceive it as a challenge and try even harder.

On the other hand, pessimists give up more easily and get depressed more often. Usually the problem lies in their habits of thinking—how they view events and their outlook. If you're more of a pessimist, then you need to develop strategies for correcting distorted thinking (the destructive things we say to ourselves when we experience a setback) and raising self-esteem and confidence. The goal is to go from helplessness to gaining personal control in your life, thereby allowing you a greater chance of experiencing success rather than failure.

FEAR OF SUCCESS

As strange as "fear of success" might sound to some, to others it's a reality. For many of us, success represents the satisfaction of completing a goal with a sense of accomplishment. However, others give up just short of accomplishing the goal. Why? Some people are subconsciously worried that they might look too good and would therefore have to face some unpleasant consequences of recognition. That's being fearful of success.

Yes, even achieving success means facing change and the unknown. With fear of failing, we are afraid of losing our reputation, pride, sense of identity, job, or money, and so we might decide not to compete. With fear of success, one is actually afraid of winning. Central to this concern are the questions: "What will this level of achievement bring in the form of new responsibility, demands, expectations, or resentment (from family members, friends, colleagues, or employers)? Can I make it, if and when I get there?" "Will people treat me differently?" Thus, a fear of success can be part of a future fear of failing.

Jane Burka and Lenora Yuen present the following additional reasons for fearing success:

1. Success may require working longer hours to live up to expectations, possibly becoming a workaholic. If you fear success, you may need to gain better control of your time.

2. You may feel undeserving of success, not good enough to have what you want. This is usually grounded in low self-esteem, but your success might have actually caused problems for others. If so, try to remedy the situation and attempt to move on. If you're stuck in guilt, consider personal counseling.

3. Possible consequences of success include jealousy of others, loss of friends, and loneliness. People who fear success tend to assume responsibility for others' feelings. The most you can ask of yourself is to be conscious of how you're handling your success when around others.

4. Some people fear being punished for their success (almost like a superstition). They might gain center stage and then be vulnerable to some form of challenge or criticism from others, revealing their imperfection.

5. Some people can't even see success having a place in their lives. They see themselves as lacking the traits success requires. Again, this is a self-esteem issue.

A promotion or career change can complicate life with new responsibilities, the challenge of once again proving one's competency, and the need to gain the approval and acceptance of a new supervisor and coworkers. The key is to view changes as challenges and opportunities, rather than obstacles, so you can enjoy and build on your success.

Your success doesn't need to bring about the adverse consequences you fear. By developing your ability fully and achieving all you can, you're showing respect for your gifts as a human being and providing a healthy role model for others. It is true that some people in your life might have difficulty dealing with your success. However, others will take pride and share your joy in your success.

PERFECTIONISM

Perfectionism is related more to unrealistic attitudes than to perfect behavior or performance. High achievers are usually not perfectionists. They realize that at times they will make mistakes or have a bad day. They usually set high goals for themselves, but they are able to tolerate disappointment. Rather than giving up in frustration, they know they can do better, and they work hard to do so.

Perfectionists usually expect more of themselves than is realistic. Everything must be perfect. Their impossibly high expectations cannot be met, but they refuse to accept anything less than exactly what they want. Therefore, they would rather not attempt to reach desired goals if perfection cannot be attained. It's not how high their standards are that makes them perfectionists, but rather how unrealistic and inhibiting their standards are for them.

Just how does one become a perfectionist? One possibility is being taught early in life that self-worth is equal to success. If you grow up learning that nothing is good enough, eventually you see all efforts as inadequate.

Later on, the perfectionist becomes stuck when facing challenges that test skills or put work or ideas on the line. This, again, reflects low self-esteem and an overwhelming need for approval. The need for approval could result in inaction caused by fear of disapproval.

Are You a Perfectionist?

Two sets of characteristics are presented here to help you determine whether you are a perfectionist. The first is a list of general indicators of

being a perfectionist, and the second is a list of beliefs that perfectionists possess.

Ann Smith lists the following indicators of perfectionism:

1. Negative self-talk prevents enjoying still and quiet moments.
2. Feeling as if you're never doing enough, having a long "To
    Do" list.
3. Obsessing about details of a task, anticipating problems before-
    hand, being unable to break tasks down into manageable pieces.
4. Being frustrated with and criticizing others' imperfection.
5. Practicing rigid, purposeless rituals in the name of
    organization, structure, cleanliness, or believing it is the right
    way (e.g., keeping the home in perfect order, ironing
    underwear, spending hours organizing activities and only
    minutes doing them). Applied to job search activities, perfec-
    tionism might lead to constantly revising your resume but
    never sending it out because it isn't good enough.
6. Feeling the need to be the best when competing, yet never
    feeling satisfied with the outcome.
7. Having an all-or-nothing philosophy, believing in absolute
    terms that things are either right or wrong, always or never,
    with no gray areas.
8. Struggling with spirituality, feeling unworthy and judged,
    needing or depending on God, but thinking you must be
    perfect to be accepted.

In addition, Burka and Yuen identify several beliefs of perfectionists:

1. Being ordinary is intolerable. Everything I do must be
    outstanding.
2. I must do everything myself. It's a sign of weakness to relieve
    myself of responsibility by getting assistance (e.g., career
    counseling).
3. There's only one correct solution to a problem, and it's my
    responsibility not to take action until I find it (resulting in
    doing nothing).
4. I must avoid any activity that would bring me into direct
    competition with others, because losing is intolerable.

5. As long as a project is incomplete, nothing has been accomplished.
6. Even small mistakes are catastrophic.

After reviewing the characteristics and beliefs of perfectionists, you probably have a better idea about your own degree of perfectionism (high, medium, low) and in what areas of your life it exhibits itself (work, family, love relationship, friends).

If you are a perfectionist to some degree, one suggestion is to imagine the worst-case scenario for your career situation. Try to visualize it—what do you see? You might visualize a difficult interview, failing once on the job, not getting along with your new supervisor, or being shunned by fellow employees. It might help to remind yourself that although these fantasies are your fears, they're most likely exaggerated. However, let's assume they're not. Once your worst fears are visualized, what can you do to prepare to confront them?

Take, for example, changing careers and failing to perform adequately once on the job because of a lack of skills. If you're interested in a specific job, then your task is to identify exactly what skills are required and at what level of expertise. You need to measure the difference between that and your present skill level. Once you identify the skills you need to gain, and how and where you can gain them, you will be ready to seek employment in that career field once again.

ANXIETY, STRESS, OR DEPRESSION

Fear and anxiety can cloud your thinking and produce a sense of dread and impending doom that reduces your ability to make decisions or take action. You may feel paralyzed and powerless because of your fears.

Many people react to fear and anxiety by avoiding anything that frightens them or makes them anxious. If a decision causes anxiety, one avoids making it. Fears are powerful. They can dictate how you live your life, limit your enjoyment or satisfaction, and cause you problems in trying to make changes in your career and life. Fears can obstruct the career change at any point in the process, from the initial setting of a career objective to the job search itself, including networking and job interviewing.

Work is an important part of our identity, so issues of low self-esteem, fears, anxiety, stress, and depression may result when adults are faced with the threat of change or loss of career. Let's take a closer look at anxiety and the stress it can cause.

Acceptance Anxiety

Changing careers entails a few types of anxiety. The first could be thought of as *acceptance anxiety*. To successfully make a career change, we need to gain the approval of those doing the hiring. For each of us, to different degrees, our sense of self-worth is bound up with the approval of others. The larger that degree, the more anxiety we will experience over being accepted for a particular job.

If we make the desired job or career change, we might continue to experience acceptance anxiety. We have some control over being accepted and liked by supervisors and coworkers, but it is far from complete. Beyond what we learn from the interview process, all we can do is to have a professional attitude, be committed to our work, and show respect for ourselves, our jobs, and others.

However, if poor interpersonal skills have hurt you in your efforts to get along with others in the past, then some corrective action on your part might be necessary. This could include personal counseling (individual or group), as well as communication courses or workshops.

Performance Anxiety

In addition to acceptance anxiety once you're on the job, there's also the possibility of performance anxiety. If you're unsure about how your skills match up to the requirements of the targeted job, you could seek feedback from experts in the field. They may be able to shed some light on the degree to which you have the required skills. Nevertheless, some people hesitate to put themselves to the test because of performance anxiety. Depending on the degree to which it exists, it could create a good deal of stress.

Frustration Anxiety

One other type of general anxiety comes into play when making a career change. Compromise is inevitable in any change; we gain something, yet we have to give up something else. The challenge is to make a change in which you value what you gain more than what you give up. Personal and financial sacrifices are often necessary to achieve your goals, dreams, and ambitions.

For example, a career changer has a job opportunity of greater interest that is more related to his or her long-range goal. However, there is an initial salary cut and less available leisure time. This person will have to weigh the pros (more interesting work leading toward overall career goal) against the cons (initial salary cut and loss of leisure time). Certainly, no one would be happy about the cons, but some people might become downright anxious over it. The thought of not getting all of one's needs met can cause frustration and anxiety.

If you currently suffer from anxiety, is it a normal amount or more severe? Try to recall a recent situation, such as a job interview, in which you strongly desired particular results. Did you experience any of the following symptoms of severe anxiety?

- Dizziness
- Heavy perspiration
- Clammy hands
- Increased heart rate
- Rapid breathing
- Faintness
- Chest pain or pressure

Such severe anxiety does have its consequences. During a job interview it can certainly affect the content of your answers and the style in which you communicate your responses. Other consequences of severe anxiety include being less productive, an inability to concentrate, overcompensating (which others can usually see through), and measuring yourself against an unrealistic standard.

Stress

Anxiety can bring on stress. Stress is what we experience when our body systems perceive and react to an event or situation as threatening or challenging. Therefore, the stress response is both psychological and physiological. The psychological stress may be experienced as anxiety, tension, depression, anger, fear, helplessness, hopelessness, or other emotions.

Physiologically, stress is experienced as a variety of bodily responses: the heart beats a little too fast, blood pressure remains elevated, the stomach fails to digest properly, muscles stay tense, and breathing remains shallow. In time, a stress-related illness can develop. Among these familiar psychosomatic or psychogenic illnesses are headaches, ulcers, lower back pain, and hypertension.

Illnesses not caused by stress can be aggravated by it: asthma, arthritis, diabetes, epilepsy, and even the common cold. This is because stress depletes the body's resources and hinders its innate ability to restore and maintain healthy functioning. If excessive, stress can prevent you from attaining your career goal by reducing your energy, immune response, and confidence. Recognizing the signs of stress is the first step in reducing it.

Fortunately, we have the ability to trigger a mechanism that reverses the stress response: the relaxation response. With relaxation of mind and body, physiological change automatically occurs: the heart rate slows down, blood pressure drops, breathing becomes calm, blood flow increases in the hands and feet, muscles release tension, and there is also a brain wave change. The processes involved in the stress response begin to return to normal functioning.

Body and mind respond equally to stress and relaxation, and with adequate amounts of each, a healthy balance will be maintained. The difficulty is that so often the balance is weighted heavily on the side of stress. We can counter this with techniques that promote deep relaxation.

Depression

At times, when unattended to, our worries and concerns can lead to being depressed. Depression is characterized by feelings of helplessness, hopelessness, inadequacy, and sadness. Some depression is to be expected in situations such as loss of one's job, a career setback, burnout with a job or job search, adverse office politics, or inability to realize one's dream.

However, we must differentiate between mild depression, which is normal in certain circumstances, and severe depression, which impedes one's ability to participate in career planning activities. There are certain "danger signs" used to distinguish among temporary, mild, and severe depressions. If you have five of the following nine symptoms over a two-week period, then you are in a major depressive episode, according to the American Psychiatric Association:

- Depressed mood
- Loss of interest in usual activity
- Loss of appetite
- Insomnia
- Psychomotor retardation (slow thought or movement)
- Loss of energy
- Feelings of worthlessness and guilt
- Diminished ability to think and poor concentration
- Suicidal thought or attempt

If you are experiencing severe depression, obtain professional counseling without delay. Even if you are only moderately depressed, you need to know how to help yourself and when and where to seek help.

Your job success and an optimistic outlook go hand in hand. A confident, upbeat outlook increases your ability to make decisions, which can improve the quality of your life in general and your career specifically. You'll be better equipped to handle setbacks, because you'll view them as challenges and work hard to rise above them.

RELAXATION AND STRESS MANAGEMENT

Relaxation is a skill. Like all skills, learning to relax involves instruction and practice. Let's review a few of the many approaches to managing stress through relaxation. To pursue any of these methods that sound interesting, get the books mentioned here or one of many others on the topic. Courses and workshops on these methods are offered frequently in many areas.

A crucial first step before attempting any of these methods is to consult a physician about your physical preparedness to attempt these techniques. People with heart or respiratory conditions, back problems, or mental health issues, as well as pregnant women, should take special precautions.

We will briefly discuss progressive self-relaxation (PSR), sensory fantasy, Hatha yoga, concentrative meditation, hypnosis, biofeedback, and systematic desensitization.

Progressive self-relaxation (PSR) involves alternately tensing and relaxing different muscle groups until you've moved through your body and achieve a state of complete relaxation. Formal PSR requires that you listen to (or follow) a detailed set of instructions (scripts). There is usually a longer set for the first few weeks of training and then an abbreviated version. The instructions can be memorized or recorded on tape and played back during a relaxation session. Professionally recorded relaxation tapes can be found at bookstores, especially those specializing in East-West psychology, and related music outlets. A good source for PSR, including instructions and scripts, is *BT: Behavior Therapy: Strategies for Solving Problems in Living,* by Spencer Rathus and Jeffrey Nevid. After learning PSR and becoming familiar with the feeling of deep relaxation, you can learn other methods, such as sensory fantasy.

Sensory fantasy involves imagining a special place that was relaxing for you. For example, you might picture yourself at a favorite beach with no one else around. The more vividly you can imagine this scene, the more involved and relaxed the fantasy will be. It's suggested that you visit this special place for 15 minutes, then slowly return to the present. Allow a few minutes to adjust to your actual surroundings. This technique, if practiced regularly, can provide a reliable and effective way of achieving a relaxed state.

Hatha yoga means mastery of body and breath. *Pranayana,* the yogic science of breath control, is at the very heart of Hatha yoga practice. It's believed that stress leads to the contraction of respiratory muscles. Breathing becomes shallower and more restricted, resulting in the intake of less air and thus less oxygen. Through controlled yoga breathing, you may be able to raise your level of vitality, feel more conscious, tone your nervous system, and generally feel better. For a description of the physiological process of breathing, including basic facts related to the anatomy and physiology of respiration, consult *The Complete Yoga Book,* by James Hewitt.

Meditation is a general term applied to the methods of steadying, quieting, or opening the mind for the purpose of expanding states of consciousness, intuitive awareness, and deeper relaxation. **Concentrative meditation** is a yogic practice intended to calm and tone the nervous system and help you relax, thus protecting against stress. This is accomplished by focusing awareness on a fixed point and steadying your mind. Yoga and meditation instruction can be found in a variety of settings: East-West psychology centers, health clubs, adult education centers, and private instruction. For further information with regard to meditation, contact the Institute of Noetic Sciences, Box 909, Sausalito, CA 94966.

Hypnosis is a method of focusing your mind and then using your imagination and thoughts to stir feelings and to alter your behavior and attitude. In hypnosis, you are altering your internal world. Putting yourself into a hypnotic state requires concentration and a tranquil environment. The result can be a more positive outlook and an improved sense of well-being. Hypnosis is simply a focused state of attention and concentration that allows you to use more of the potential and power of your mind.

Your success with self-hypnosis will depend on the nature of your problem, your ability to be hypnotized, and your level of motivation to perform self-hypnosis. The technique seems to work best with relieving anxiety and nervous anticipation (such as at job interviews). If you think you might benefit from hypnotherapy, you should discuss it with your psychologist, physician, or other health care professional. They should be informed enough to discuss with you the pros and cons of this approach in helping you better attain your goals. If your health care professional doesn't seem knowledgeable enough about hypnotherapy to give you a recommendation for or against it, then consult one of the following professional associations for referrals to trained hypnotherapy professionals: American Society of Clinical Hypnosis, 2200 E. Devon Avenue, Suite 291, Des Plaines, IL 60018; or Society for Clinical and Experimental Hypnosis, P.O. Box 26225, Indianapolis, IN 46226.

Biofeedback is a treatment technique in which people are trained to improve their health by using signals from their own bodies. In the term *biofeedback,* the *bio* refers to the biological organs, the human being, and the *feedback* is provided by safe electronic instruments. These instruments are attached to various parts of the human body to measure the strength or intensity of a particular biological signal by a light, a meter, or a tone. For clients, the biofeedback machine acts as a kind of sixth sense that allows them to "see" or "hear" activity inside their bodies.

Once the professional you're working with has ascertained the status of the activity in your muscle or autonomic system, he or she then guides you in your efforts to alter the sounds or image—by finding ways to alter physiological processes within your body. You might use muscle relaxation, breathe more slowly and deeply, or simply think relaxing thoughts to alter these processes. It's a process of trial and error.

Many clients participating in biofeedback training who practice the skills of relaxation and stress management achieve significant symptom reduction and are able to reduce or eliminate related medication (biofeedback therapists work in conjunction with your personal physician). Clients often report a renewed sense of physical and mental well-being and improved self-image. If you think you might benefit from biofeedback training, you should discuss it with your physician or other health care professional. For further assistance, contact the Association for Applied Psychophysiology and Biofeedback, 10200 W. 44th Avenue, Suite 304, Wheat Ridge, CO 80033.

Systematic desensitization through visualization is an approach to help you clearly define the target situation that is causing anxiety, such as a job interview, and imagine yourself going through a series of steps of graduated difficulty, with each more closely approaching the situation you fear. At every step, relaxation techniques are used to help you cope with whatever is fearful for you at that stage. When you are able to imagine yourself in the frightening situation and remain completely relaxed for several minutes, you can then move on to the next step. Eventually you will be able to remain completely relaxed as you picture yourself in the target situation. The desensitization process can rarely be accomplished in one sitting, or even in a few. A desensitization session should not last longer than an hour, and because several sessions may be required to overcome your fear, you may need a considerable length of time to complete a desensitization program. Figure 4.1 details an example of the desensitization process.

FIGURE 4.1

Overcoming Anxiety About the Job Interview
Through Desensitization

APPROACHING THE INTERVIEW

1. Construct a hierarchy of fears by writing each incremental step in the job interview process on a 3 × 5 card. Each step should be only slightly more unsettling than the one before. Here is an example list of incremental steps:

   • Getting up, showering, dressing, and having breakfast

continued

- Leaving home, driving downtown (on the expressway, if applicable) or using public transportation
- Arriving at the office building where the interview will be conducted, parking in an indoor garage (if applicable)
- Entering the building, standing in the lobby, verifying the interview office location, taking the elevator to the appropriate floor
- Exiting the elevator, walking down the hallway, finding the office where the interview is to take place
- Entering the office, announcing yourself to the receptionist, having a seat
- Waiting to be called in for the interview

2. Number the cards 1 to 7, 1 for the least frightening step and 7 for the target situation. Begin each desensitization session by relaxing, using one of the methods previously discussed.

3. Once relaxed, read the first card in your numbered series. Try to accurately imagine the situation on the card. Develop a detailed scene using all your senses: see yourself in the situation, hear the sounds you might hear if you were actually there, feel the sensation, and smell the odors. Maintain this scene in your mind until you begin to feel frightened, then stop your imagining.

4. As you begin to feel fear, make your mind go blank or picture a peaceful, relaxing scene. Continue to practice your relaxation technique until your fear is replaced by a feeling of calm. This could take 2–10 minutes. If unable to achieve calm in 10 minutes, back up to the prior scene, or create an incremental step between the prior step and the current step that you can handle.

5. Try to imagine the same feared situation again. Most likely you'll be able to keep it in mind longer now. When it does become uncomfortable, put the scene out of your mind and relax yourself again. Repeat this process until the situation no longer evokes fear.

6. When you are able to think about the situation for three consecutive times (for several minutes each time) without feeling any fear, then move on to the next card in the series and repeat the process. Continue through the cards using steps 2–5. As a result, you will be able to contemplate the target situation while remaining completely relaxed.

RESPONDING TO INTERVIEW QUESTIONS

1. Write out every possible question you can anticipate that would make you uncomfortable.

continued

2. Develop an answer for each, actually writing them out, then summarize your responses on index cards.

3. Study each question and related responses until you are comfortable in answering them.

4. Now you are ready to proceed in one of the two following ways:

- Order your cards from easiest to most difficult, and use the desensitization approach just described. During your relaxed state, visualize yourself a success in all ways: appearance, speaking voice, and content of answers. You can even envision a positive response from your interviewer, using a tone that indicates you did well.

- Have someone role-play an interview with you, asking the questions in order of difficulty. This will make the desensitization more realistic for you.

Overcoming Distorted Thinking

We've just taken a look at a variety of approaches to help you learn how to relax. Relaxation is a first step in dealing with anxiety, stress, and depressive moods caused by fears and related issues associated with changing careers. These methods, however, don't require paying attention to the thoughts that create your fears. We will now consider the principles of cognitive therapy, which helps to eliminate fears by challenging the irrational beliefs and illogical distortions that cause them.

Cognitive therapy argues that how you think largely determines how you feel and behave. Your emotional and behavioral responses to a situation are largely determined by how you perceive, interpret, and assign meaning to that event. Cognitive therapy attempts to change the way you think about events, in order to change the way you feel and behave. For example, someone who was laid off from a job after ten years could feel overwhelmed with depression and a sense of unfairness. Or the person can decide that this is the "kick in the pants" he or she needed to start a new career.

People form concepts about themselves, others, and how the world operates. These concepts are reinforced by further learning experiences, and they, in turn, influence the formation of other beliefs, values, and attitudes. Cognitive therapists take the approach that it is these beliefs, values, and attitudes that are usually the driving force behind both emotions and behaviors.

When one suffers from distorted or faulty thinking, the results could be disturbed feelings (of discouragement, frustration, or depression) and undesirable behavior. Cognitive therapists believe that you can get better by learning a new set of cognitive skills.

This approach works well with the types of problems and issues that face those wanting to make a career change. Cognitive therapy can be of value in helping career changers to identify and overcome their roadblocks and to relieve inner conflicts that are impeding progress toward their career goals. For example, potential career changers might exaggerate current career problems, disqualify their positive attributes, or think in ways that increase their fears and limit their positive response to possible career transitions. Through cognitive therapy, you can learn to recognize distortions in your own thinking and then substitute a more natural, accurate perception as an alternative for these thoughts.

Three Common Forms of Career Change Negative Thinking

Most negative thinking that occurs in career planning falls into one of three categories.

1. Unrealistically high expectations for performance that can result in self-condemnation, anxiety, and guilt (should, ought to, and must statements):
   "I should not make mistakes."
   "Everyone must like and accept me."
2. Viewing oneself in a limiting way, in a self-deprecating manner:
   "I can't change careers; I'm not smart enough to be successful in a job like that."
   "If I change, I'll probably fail, because I'll be unable to achieve the support of my coworkers and my supervisor."
3. Unrealistic expectations of other people or of life itself:
   "I keep getting rejected in my job search. I'm not meant to be successful."
   "Why continue with my job search—other employers will also reject me."
   "Life shouldn't be this tough; getting a job should be easy."

As you become more aware of these areas of distorted thinking, try to be aware of how they apply to what you're thinking or feeling. In the area of career change, being held back by distorted thinking is a serious problem. Much of people's anxieties, fears, guilt, low self-esteem, and irrational behavior is generated from beliefs, attitudes, and expectations that are often unconscious and unexamined yet play a large role in career changers' lives.

An important strategy that can be applied to a situation like this is reality testing. Most fears in the career change process originate from exaggerated views of what success really is, misconceptions about how many people do actually fail at a particular job, and not recognizing the extent to which your dedication, a solid work ethic, and good career planning can reduce the possibility of failing. Therefore, it makes sense to examine your thoughts in the light of reality and rationality.

Steps in Applying Cognitive Therapy

Five general steps can be taken in cognitive therapy, with a professional therapist, to challenge possible unrealistic and irrational thinking:

1. Identify the feeling (e.g., fear of failing).
2. Identify the thoughts, beliefs, and attitudes that are associated with the feeling.
3. Examine the thoughts in the light of reality and rationality.
4. Ask questions:
   a. Is there evidence of the truth of this belief?
   b. If there is no evidence, are there any other explanations?
   c. As bad as it seems, how is it in light of other terrible things that could happen?
   d. How likely is it that the dreadful consequences will occur?
   e. How reasonable are your expectations or standards for judging performance?
5. Assign homework to test the validity of beliefs or ideas.

By following these steps, you might discover that you had an inaccurate view of your own ability, were using an unrealistic measuring stick to assess potential, or were overplaying the impact of changes in your lifestyle.

As effective as cognitive therapy can be, keep one thing in mind: When confronting long-held beliefs, ideas, values, or attitudes, you will often experience painful thought confusion. This confusion may give rise to anger, guilt, or helplessness and probably strong resistance to future introspection and exploration. Introspection and exploration can be thought of as a journey into unfamiliar territory. Whenever you travel into unfamiliar territory, it's not a bad idea to have a guide (professional personal counseling). The therapist is not someone who will do things for you, but rather someone who will help point things out, like road signs along the highway. You will still be the one to make the decisions and to take the necessary action.

Thus far, we've looked at an overview of cognitive therapy and identified general steps in dealing with distorted thinking. Now let's examine two specific techniques that can be used within the context of cognitive therapy, constructive self-talk and the ABC method.

Constructive Self-Talk   One thing you might inadvertently do as you deal with the anxiety and stress of a career change is make negative statements to yourself that promote a self-fulfilling prophecy. Here is an example of negative self-talk and a more constructive approach:

- **Old self-talk:** "I don't have enough patience to make it through the job search any longer. I can hardly take another rejection."

- **New self-talk:** "I *have just enough patience* to make it through the job search for tomorrow. I can handle one more possible rejection. If it occurs, I plan to . . ."

Take the job search and break it down into more manageable pieces. Take one day at a time. This positive approach assesses what you have left to work with, not what you have lost. When the going gets tough, you will benefit most from actually saying to yourself, out loud, while you *visualize* it, "I have just enough   (of the resource I need)   to   (reach my goal) ."

A worthwhile new habit is to learn how to encourage, not discourage, yourself. Of course, you have to believe that you do have the inner resources you need. The word *believe* might trouble you if you find it difficult to truly believe in yourself. Recognize that self-esteem is the core of self-belief, and you can do something about raising your self-esteem.

The ABC Method   ABC is a method developed by Albert Ellis, the founder of Rational Emotive Therapy (RET), which has much in common with cognitive therapy. When you encounter adversity, you react by thinking about it. Your thoughts then quickly form beliefs that have certain consequences. The beliefs are the direct cause of what you feel and what you do next. Your beliefs can be the difference between objecting and giving up, on the one hand, and positive thinking with constructive action, on the other.

The first step in applying the ABC method is to see the connection among adversity, belief, and consequence. Let's take, for example, a frustrated job searcher who has been experiencing a number of rejections following interviews.

A. **Adversity:** The most recent rejection

B. **Beliefs:**

I'm really not that good; everybody can see it, thus the rejection.
I must come off terribly during the interview process.
Most likely the type of job I'm pursuing is not a good match for me, so I'll never get hired.
Why go on with this career change effort? Life just isn't fair.

C. **Consequence:** This distorted thinking becomes a self-fulfilling prophecy, resulting in anxiety, stress, or depression.

By applying some cognitive therapy techniques, our job searcher can find the link between unfounded beliefs and the consequences. Distorted thinking leads to inaction and dejection, whereas more explanation can create energy and help bring about more positive results. Therefore, changing habitual beliefs becomes a priority. Two general ways to alter distorted thinking and beliefs, once you're aware of them, are to distract yourself when they occur and to dispute them, which is more effective in the long run, because you're less likely to experience a recurrence.

Disputation entails giving your distorted thoughts and beliefs an argument. By effectively disputing the beliefs that follow adversity, you can change your automatic (immediate) reaction from dejection and giving up to positive action.

- **Belief:** I must come off terribly during the interview process.

- **Disputation:** Not necessarily. The competition is also excellent, so of course I have some "no's" to go through before I reach that one, all-important "yes."

For an excellent discussion of the disputation technique, see *Learned Optimism,* by Martin Seligman.

The next chapter offers strategies for increasing your self-esteem, which can have a positive impact on your career planning efforts.

CHAPTER 5

INCREASING YOUR SELF-ESTEEM

✮

A KEY INGREDIENT IN CAREER PLANNING

Self-esteem is a major factor in success or failure, in every aspect of your life, and especially in your career. Our self-concept influences all of our significant choices and decisions and therefore helps to shape the kind of life we create for ourselves. This includes how we view the world around us and what we consider to be potential career choices.

The development of your self-confidence and self-acceptance is related to how your parents, teachers, friends, and others around you reacted to you as you grew up. In addition, much of your own present sense of self-confidence comes from your career. A job well done can be self-satisfying and also generate positive feedback from those around you: supervisors, coworkers, family, and friends.

Low self-esteem leads to feelings of inadequacy, insecurity, self-doubt, lack of assertiveness, fear of failing, irrational beliefs, procrastination, and depression, all of which adversely affect one's efforts in changing careers.

The link between self-esteem and your career is so strong that any serious self-esteem issues should be the primary focus of counseling before any career planning work is done. Before undertaking career-related self-assessments (interests, values, skills, and related preferences), self-esteem issues must be addressed.

Adults with low self-esteem are likely to misjudge themselves. They are less likely to own their skills or feel entitled to their interests and dreams. Therefore, career planning efforts should be put on hold for a while, if possible, until a healthier frame of mind can be developed.

Living Consciously, Responsibly, and Authentically

In *How to Raise Your Self-Esteem,* Nathaniel Branden states that we can increase our self-esteem by living our lives consciously, responsibly, and authentically.

Living Consciously

Living consciously is the basis of self-confidence and self-respect. To live consciously means to attempt to be aware of everything that leads to our actions, purpose, values, and goals and to act appropriately. Living consciously means taking responsibility for being aware of the decisions we need to make. In any given situation, living consciously means generating a state of mind that fits the task at hand.

In the situation of changing careers, living consciously could mean facing any current unhappiness and feelings of depression and the need to change, facing fears about changing careers, and then taking appropriate actions to help resolve these difficulties rather than denying and burying them. When you learn to accept fear, you cease to be a slave to it. You cannot overcome a fear whose reality you deny.

Living Responsibly

Living responsibly means realizing that you are responsible for your choices and actions: how you spend your time, the level of consciousness you bring to your work, how you care for your body, the relationships you choose to enter or remain in, how you treat others, the meaning you give to your existence, your own happiness, and your life (materially, emotionally, intellectually, and spiritually).

Being responsible, in this context, means being the main causal agent in your life, not the recipient of blame or guilt. It's saying to yourself, for example, "Why do I make myself so lazy when it comes to my job search?" rather than, "Why am I so lazy?" This is not to say that one never suffers through the fault of others, or even accidents, or that you are responsible for everything that happens to you. You need to know what is within your control and what is not.

Where does your responsibility start and end in comparison with others you are dealing with? If you take responsibility for matters beyond your control, your self-esteem will be at risk. You'll fail to meet your own expectations. Likewise, if you fail to take responsibility for matters that are within your control, your self-esteem again will be at risk.

It is through actions that an attitude of self-responsibility is implemented and expressed. Ask yourself, "What actions will bring me closer to my goals and advance my career?" By living consciously and taking responsibility, you gain greater control over the direction of your life.

Living Authentically

Good self-esteem also demands congruence, living authentically. To live authentically means being truthful to yourself and others. Honesty consists of respecting the difference between the real and the unreal. Yet many of us have shut down our inner self and have chosen to become unconscious. Thus, it takes courage and independence to attain authenticity, to face the good with the bad in our lives.

Living authentically incorporates the following traits and qualities:

- You're usually honest with yourself and others.
- You strive to be truthful when communicating with others.
- You're open about what it is that you love, admire, and enjoy.
- If experiencing hurt or anger, you usually talk about it with honesty and dignity.
- You honor your needs and interests by standing up for yourself.
- You don't mind others' seeing your excitement.

- You can acknowledge when you're wrong.

- You present the self you feel on the inside the same as the self you present to the outside.

To grow in self-esteem means leaving our comfort zone and entering the unknown. This entails risk, but all change involves some degree of risk.

The Reactions of Those Close to You

As you succeed in increasing your self-esteem by living more consciously, responsibly, and authentically, others around you will either adjust to your new self or attempt to maneuver you back into your old self-concept. This is because people are used to dealing with you in a certain way, and your change is making them readjust. Some relationships will remain intact, but others will not. Again, a part of change is letting go, and being realistic means accepting the fact that we can't have everything.

Healthy individuals with high self-esteem are not always liked, because they are usually more independent, outspoken, direct, and self-assertive. This can bring out envy and hostility in certain people, especially conventional types. Most people are somewhat insecure. If you're insecure and not very happy, it's hard to recognize and accept others who are secure and happy.

Don't confuse liking yourself and appreciating your own self-worth with being selfish and self-centered. It's the way you handle yourself with others that determines whether you are acting in a selfish or self-centered manner. Therefore, it is worthwhile to monitor yourself. The best guide for you to follow could be that if you live your life consciously, responsibly, and authentically (and treat others with respect), you must be on the right track.

GOAL SETTING

The Importance of Decision Making

Even though much that happens in our lives is by chance, it's important to recognize the power we do have to influence and control situations and events in meeting our goals. One way to illustrate this is to think back to some recent, positive development you experienced on the job. Was it the result of chance, or had you taken specific action that helped to bring about the positive result? Chances are that you made a decision along the way that influenced the positive outcome.

It might be helpful to take a look at your decision-making style at this point. Is the process you use satisfactory to you? When you review past major decisions, such as choice of education, spouse or significant other, job, or a major purchase, what conclusion are you able to make about how you went about your decision making?

Effective decision making is influenced by information gathering, timing, and willingness to take a risk. Adequate information allows you not only to determine your alternatives, but also to assess the pros and cons of each. If you did not have enough information in a particular decision, how did it affect the outcome? What might you do differently in the future? Your timing might have been just right, or perhaps it was off. You might have made a decision too quickly, only to regret it later, or too slowly and missed out on valuable options. What might you do differently in the future to be better prepared and therefore respond in a more timely manner? In your past decisions, how much of a challenge were you willing to take? Perhaps too much, and you paid the price with negative results. Or maybe you accepted too little challenge, deciding to play it safe and yet paying a price for that as well, in terms of less satisfaction.

You might also ask yourself, "Have my decisions been consistent with my values?" Your overall satisfaction and happiness will be enhanced when your decision making matches as closely as possible with the things, ideas, or beliefs that you value the most. Obviously, decisions most closely in line with your values have a greater chance of being carried through to completion.

Decision-Making Styles

Which style do you believe characterizes most of your important decisions? If after identifying your decision-making style you are not pleased with the way you have made decisions in the past, you now have an opportunity to change your style and apply some of what you learned here to present and future decisions. Following are some decision-making styles:

Planned:	Gathering information and applying a methodical, deliberate, and judgmental approach that is balanced between cognitive and emotional factors in weighing the facts
Agonizing:	Too involved with gathering information and analyzing the alternatives, getting lost in the data, so much so that it's difficult to make up your mind
Impulsive:	Take action too quickly, usually the first alternative, based largely on emotion without gathering necessary information
Intuitive:	Somewhat mystical, based on what "feels right," non-verbalized emotion
Avoidance:	• **No decision:** Fatalistic, leaving to fate—"It doesn't matter what I do."
	• **Procrastinating:** Delaying, keep putting off, can't get started
	• **Accommodating:** Compliant, let someone else decide—"Whatever you say is fine with me."

Whichever decision-making style you normally use, try to adopt the planned style: gathering information and weighing the pros and cons of each alternative. This is important especially when it comes to your career, because the process requires time and thoughtful study. Following is a decision-making model that can help you carry through changes and increase the possibility of becoming a more effective decision maker:

1. Identify the decision that needs to be made precisely and completely.
   What is the problem?
   How important is the decision?
   How soon must you decide?
2. Gather information and evaluate the quality of your data.
   Is it complete?
   Is it unbiased?
3. List possible actions that you might take.
   Brainstorm—identify every possible action.
   Discard those that are obviously unacceptable.

4. List the advantages and disadvantages of alternative choices.
   What are the probable outcomes of each?
   What are other possible outcomes?

5. Weigh the pros and cons of the various actions carefully.
   Which are consistent with your values?

6. Develop strategies to follow (similar to goal setting).

The Role of Risk

All change involves some risk. The risk is the uncertainty of not knowing the outcome of the intended change in advance. This in turn could create anxiety that results from fearing the unknown.

Growth simply cannot occur without your taking chances. Growth takes you to uncharted territory, creating uncertainty and potential danger. This is part of the process of change. However, this doesn't mean you have to go out on a limb. Through examining your needs, recognizing your self-worth, accepting that you deserve the very best you can attain for yourself, applying a sound goal-setting strategy (see next section), and taking the responsibility for acting, you'll be able to approach taking risks in a sensible and viable manner, which will lead to the accomplishment of your goals.

The first step in deciding whether to attempt the risk of changing careers is to admit to yourself what degree of unhappiness your current position holds for you. Are you where you'd like to be? Do you think your career should be more than it is, that you should feel more satisfaction than you are? Think about times in the past when you have risked, whether at work, with family, or in a love relationship. Look to see what you feared and how you felt before taking the risk. What actions did you take that helped you push through your fears? Think about how these past experiences can help you with your current risk of changing careers.

Setting and Accomplishing Your Goals

Part of undertaking change is risking, and part of risking is dealing with the unfamiliar, thus creating fear and anxiety. This makes it important to understand what you can and can't control and to be realistic about what you can and can't achieve. You can get beyond fears and anxieties by exercising good, sound planning and taking smart, calculated risks.

Applying goal-setting criteria is a method you can use to accomplish more of what you want. Goal setting, if you take it seriously, is a process of taking greater control over your life. Three basic guidelines for goal setting are breaking a goal into smaller steps, staying flexible, and challenging yourself.

Breaking a Goal into Smaller Steps   Over time, achieving a series of small successes can lead to your feeling better about yourself as a result of accomplishing your goals. Therefore, start small. Break down larger goals into more manageable pieces.

Let's take the goal of revising your chronological resume into more of a functional/chronological combination. This is a good goal example because revising resumes often feels overwhelming at first. Because you're changing careers, this format (emphasizing your functional skills, with a chronological work history at the end) will serve your purposes more effectively than the chronological format, which emphasizes your past job titles and employers. Let's assume you have established an objective and have done some preliminary research into the skills required for the position you intend to apply for. In addition, you've assessed your skills from past positions.

First, we will break up this ambitious task into smaller, more manageable steps:

1. Purchase, or borrow from a library, a resume guide that emphasizes functional resumes, such as Yana Parker's *Damn Good Resume Guide.* Spend a couple of days looking it over, noting resume examples that are for jobs similar to your objective. Specifically, note the major skill categories being emphasized and the action verb statements in each.

2. Identify the three to five major functional skill categories you wish to emphasize. This is where your skill assessment comes in handy, as you combine the skills you now have with the major transferable/functional skill categories that relate to your job objective.

3. Develop two to four skill statements, using action verbs, for each of your three to five major skill categories.

4. Develop a chronological section that includes past job titles, employers, and dates. No description is necessary here. This

section shows potential employers that you are not trying to hide gaps in your work history.

5. Develop your education section with the usual information, including special honors.

6. Include other relevant information (professional association membership and activities, honors, related accomplishments).

7. Have your resume professionally typed and printed.

Does changing the format of your resume seem less overwhelming to you now? Would you feel more inclined to give it a try with this approach? The idea here is to enhance the likelihood of your accomplishing your goals by taking each goal one manageable step at a time.

Even a long-range goal such as your job search can be broken down into month-to-month, week-to-week, and day-to-day manageable steps. The steps related to the job search, in addition to updating your resume, could include the following:

- Read up on interviewing skills and job search methods.

- Attend networking-related meetings and seminars.

- Contact employers.

To break these goals into smaller steps, you need to sit down and figure out specifically what it is you want to do, how long it would take, and when you want to do it and then put together your plan.

Staying Flexible   As you go about accomplishing your goal, remember that sometimes circumstances and events alter your situation. You will need to readjust your goal—either the time you've allowed yourself, the method you intended to use, or other aspects. You must remain flexible so that when legitimate factors arise, you can alter the original goal to meet the new situation. In fact, if you're working on a long-range goal of a month or more, you can expect, at the very least, to make some weekly adjustments. These adjustments are usually minor and don't deviate from your original plan by a day or more, unless some major interruption occurs.

Challenging Yourself   Try to include some challenge in your goals. When you're first starting out, it could be a small challenge. As you get more into it, gradually increase the challenge. In goal setting, the possibility of failure actually has a positive side—it provides a challenge. Your level of satisfaction and accomplishment will usually be directly proportional to the amount of challenge you create. The accumulation of small successes can add up and help you feel better about yourself.

Criteria for Goal Setting

James McHolland presents the following criteria to assure that goals are achievable. As you set a goal, be sure it meets each criterion.

Desirable Do you really want to accomplish this goal? If you don't want to, the odds are pretty good that you won't. This criterion is not a *should* or a *have to,* but rather a *want to.*

Believable Do you believe you can accomplish your goal? Is it realistic? Believing is a powerful aspect of goal setting. You want to set goals that are within your reach.

Achievable Do you see this goal as being possible to achieve? Do you have enough time to accomplish your goal? If you're not organized about your time, create a weekly schedule: block off all work hours, travel hours, family responsibilities, and so forth. Once a week, figure out what you need to accomplish during the following week. Estimate the time each goal will take, and plug them into the open slots of your schedule. Being organized with your time is a key ingredient in helping to ensure the accomplishment of your goals.

Measurable Is your goal stated in specific and concrete terms, so that it is clear when you have accomplished your goal? Stating that you will "work on your resume" is not specific and concrete. However, stating that "for the next three days, I will spend two hours per day developing skill statements of two major skill categories" is both specific and concrete. In this way, it will be clear when you've accomplished your goal.

Focused Is your goal presented without an alternative? Statements like "I'll do some work on my resume or call for two information interviews" are not acceptable. Decide which you want to do more, set it as your goal, and then do it. Being clear and focused about your goal setting helps to ensure success.

Values-Oriented Is the goal consistent with your value system? Maybe a high value of yours is family, and you have plans to be with them during the next day. Even though you hold changing careers high as a value, it might not rank as high as your family and your plans with them. However, you mistakenly planned to work on your resume on the same day, which might create a conflict with your family plans. It may be best to reschedule the resume writing goal to avoid a values conflict with your family plans.

Noninjurious Is the goal noninjurious to yourself and others? This criterion usually pertains to physical goals, such as exercise and diet plans. However, other goals could be injurious to self or others in physical or emotional ways. Perhaps your career goals are running you into the ground, causing undue additional stress. It would seem wise to reorganize the focus of your career planning efforts and establish a healthier pace.

Independent Are you depending on anyone else for the accomplishment of your goal? If so, you've just opened the door to not accomplishing your goal. State your goal in an independent manner, and rely on no one but yourself. Take full responsibility for accomplishing your goal.

If for some reason you don't accomplish your goal, try to figure out what happened. What kept you from accomplishing your goal? Review the

---

CAREER CHANGER UPDATE

★

Larry, usually an excellent planner, goal setter (life- and work-related), and achiever, lost track of his goals upon starting a national position in corporate America, due to a heavy workload. He felt that work had taken over his life, and he lost focus of the other areas of his life, which got left out of his planning. These included family, friends, and leisure activities.

Now, as he begins to refocus and undertake a new job search (hopefully leading to a position that allows more balance in his life), he intends to resume his goal setting and planning. Larry plans to revisit his goals at least every week to see how things are going and if any adjustments need to be made.

criteria to see if the mishap can be explained by having not met certain criteria that you thought would be met. Make a note of the mishap, and as you set future goals, consider these experiences and pay particular attention to related criteria. Learn from your mistakes, use the criteria in a positive, not a punitive way, still helping to ensure future successes.

One suggestion is to keep a daily journal of what you accomplish. Evidence of small, steady actions recorded in your journal can help validate your progress. You'll be able to refer to it and see how your small, successful steps can add up. Keeping a daily journal is a method to help you see your real progress and increase your self-esteem. In the journal include the date, what was accomplished, and a few words about how you felt about it.

When you do accomplish your goals, it's a good idea to reward yourself in some manner. Perhaps you will allow yourself some small luxury that you seldom pursue. This could range from buying a new compact disc to dining at a French restaurant with someone special, and many things in between.

DEVELOPING YOUR SUPPORT SYSTEM

A support system is a set of people who will listen, understand, and offer suggestions and feedback about your career changing and job search experience. Members of your support system should not make decisions or take actions for you. Rather, they serve as a sounding board for you to bounce ideas off of and receive additional points of view and insight.

Seeking support does not mean you're a failure, incompetent, or weak. It means that you've realized it's unrealistic to expect yourself to go through this experience alone. As long as you fulfill your responsibilities for your career change and don't expect others to do things for you that you should be doing for yourself, there's nothing wrong with seeking encouragement, feedback, and support from others along the way. In fact, at times you might get stuck in a step of the process, and members of your support system can help to get you back on track.

Choosing the Right People

Many different individuals can be part of your support system. However, not everyone has the right qualities to serve your best interests. Probably the most important quality to look for in potential support system members is being an objective listener. In addition to the person's being a good listener, it is important to find someone who is mostly on your side and tries to see things from your point of view.

Of course, if you become unrealistic and irrational, a solid support system member will recognize this and point it out to you in a noncritical and nonjudgmental manner. Criticism and judgment are not supportive, as they tend to reinforce your critical view of yourself. In addition, unconditional praise is not really supportive either.

It's important for you to recognize the various strengths that your support system members have to offer. Examples follow of different strengths members could offer:

- Someone who is good to brainstorm business-related ideas with
- Someone who is adept at planning the job search strategy (from resume writing to networking to job interviewing)
- Someone who can listen when that's all you need and want
- Someone to schedule free time with to break up the stress a career change/job search can generate

People to exclude from your support system are those who have their own issues to deal with. This prevents them from being supportive in the way you might like. They could be competitive, jealous, threatened, or indifferent.

Gaining Family Support

Support of family members is most important for a career changer/job searcher, for you are never a career changer on your own. Those in your immediate family feel the impact as well, especially if you are married with children. Spouses, children, and significant others might be used to a certain lifestyle. It could be difficult for them to sacrifice in this area while you go about your career change. So this process is difficult for them as well as you. Career change can take time, especially if additional education or training is necessary. Family members' patience may waiver at times if they don't fully realize the ordeal that this is for you.

The best way to gain family members' support is through communication. Keep them aware of your career change, every step of the way. Let them know the goals you plan to accomplish on a daily, weekly, even monthly basis. This shows some sense of direction and responsibility on your part, which can serve to help all of you. When your family members see you motivated and accomplishing your goals, it will be easier for them to make necessary sacrifices and be supportive toward you. Don't be afraid to let them know how they can help you and that you realize the impact this has on them as well.

The hardest time will occur when you become stuck and are unsure of your next move. If family members are in the dark, it will be hard for them to remain patient and supportive. Be open about being stuck, but try to develop a plan to get unstuck and start taking steps in that direction. When family members see positive steps, even small ones, and are kept informed, they will usually hang in there with you. It's your responsibility not to be unreasonable, however, in your expectations of them. Be fair to yourself and them as well.

The economic benefit of being recently remarried helped Zephree to be able to afford a significant cut in salary in changing careers. Ed claims he would never have made it without his wife's income. Vincent credits his wife's emotional support as being most helpful. He adds, "If your spouse (or significant other) isn't behind you, you're not going to make it." Vincent's wife's encouragement along the way to the opening of his bookstore proved to be the caring and support he needed as he moved through his career transition.

Sandra got help from numerous family members with her publishing business. From her packaging needs to delivery and distribution services, family proved to be a key to Sandra's success.

Support Groups

There's something to be said about being part of a group that is going through the same life experience as you. Usually, career change support groups will consist of members at various stages of the process. Some will be just starting out on a job search, others will be well into the process, and still others will have completed the process and will soon be moving on. The members represent a wealth of experience that you as a member can tap into, as well as sharing what you know with them. Ten heads are surely better than one when it comes to problem solving.

Career change support groups can be found in a variety of settings:

- Adult continuing education centers
- Community colleges (most serve nonstudents)
- Universities (especially noncredit programs)
- Places of worship (churches and synagogues)
- HMO/hospital self-help/education programs
- Career counselors in private practice
- Social service agencies (e.g., Jewish Vocational Service)
- Community mental health centers

A few phone calls to career counselors in your area will help you identify related groups. In addition, you can contact the following national clearinghouses for support groups in your area: American Self-Help Clearinghouse, Northwest Covenant Medical Center, 25 Pocono Road, Denville, NJ 07834; and National Self-Help Clearinghouse, 25 W. 43rd Street, Room 620, New York, NY 10036.

Group members can be sources of valuable information, insights into the process, and contacts for you to expand your network. It helps you avoid feeling alone as you go through the often difficult career change process. Of course, you must be brave enough to join one. Seeking out help can be hard for some. They don't like to admit that they need it. It is not a weakness. The only related weakness here is being too stubborn to realize that it's unrealistic to go through a career change on your own and, therefore, choosing not to seek help from others.

GETTING PERSONAL OR CAREER COUNSELING ASSISTANCE

You may find that after reading all the suggestions in this chapter and in Chapter 4, you're still somewhat stuck. Nothing seems to be helping you get back on track. You may be experiencing any of the following:

- Significant lack of confidence and self-esteem
- Continuing indecisiveness and procrastination

- An unwillingness to make a commitment toward one goal and having to then let go of other possibilities

- Your fears of change, failing, or success are controlling you, and you're stressed out

- You meet the clinical definition of depression provided earlier and see no change over a period of months

- Problems that are not directly career change related (substance abuse or difficulties with spouse or significant other) that can negatively impact your career change process

In this case, you should consider pursuing either personal mental health assistance or professional career counseling, depending on your unique situation.

Personal Mental Health Assistance

One of the first issues you will want to know about a counselor or therapist is his or her approach to counseling. This can refer to either a formal counseling technique, following a certain theoretical approach, or simply the person's own way of viewing problem solving.

Most effective counseling professionals combine features from different approaches to counseling, depending on the problem that the client may have at a given time. However, some counseling professionals do identify with a specific approach. Ask the counseling professional, "How do you see the problem I'm dealing with?" or "What form of counseling/therapy will you be using?"

Following are some suggested sources for information about and referrals to reputable counseling:

1. Check with family and friends with whom you're willing to be open.

2. Ask your personal physician.

3. Contact related professional associations. (See Appendix C.)

4. Contact directors of counseling centers at local universities, colleges, and community colleges. (Often community college counselors will see nonstudents at a reduced rate as compared with those in private practice.)

5. Contact local universities that have a graduate-level counseling psychology training program. Many of their faculty will have private practices, as well as be familiar with professional and community resources.

6. Contact the psychiatry department of local medical schools.

7. Contact faculty from undergraduate psychology departments at local universities, colleges, and community colleges.

8. If your city or state has community mental health centers, you could get help there. They might also be able to make a referral for you.

9. Your priest, pastor, or rabbi sometimes can provide services and make referrals as well.

10. The phone book has listings of counseling professionals in your area.

If you do pursue counseling, you should be able to decide after six to eight visits whether it is "working." At this point, trust is important because you will be starting to reveal more and more about yourself. You might begin to feel a sense of relief and a sense of hope. Your problems might not feel "solved," but you should be starting to feel that they could be. You should feel in control of your counseling. "In control" means you're an active partner in this process. Self-disclosure needs to evolve at a pace that is comfortable for you. You may talk about whatever you wish; the subject is up to you. Your rapport with your counselor or therapist is crucial to your success in the counseling process. You should feel that you're being helped and that you are responsible for your progress.

Your sense of personal comfort with your counseling professional is most important. Ask yourself the following questions:

- Can I trust this person?

- Does he or she remember what I said?

- Does he or she have a sense of me as an individual?

- Am I being understood?

These questions will better enable you to assess the "fit." Don't feel compelled to stay in a situation that you feel isn't working. Seek out additional referrals and check them out. In addition to evaluating your professional counselor, be sure to do some self-evaluation as well. Are you being honest with yourself and the counselor? Do you sense that you're dealing with your important issues? Discomfort can be a healthy sign in this process, to a degree. It could indicate you're really facing your issues and being responsible about owning them and doing something about them.

Career Counseling Assistance: NCDA Consumer Guidelines for Selecting a Career Counselor

Career counseling requires the expertise of a trained professional. Be skeptical of services that promise you more money, quick promotions, better jobs, resumes that get speedy results, or an immediate solution to a career problem. Career issues are usually complex and require a multifaceted approach by a career counselor who has extensive education, training, and experience.

The following guidelines, developed by the National Career Development Association (NCDA), can assist you in making this selection.

Credentials of the Professional Career Counselor   A Nationally Certified Career Counselor (NCCC) signifies that the career counselor has achieved the highest certification in the profession. Further, it means that the career counselor has

- Earned a graduate degree in counseling or in a related professional field from a regionally accredited higher education institution
- Completed supervised counseling experience that included career counseling
- Acquired a minimum of three years of full-time career development work experience
- Obtained written endorsements of competence from a work supervisor and a professional colleague
- Successfully completed a knowledge-based certification examination

---

PROFESSIONAL COUNSELING ORGANIZATIONS
Related Internet Sites
- National Board for Certified Counselors: http://www.nbcc.org
- National Career Development Association: http://www/ncda.org

---

Other professional counselors may be trained in one- or two-year counselor preparation programs with specialties in career counseling and may be licensed by state counselor licensure boards or certified by the National Board for Certified Counselors.

What Career Counselors Do   The services of career counselors differ, depending on competence. A professional or Nationally Certified Career Counselor helps people make decisions and plans related to life/career directions. The strategies and techniques are tailored to the specific needs of the person seeking help. It is likely that the career counselor will do one or more of the following:

- Conduct individual and group/personal counseling sessions to help clarify life/career goals.

- Administer and interpret tests and inventories to assess abilities and interests and to identify career options.

- Encourage exploratory activities through assignments and planning experiences.

- Utilize career planning systems and occupational information systems to help individuals better understand the world of work.

- Provide opportunities for improving decision-making skills.

- Assist in developing individualized career plans.

- Teach job-hunting strategies and skills and assist in the development of resumes.

- Help resolve potential personal conflicts on the job through practice in human relations skills.

- Assist in understanding the integration of work and other life roles.

- Provide support for persons experiencing job stress, job loss, and career transition.

Ask for a detailed explanation of services (career counseling, testing, planning employment search strategy, resume writing). Make sure you understand the service, your degree of involvement, and any financial commitment.

Fees   Select a counselor who is professionally trained and will let you choose the services you desire. Make certain you can terminate the services at any time, paying only for services rendered.

Promises   Be skeptical of services that make promises of more money, better jobs, resumes that get speedy results, or an immediate solution to career problems.

Ethical Practices   A professional or Nationally Certified Career Counselor is expected to follow ethical guidelines of such organizations as the National Career Development Association, the American Counseling Association, and the American Psychological Association. Professional codes of ethics advise against grandiose guarantees and promises, exorbitant fees, and breaches of confidentiality, among other things. You might wish to ask for a detailed explanation not only of services offered, as suggested earlier, but also of your financial and time commitments, and a copy of the ethical guidelines used by the career counselor you are considering.

Package Deals and Contracts   The fact that an organization offers a package deal, in the form of a contract with a large up-front fee, in itself does not mean it is unethical. A recent survey of California career counselors revealed that the average number of appointments for career counseling clients was four to five. Most likely this means two things are occurring, since testing and assessment alone should take three to five appointments and resume writing, two to three appointments, and the job search process as a whole benefits from periodic meetings over numerous months.

First, career counseling clients are choosing, in many cases, not to complete the process with the counselor. They're either completing it on their own or deciding to stay put in the current career situation. Career changers who are good at pencil-and-paper tasks might be less comfortable with face-to-face encounters with employers and tend to drop out of counseling. Second, career counselors may be having a difficult time maintaining a financially viable practice, continually having to market for new clients due to a quick turnover.

Therefore, a package deal with a competent and ethical career counselor locks the career changer into the process. People are less likely to drop out if it's already paid for. This is to their advantage, especially if they would have dropped out otherwise. A package deal also helps the career counselor to pay bills and maintain the practice. However, not everyone who offers a package deal is necessarily competent or ethical. That's why it's important to ask questions such as the following:

- What will be done, and by whom?
- Is there a cut-off point with regard to refunds? (If so, don't expect much after that date.)
- Is there an upper limit in the amount of time they will spend with you? Per week? For X number of months?

If there is a contract, don't sign it until you understand everything clearly and agree. (Have your lawyer take a look, as well.)

Obtaining a Career Counseling Referral   The following are sources that you could contact for a referral to a career counselor:

National Board for Certified Counselors: Call or write for a list of National Certified Career Counselors (NCCC) in your area: National Board for Certified Counselors, 3 Terrace Way, Suite D, Greensboro, NC 27403.

Your network of contacts: Ask around, including family and friends, if anyone knows of a qualified career counselor.

Local college career counselor: Contact career counselors at local community colleges (they may offer services through the college to members of the community at a reduced or reasonable fee, compared with private-practice career counselors) or universities for referrals to private-practice career counselors who offer their services to the public. In fact, they themselves might also have a private practice, in addition to the college position.

Local college placement office: Professional staff (directors or assistant directors of placement) will know of those in the community doing career counseling. Their offices can be known by a variety of names:

- Placement Office
- Career Placement Office
- Career Planning and Placement Office
- Career Planning and Development Office

The university you graduated from might have services for its alumni. If you do not live in the area, you might still call the university for a referral to someone near you, or they may have (or be willing to set up) a reciprocal agreement with a university placement office closer to where you live.

Social service organization staff: Contact places such as the Jewish Vocational Service, Forty Plus, Operation Able, women's centers, and so forth. They might either provide the services you're looking for or provide a referral.

Churches and synagogues: Some local churches and synagogues may offer support groups, resources for researching career ideas and employers, and individual counseling.

Public libraries: Librarians in business reference sections or educational and job information centers (more than 100 nationwide) offer workshops, lectures, resource materials, and computer use, as well as possible referrals to career counselors and related resources in the community.

Other options: You can also try the following for a referral: your physician, your HMO staff, your employment assistance program staff, and the *Yellow Pages.*

Your First Contact with a Career Counselor Richard Bolles suggests making a visit to a potential counselor and leaving your wallet at home. When calling to make the appointment, Bolles recommends saying up front that this is an exploratory visit and you don't expect to be charged. If you are able to arrange such a meeting, we support you in that effort. We definitely agree with Bolles's position here, especially for package deals. Those offering package deals for a large fee but without a free initial appointment should be avoided.

However, for the individual counselor operating on an hourly appointment basis, offering free initial appointments might not be practical from a time perspective. Perhaps the counselor can give you 10 to 15 minutes on the phone to answer some questions and follow that up with service and fee information in writing. Moreover, Mary Burton and Richard Wedemeyer suggest that meeting the potential counselor for one session (and paying) is a worthwhile investment.

Regardless of how ou make contact, you want answers to these basic questions:

- What are the specific services offered?

- Who is going to provide the services, and how long have they been doing it?

- What are the fees for these services?

- Can I pay as I go?

In addition, request the names of current or past clients that you may speak with. Counselors need the permission of the client before giving out personal information, so a short amount of time is needed here.

Don't expect any guarantees. You can expect a lot of homework and a good coach who can guide you through the self-assessment phase and the job search as well (including resume writing, interviewing skills, and job search methods). He or she can lend objective insight and support but cannot get you a job. You will have to go face to face with potential employers and convince them of your value. You might be capable of going through the career planning process on your own, but if you need help, then get it.

CHAPTER 6
STRATEGIES FOR IDENTIFYING
CAREER OPTIONS

★

Perhaps the most difficult part of the career planning process for most career changers is identifying a target career. Often, adults feel ashamed to admit that they are confused about their career options. They wonder how someone at age 30, 40, or older could still be unsure about what to pursue in terms of a career. If you share this confusion, remember that as adults pass through different developmental stages, what once fit for them, assuming something did, may no longer. Adults continue to change in terms of likes and dislikes, values, and even in approach to and philosophy of life.

You might realize that your former career no longer fits but still be confused as to what other occupation would be more appropriate. The first step, if you're confused, is to allow yourself to be confused! If you can allow yourself to be confused, you can then relax and get on with your career planning process more effectively.

This is where assessment and testing come into the process. One effective and successful approach for adult career changers, based on my over 20 years in the career planning field, is a combination of an Analysis of Life Experience Exercise and testing. The exercise incorporates identifying and prioritizing enjoyable experiences from all aspects of your life, including home and family, education, career, social, and leisure, and then taking a closer look at those you ranked the highest with regard to what interests were involved, skills used, values reflected, and personality preferences exercised. These become the nuts and bolts for generating career option ideas.

Two key tests, or inventories, are the Strong Interest Inventory (SII) and the Myers-Briggs Type Indicator (MBTI). These popular inventories show how similar your interests (SII) and your personality preferences (MBTI) are to those of people working happily, to some degree, in many different occupations (more than 100 on the SII and more than 200 on the MBTI).

The jobs scoring the highest for you on these inventories usually match up well with those generated from the Analysis of Life Experience Exercise. It is a powerful confirmation to see that your effort on the life experience exercise pays off with some viable possibilities. Often, testing alone leaves career changers wondering, "Well, what now?"

One potential problem with the SII and MBTI, however, is that they can be easily misinterpreted. Sometimes they are not interpreted at all; some counselors merely hand their clients the results. Not only is this a detriment to the client, but it is also unethical career counseling. The major area of concern is that career changers will walk away thinking that these inventories are telling them they *should* go into one of their higher-scoring occupations. The inventories are not recommending a career direction. They simply indicate that your interests or personality preferences are similar to those of people happily employed in certain occupations and that perhaps you would enjoy the same occupations. The career changer must investigate these occupations further to verify whether or not they are viable career options.

No career decision should be made based on only one source of information, even if that source is as reputable as the SII or MBTI. However, after combining different, reliable sources that cover your interests, personality preferences, skills, and values, it's not unusual to begin to see certain patterns or themes in your results. Seeing these patterns can help to lessen your confusion and help you to focus on identifying meaningful career options.

In this chapter, we will focus on actual assessment results for a career changer whom we'll call Tony. This example will illustrate how to

- Complete the Analysis of Life Experience Exercise, of which a major component is identifying your skills

- Gain insights into your SII and MBTI results

- Clarify your life and work values and understand their impact in your career decision making

The goal is to identify career options in which most of your preferred criteria are somewhat in balance.

ANALYSIS OF LIFE EXPERIENCE EXERCISE

The following exercise is similar to exercises found in *What Color Is Your Parachute?*, by Richard Bolles (also published separately as *How to Create a Picture of Your Ideal Job or Next Career*); *Job and Career Building*, by Richard Germann and Peter Arnold; and *Career Satisfaction and Success*, by B. Haldane.

To work through the exercise, you'll need a supply of paper and a pen or pencil (or word processor if you prefer) to record your answers.

Identifying Your Significant Life Experiences

The key to success in this approach is being able to identify your most significant life experiences. The whole process depends on this first step. Here we define *significant* to mean any experience in which you have accomplished something and enjoyed it (both aspects are required) from any area of your life: learning (formal education, formal training, or informal education), work, family, leisure, and social. Don't confuse *significant* with *grandiose* experiences, in which perhaps you were presented with an award or some type of honor. Your significant experience can be anything, as long as you enjoyed it, accomplished something, and were an active participant (rather than an observer). The average adult usually comes up with 35 to 40 significant life experiences.

The next step is to prioritize your experiences according to which ones you enjoyed the most. You will consider your top 10 or 12 experiences and ask yourself the following questions: Why are these my most significant experiences? What interests are involved? What skills am I using? What special knowledge am I applying? What preferences are indicated? What values are reflected? You will also look for patterns or themes among your top experiences. Examples of patterns include helping others, being creative, managing or leading others, teaching/training others, problem solving, and experiencing adventure.

The best way to identify experiences is to refer to a list of skills. Bolles lists transferable skills, organized in the three categories of Things; People; and Information, Data, and Ideas. We've also provided a Sample List of Transferable/Functional Skills on page 130 for you to refer to. Along with the printed list you'll be using, you will need a piece of paper—your Life Experience Brainstorming Work Sheet—for listing the various areas of your life that your experiences could come from: learning/education, work, family, social, leisure, and so on. Fill in pertinent information within each of these. For example, list formal (names of schools attended) and informal learning experiences, job titles (all the way back to high school, if you want), and hobbies and leisure activities.

Take, for example, your own college experience. Examine classroom activities such as papers, presentations, and group collaborations, as well as outside experiences like clubs, organizations, athletics, arts, and student government. Likewise, a job could be broken down into separate major aspects. You'll be referring to this work sheet to help you focus "in" during the experience brainstorming phase. Tony's (our case-study client) Life Experience Brainstorming Work Sheet is shown as an example in Figure 6.1.

Now you're ready to identify experiences. Start with the major skill category you think you most enjoy (refer to the sample list provided). Let's take management skills. Focus on one skill at a time. For example, in this category is the skill of being persuasive. Ask yourself, "When have I used persuasive skills and enjoyed using them, as well as experienced a sense of accomplishment?"

First consider your education. Can you recall any education experiences in which you used persuasive skills and enjoyed it? Perhaps you gave a persuasive speech in your freshman Introduction to Speech course, on the importance of having the right to vote. You enjoyed giving the speech and felt you accomplished something, because in high school you were somewhat shy and would never have pictured yourself getting up in front of 20 people and giving a persuasive speech. As you identify significant experiences, name each one and record it on a sheet of paper or on your computer (e.g., High School "Right to Vote" speech). Continue with the

FIGURE 6.1

Tony's Life Experience Brainstorming Work Sheet

EDUCATIONAL EXPERIENCES

- **Duke University, Durham, North Carolina,** 1982–1986
  B.A., Majors in Finance & Economics
  President of National Honor Society
  Cooperative Education/Work Program—Jewel Food Stores
- **University of Illinois, Chicago,** 1988–1990
  M.B.A., Emphasis in Marketing
  Marketing Club, Committee Chairman—Marketing Symposium
  Team Leader—Management Consulting Club, International Business Club

BUSINESS EMPLOYMENT EXPERIENCES

- **TSI Marketing Consultants:** Broadcast Media Sales Representative, 1992–1993
- **Raymon Associates, Inc.:** Assistant Account Manager and then Account Manager at Sales and Marketing Organization, 1990–1991
- **Sitman Corporation:** Senior Treasury Administrator, 1987–1988
- **Crane Industries:** Financial Analyst, 1986–1987

FAMILY-RELATED EXPERIENCES

- Religious Activities

SOCIAL-LIFE EXPERIENCES

- Youth Group Advisor

LEISURE-TIME EXPERIENCES

- Health/Fitness
- Traveling

education category until you've identified all other significant experiences in which you used persuasive skills and enjoyed using them.

The experiences you identify should be specific, rather than general. If you can describe *what* you did, *how* you did it, and what the *outcomes* or *results* were, you most likely have identified a specific experience. You'll see later that the description of how you did something leads into the identification of the skills you used. In our example, identifying the speech course is too general, but identifying the actual speech you gave is specific.

In some cases, however, a general experience may be worth including, if you can describe *how* you went about doing what you did. You may remember a certain activity/project that was repeated year after year, though it's difficult to recall the specifics of any one particular year. Yet, you're still able to describe, in general, *how* you went about doing what you did.

When you've completed the education category, continue brainstorming experiences in which you used persuasive skills from the remaining categories. For example, in a particular work experience, you may have persuaded your supervisor or a group of coworkers to proceed on a certain project using your ideas. Perhaps you recall persuading your family to have a long-overdue dinner together. Maybe you recall persuading a reluctant friend to join you in a game of tennis. Generate as many experiences as possible in which you used a certain skill and enjoyed using it from each major life category, and then go on to the next major skill category and do the same.

An alternative to using skill terminology as a catalyst for remembering experiences is simply to start off by thinking about enjoyable experiences you've had that you're able to recall off the top of your head. After all, we're more likely to remember the activity, in some instances, than skills used. When you've come up with all the experiences that you can remember, from the various areas of your life, you can then use the skill terminology to help brainstorm additional experiences that are a bit more difficult to recall.

You're probably thinking, "This is a lot of work." This is true; however, it's well worth it.

When you try this exercise, you'll quickly realize that it takes intense mental concentration. Don't be surprised if you're feeling wiped out in less than an hour. If that occurs, rather than sabotaging your career planning efforts by working at less than full capacity, put it down and come back to it when you can give it your full and fresh attention. How long can this take? Perhaps as many as 10 to 12 hours. People who work full-time and are motivated about their career planning efforts seem to finish within two weeks. Many people take longer, depending on the time they have and their motivation level.

It's difficult to remember everything from your past that might fit here. Looking at photo albums can sometimes help you to remember enjoyable experiences. Family members and friends might be able to help you recall experiences.

Sample List of Transferable/Functional Skills

CLERICAL SKILLS
bookkeeping
classifying
collecting
compiling
computing
examining
filing
organizing
recording
word processing

COMMUNICATION SKILLS
editing
explaining
influencing
interpreting
listening
mediating
promoting
speaking
translating
writing

CREATIVE SKILLS
designing
developing
establishing
illustrating
imagining
improvising
inventing
performing
revitalizing
visualizing

FINANCIAL SKILLS
accounting
administering
allocating
auditing
balancing
budgeting
calculating
forecasting
investing
projecting

HUMAN RELATIONS SKILLS
advising
assisting
counseling
empathizing
facilitating
guiding
listening
motivating
representing
serving

MANAGEMENT SKILLS
communicating
coordinating
decision making
delegating
directing
evaluating
leading
negotiating
persuading
planning

PROBLEM-SOLVING SKILLS
analyzing
decision making
diagnosing
examining
executing
planning
proving
reasoning
recognizing
validating

PUBLIC RELATIONS SKILLS
conducting
consulting
informing
planning
presenting
promoting
representing
researching
responding
writing

RESEARCH SKILLS
assessing
calculating
collecting
diagnosing
evaluating
examining
extrapolating
interviewing
investigating
synthesizing

SELLING SKILLS
communicating
contacting
educating
informing
organizing
persuading
planning
presenting
promoting
scheduling

TECHNICAL SKILLS
adjusting
aligning
assembling
drafting
engineering
installing
observing
operating
programming
repairing

TRAINING SKILLS
adapting
communicating
demonstrating
enabling
encouraging
evaluating
explaining
instructing
planning
stimulating

Upon completing the experience brainstorming exercise, you're ready for the next step. From your list of experiences, however long, attempt to identify the ten experiences in which you felt the most enjoyment and accomplishment and list them in that order.

Your Top 10 should represent some variety. If your Top 10 includes more than two experiences that are somewhat the same, consider adding one or two more experiences. This might help to add some meaningful variety to your Top 10. However, you do want to note the intensity of the type of skills/experiences that had multiple Top 10 entries.

Let's turn now to our case study, beginning with a brief description of Tony. As we progress through the assessment process, much more information about Tony will be added. Tony is a 31-year-old Caucasian, with a bachelor's degree in finance and economics and an M.B.A. with an emphasis in marketing. During the five years previous to seeking career counseling, Tony has had five positions in the areas of media sales, account management, and finance (not a top interest). Generally speaking, all positions lacked creative input (which is a top interest). The two positions held since he finished his M.B.A. did not utilize the knowledge gained from it, which Tony values. Tony is a likable person with an outgoing and energized personality. Tony's primary goal when starting career counseling was to further validate his creative interest in advertising/marketing or identify any other possibilities. Tony's Top 10 life experiences are shown in Figure 6.2.

Writing Descriptive Stories of Your Top 10 Experiences

When you have identified your Top 10 experiences, you're ready to write a description of each. You'll need at least one sheet of paper for each experience, with the title of the experience at the top of the page. For each experience, describe *what* you did (usually an introductory paragraph), *how* you did it (the main body of the story, giving a detailed, step-by-step description of what you did), and what the *outcomes* or *results* were (a concluding paragraph). If you haven't realized up to now why your experiences needed to be specific, you will at this point, as you try to describe step by step what you did. When an experience is too general, it's impossible to generate a step-by-step description. Leave space in the margin for the next step—identifying skills.

People often ask, "How long should each written description of an experience be?" The answer is that it should be long enough for you to

---

FIGURE 6.2

Tony's Top 10 Life Experiences

1. **TV Game Show Contestant:** Tested knowledge, sense of showmanship
2. **Teaching Niece Multiplication Tables:** Helped her overcome anxiety
3. **Church Youth Group Advisor:** Related specifically to role of coordinating talent show
4. **Vitamin Product Class Presentation:** For undergraduate management class, researched product, wrote, acted, and videotaped
5. **Snack Product Commercial:** For business school (M.B.A.) course, put together commercial targeted for a college population and was master of ceremonies
6. **Learned to Use Computer:** When working as a financial analyst
7. **Service Desk Manager:** In food store the day of the Super Bowl; able to handle crowd through speed and versatility
8. **Trip to Europe:** Specifically, time spent backpacking; experienced different culture, language, and people
9. **Developed a Gourmet, All-Natural Cat Food Business Plan:** Presentation for a business school (M.B.A.) course
10. **Skydiving:** Overcame fear

Because number 9 is similar to 4 and 5, we will include entry number 11 to add variety:

11. **Creative Writing Class Paper:** Focused on relationship with brother

---

be able to identify the skills you used, as explained in the following section. Average length is about two handwritten pages, though some can be less and others more. Tony's description of experience number 4 (annotated with skills) is shown in Figure 6.3.

Identifying Your Transferable/Functional Skills

At this point, you are ready to identify your transferable/functional skills as they relate to your Top 10 experiences. Using as a reference the first skills listing provided in this chapter, the skills listed in *What Color Is Your Parachute?*, and/or any other relevant listing you might have, consider carefully the skills used in each experience. Feel free to add descriptive terms to the list entries to better express how you used the skill or skills involved.

FIGURE 6.3

Tony's Top 10 Experience Descriptive Story

All the students in my Executive Management (undergraduate) class were assigned to a group and asked to come up with a presentation on an actual company. I and two other students worked together. We brainstormed ideas and decided to put on an informational play about a particular vitamin company. We had to write our own parts and be prepared to answer questions.	Communicating with others, generating ideas
One aspect of my responsibility was to give a financial report on the company for the last 4–5 years. I went to the business reference section of the university library and looked over the company's annual reports and related information (product lines, etc.).	Researching, compiling, gathering information by studying resources
To get an idea of the company's financial status, I looked at information regarding net income over the past five years, in order to spot any trends, as well as gross profits and expense figures.	Computing, working with numbers, analyzing information, breaking it down
Once I completed taking notes from the resource materials, I sat down to prepare my 3-minute presentation. I wrote it out much as one would if preparing a speech. I also included five graphs, which the university service made into overheads to be used during my presentation.	Organizing thoughts, planning out a step-by-step process, business-related writing, visualizing
I then memorized the presentation, word for word, paragraph by paragraph, and studied it for quite a while. The presentation was made to our class, and my 3-minute segment went well. It generated positive responses from the instructor and my fellow students.	Keeping track of details, memorizing, communicating to a group, making a presentation

Simply read through your descriptive stories, and as you identify skills used, write them in the margin, as shown in Figure 6.3. But note: List only the skills you enjoyed using: as many as you can for each experience. Try for 10 to 15, but some experiences might have more or less. Don't shortchange yourself; after all, this is for you. Then prioritize the skills within each experience to identify those you enjoyed most and would like to use in your next career. Draw up a short list for each experience, reflecting these choices.

When this step is completed, you should have ten lists of skills (or more, if you include more than ten experiences), prioritized in order of those you enjoy using the most. Now look at the top entries in each list and ask yourself which of these skills are essential for you to use in your next career. Mark those you consider essential. By essential, we mean that even though your career choice has yet to be identified, when it is, it's essential that you get to use that skill. However, in the interest of forcing you to make some differentiation among your top skills, try not to include more than four or five from each of your ten lists. If a skill appears in more than one experience, list it only once. These 30 to 40 top skills will be the ones we'll focus on in the next step of this process.

Tony's prioritized list of the skills identified in the story follows, with essential skills marked with an asterisk:

- Generating ideas*
- Making a visual presentation of information*
- Communicating with others, or group*
- Making presentations*
- Analyzing information, breaking it down*
- Business-related writing
- Keeping track of details, good memory
- Organizing thoughts, planning out a step-by-step process
- Researching, compiling, gathering information by studying resources
- Computing, working with numbers

Formulating Your Personal Transferable/ Functional Skill Clusters

At this stage of the exercise, we organize your top transferable/functional skills in a way that will be more personally relevant by using personal skill clusters. Personal skill clusters are natural groupings of your preferred skills.

Clusters can be similar to the patterns or themes that your Top 10 experiences generated (refer to Sample List of Transferable/Functional Skills for categories). The patterns or themes of Tony's experiences follow:

TEACHING/TRAINING/ ADVISING

2: Teaching Niece

3: Youth Group Advisor

BUSINESS/CREATIVE

4: Vitamin Presentation

5: Snack Product Commercial

9: Cat Food Business Plan

NONBUSINESS CREATIVE

11: Creative Writing Paper

BUSINESS/OPERATIONS

6: Learned Computer

7: Service Manager

ADVENTURESOME/FUN

1: Game Show Contestant

8: Backpacking in Europe

10: Skydiving

To create your personal skill clusters, make small strips of paper, just big enough to write a skill name on, and clear off a table for space to work. Write the name of each essential skill that you identified on a separate strip of paper. Now try to form subgroups, or clusters, of similar skills. Think of the strips of paper as pieces of a puzzle. See if you can form three to six clusters of related skills. Check to see if any central theme might be related to your transferable skills. Arrange your clusters around each other by how they relate to one another.

Look at the example from Tony's skill clustering in Figure 6.4. He identified a major cluster of problem-solving skills that fed into two other clusters: creative and management/supervision. In addition, the cluster of human relations skills fed into all three of the previously mentioned clusters. Also, a central theme of instructing/teaching/guiding and training intersected all four clusters. The numbers in parentheses indicate the intensity—that is, in how many of Tony's Top 10 experiences that skill was identified as essential. If you have trouble with this step, consult with a career counselor.

Your Specific Content/Special Knowledge

We will call your favorite *subjects,* or fields of knowledge, your *specific content/special knowledge* skills. This category represents a second type of skill to add to the transferable skills. In this step, you identify subjects you've learned about and liked best from your formal education (high school and college), on-the-job training, self-study, and continuing education activities. We've provided a Sample List of Specific Content/

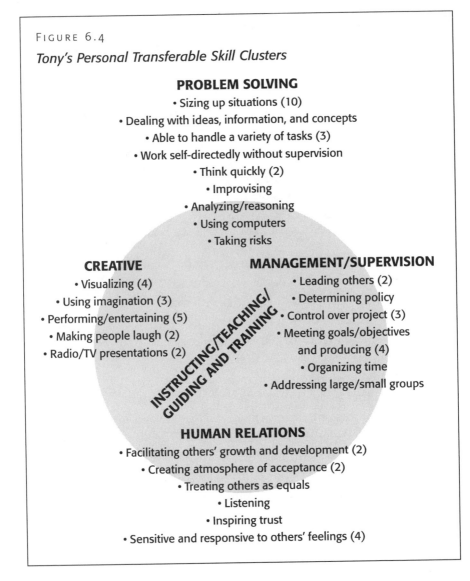

FIGURE 6.4

Tony's Personal Transferable Skill Clusters

PROBLEM SOLVING
• Sizing up situations (10)
• Dealing with ideas, information, and concepts
• Able to handle a variety of tasks (3)
• Work self-directedly without supervision
• Think quickly (2)
• Improvising
• Analyzing/reasoning
• Using computers
• Taking risks

CREATIVE
• Visualizing (4)
• Using imagination (3)
• Performing/entertaining (5)
• Making people laugh (2)
• Radio/TV presentations (2)

INSTRUCTING/TEACHING/ GUIDING AND TRAINING

MANAGEMENT/SUPERVISION
• Leading others (2)
• Determining policy
• Control over project (3)
• Meeting goals/objectives and producing (4)
• Organizing time
• Addressing large/small groups

HUMAN RELATIONS
• Facilitating others' growth and development (2)
• Creating atmosphere of acceptance (2)
• Treating others as equals
• Listening
• Inspiring trust
• Sensitive and responsive to others' feelings (4)

Special Knowledge Skills, or you can use the subjects sample list in *What Color Is Your Parachute?*

Be sure to review the categories you generated in your Life Experience Brainstorming Work Sheet (work, education, family, leisure, social, etc.), as well as your Top 10 life experiences, for related specific content/special knowledge skills. When you've identified those that apply to you, prioritize your specific content/special knowledge skills according to those you would most like to see involved in your next career.

Tony's favorite specific content/special knowledge skills are shown in Figure 6.5.

Sample List of Specific Content/Special Knowledge Skills

advertising	history	public opinion
alcoholism	house building	quality control
bicycles	income taxes	real estate
biology	interior decorating	recreation
business management	Japan	religion
community organizing	journalism	retail
crime	kayaking	safety
customer service	labor relations	science
diets	linguistics	sociology
diseases	marketing	sports
earthquakes	massage	teaching
employee relations	mathematics	technical writing
environmental planning	meditation	theater
fiber optics	opera	toys
financial planning	outdoors	training
fund-raising	periodicals	utilities
gardening	philosophy	video recorders
geography	photography	waste
government agencies	poverty	water resources
health care	psychology	wildlife

Additional Related Information

Personal Problems You Prefer to Deal With   In this part of the exercise, you'll be considering which personal problems you may want to help others with. These can include areas such as personal growth, health, education, career counseling, finances, relationships, or religion. Again, be sure to review the life experience categories generated from the Life Experience Brainstorming Work Sheet, as well as your Top 10 life experiences, for suggestions. You can refer to the list of personal problems in *What Color Is Your Parachute?* Identify those that you have knowledge of and prioritize them according to which you would like to see involved in your next career. Tony's results are shown in the lefthand column of Figure 6.6.

Products to Deal With or Help Produce   Think about whether there are any particular products or *things* you might like to work with or help create. You can refer to the products list provided in *What Color*

FIGURE 6.5

Tony's Favorite Specific Content/Special Knowledge Skills

1. Broadcasting (talk show/news host)
2. Psychology (human behavior)
3. Positive Mental Attitude (how to achieve one)
4. Religion
5. Marketing (advertising/creative)
6. Acting
7. Management
8. Finance (planning corporate investments)
9. Marketing (research and development)
10. Marketing (packaging and distribution)
11. Account Management (advertising field)
12. Philosophy (meaning of life)
13. Political Science (politics)
14. Computers (word processing and Lotus)
15. Law (for the benefit of the public interest)

Is Your Parachute? or the one that follows. Refer again to your Life Experience Brainstorming Work Sheet and Top 10 list for indications of products with which you may want to work. Check off those that apply to you, and prioritize them in order of how important it is to you that they be involved in your next career. Tony's preferred products are shown in the righthand column of Figure 6.6.

We have now identified three additional areas—specific content/ special knowledge, personal problems/services, and products—which we will combine with your top transferable/functional skills as well as recalling the patterns and themes related to your Top 10 experiences, in order to generate job/career ideas.

Sample List of Major Categories of Products

appliances	computers
artistic	cosmetics
books	electronic equipment
building materials	food
clothing	furniture

gardening	office equipment
health	sports/recreation
housewares	stereos
magazines	television
medical	toys
games	transportation

Generating Career Ideas

A crucial step in the career planning process is generating ideas and options based on one's self-assessment results. If you've actually made it to this point in the process alone, you're to be congratulated. Many career changers have difficulty completing this type of exercise on their own. Even if you have been able to generate the information up to this point by yourself, it's not a bad idea to brainstorm specific career-related ideas and opinions with a career counselor.

Career options can be generated by combining your top-ranked transferable/fuctional skills with your top-ranked specific content/special knowledge, personal problems/services, and products as well as the patterns and themes represented by your Top 10 experiences. For our example, we

---

FIGURE 6.6

Tony's Preferences in Two Additional Areas

PERSONAL PROBLEMS/SERVICES TO HELP OTHERS	PRODUCTS TO WORK WITH
1. Worship	1. Greeting Cards (creative)
2. Acceptance (self and others)	2. Books (production, contents, editing)
3. Psychological Healing (self and others)	3. Magazines (same as above)
4. Life/Work Planning	4. Newspapers (same as above)
5. Broadcasting (news to public)	5. Health Foods
6. Personal Insight (through therapy)	6. Vitamins
7. Hospital/Health (administrator)	7. Computers
8. Nursing (animals)	8. Toiletries
9. Stewardship	9. Products (manufacture of)
10. Ethics	10. Money

will concentrate on Tony's skills in problem solving through creative means, incorporating the management of others (including training activities) and projects. This captures most of Tony's preferred transferable/fuctional skill areas.

One area that stood out in many of Tony's preferences is that of marketing/advertising. Tony's disappointment in previous marketing positions was due to the fact that he hadn't had a chance to utilize his M.B.A. knowledge, especially in creative endeavors such as marketing plans for products (including production of commercials). The results here certainly confirmed Tony's interest in the marketing field. This career area involved his special knowledge areas 5, 9, and 10 from Figure 6.5 (advertising/creative, research and development, and packaging and distribution); area 2, psychology (human behavior), would be involved as well. In addition, one of the four major themes from his Top 10 experiences was the creative side of the marketing business.

Through career counseling it was suggested to Tony to consult some written resources. When he looked in the career resource books described in Chapter 7, the career options he identified included the following:

- Advertising Manager
- Advertising Agency Manager
- Creative Director
- Market Research Analyst
- Brand/Product Manager

Management positions were emphasized because they incorporate many of Tony's preferred skills (leadership/supervision, human relations, and training). Tony believed that even though his life experience exercise information indicated interest in psychology/counseling, this interest could be satisfied through a management position. However, it was pointed out during career counseling that the position of industrial psychologist combines the interest in psychology and business and thus was an additional possibility. (Note that at this point, we don't know whether Tony is currently qualified for any of these positions. That information will be developed in the research phase in Chapter 7.)

In addition to these marketing-related options, public relations and fund-raising were suggested to Tony, through career counseling, because of the importance of dealing with people in promoting a product, service, or organization through presentations and writing. Even though writing did not appear as one of Tony's most preferred skills, it did have a heavy emphasis in his Top 10 experiences (4, 5, 9, and 11; see Figure 6.2).

Tony also had an interest in communications, specifically as a newscaster or talk show host. This was evidenced by Tony's specific content/special knowledge areas 1 and 6 and by area 5 in services. In fact, there were a number of performance/presentation-related Top 10 experiences (1, 4, 5, and 9). In addition, publication editor for greeting cards, books, magazines, or newspapers was suggested, as a result of career counseling, based largely on their ranking 1 to 4 as products that Tony most preferred to work with. One additional position in this area that related to Tony's marketing background is that of circulation manager.

Through career counseling it was suggested to Tony that these various areas—marketing/advertising, brand/product management, public relations and fund-raising, radio/TV talk show host, and publication editor—could be focused in any of the following areas of interest:

- Religion: #1 Service; #4 Special Knowledge
- Personal growth/motivation: #2, 3, 4, and 6 Services; #2, 3, and 12 Special Knowledge
- Health foods, diet, and exercise: #5 and 6 Products; #7 Service

Therefore, any marketing of products or organizations (public relations and fund-raising) could be related to these areas. Likewise, any publications or radio/TV talk shows could also be focused on these topics.

The list of options generated here is not meant to be exhaustive, but rather attempts to identify the major career paths that seem to stand out. Yet, so many possibilities can still be overwhelming at first. The next phase of the assessment process, testing, will help Tony to focus in and narrow down options more effectively to those possibilities of greatest interest and preference. Try not to compare yourself with Tony's results. You might not have as many interests as he does (most of us don't), and thus you will have fewer options to consider.

UNDERSTANDING YOUR STRONG
INTEREST INVENTORY RESULTS

The Strong Interest Inventory (SII), based on the personality theory of John Holland, is targeted for teens and adults. The SII measures interests in a wide range of career areas, including professional, technical, nonprofit, and vocational-technical. It's used to assist in making education and career decisions.

Subtests include sections on occupations, school subjects, activities, leisure activities, types of people, preference between two activities, and individual characteristics. Three major categories of scores are generated: 6 General Occupational Themes (GOTs); 25 Basic Interest Scales (BIS); and 207 Occupational Scales (OS), made up of 105 female scales and 102 male scales.

Probably the most-used interest inventory, the SII is perhaps also the most misinterpreted. If one's results are not interpreted appropriately, they can actually do more harm than good. In this section, we will discuss the SII to help you understand its three sets of scores and how to use the results for identifying related career options.

If you've taken the SII, then perhaps some insights gained here will shed some new light on your results. If you've never taken the inventory, you can use the guidelines provided here if you take it in the future. The SII is usually available only from career counseling professionals.

Holland's General Occupational Themes

Much of the SII is based on Holland's theory of vocational type. Part of Holland's theory suggests that work environments attract people with similar interests and, in a sense, become people environments. Holland's research showed that vocational-related interests could be grouped into six broad categories and that each category can be described by a General Occupational Theme (GOT):

1. **Realistic:** Physical performing, outdoors, things and objects, mechanical activities
2. **Investigative:** Science and math related, analytic and abstract reasoning activities

3. **Artistic:** Any aspect of the arts (painting, drawing, sculpting, etc., theater, dance, singing, writing, playing a musical instrument) as well as just being creative in the sense of using your own ideas to do things

4. **Social:** Working primarily with people in a helping and guiding (social service) context such as teacher, counselor, or clergy

5. **Enterprising:** Working primarily with people but in a leadership context, using persuasive skills, often with a business/sales emphasis

6. **Conventional:** Highly ordered and organized, interested in structured activities, like to know what's expected of them, often related to jobs involving office/clerical activities in business-related fields and usually not in a leadership role

Holland's theory suggests that people can be described in terms of the Holland GOTs, as can work environments and the people within them. Therefore, if you can identify which of the GOTs you relate to most strongly, then you could match your results to those of satisfied workers in different occupations for career options to consider. Holland's theory states that if a work environment suits your personality, you're likely to experience greater success, stability, and satisfaction in it.

HOLLAND'S GENERAL OCCUPATIONAL THEMES RELATED SELF-ASSESSMENT TOOL

Related Internet Site

- The Career Key   http://www.ncsu.edu/careerkey/about_career_key.html

---

Major work activities that jobs consist of can be described by the Holland GOTs. One-, two-, or three-letter codes can be used to describe related activities. The first letter would be the area of heaviest emphasis in that job, the second letter the second strongest area, and so on. Usually the most important areas of a job can be described by the first two letters of its GOT code, and the third letter describes an area of lesser importance.

Let's look at the example of landscape architect. Its three-letter GOT code is AIR: Artistic, Investigative, and Realistic. Artistic, being the strongest theme, involves the design/creative aspect of being a landscape architect. Investigative is related to the scientific aspect, that of plants, soil, degree of sunlight, and weather conditions. The Realistic aspect relates to the instruments and tools used by a landscape architect.

Therefore, in addition to matching GOTs with persons happily employed in different occupations, you could match up to the major activities involved in occupations.

Much of the information about interpreting your SII results can be found in the *User's Guide for the SII* by Jo-Ida Hansen. Most career counselors will have this book. Your six GOT scores are based on a small percentage of the 325 SII items you responded to; therefore, they might not be reliable. If you sense that they are inaccurate, don't be surprised. There is an alternative way to calculate these scores, which we'll discuss later in the chapter.

Your numerical score for each GOT indicates how much interest you have in each, as compared with the same and opposite sex in the general population. Because men and women score somewhat differently on some of these themes, a descriptive statement is added to your score, which is based on a comparison with your same sex in the general population. Research has shown same-sex comparisons to be somewhat more accurate. Therefore, for a combined comparison (with your same and opposite sex in the general population), you have the numerical score, and for comparison with your same sex only, you have the descriptive statement.

The range for GOT scores is roughly from 30 to 70, with the average person scoring 50. However, the percentage of your Like responses (on the SII, one chooses from Like, Indifferent, and Dislike response possibilities) can influence your GOT scores: a greater number of Like responses increases the chance of your having higher GOT scores, and vice versa. (When you receive the results of your test, you can check your percentage of Like, Indifferent, and Dislike responses on page 6, lower left, of the Profile Report. The same information can be found on other report formats for the SII.)

Tony's GOT scores are reported here, in order of the highest scoring.

Social:	(55) Moderately High
Investigative:	(55) Average
Conventional:	(47) Average

Artistic:	(41) Moderately Low
Realistic:	(36) Very Low
Enterprising:	(33) Very Low

This reporting format, with three separate sets of scores reported from highest to lowest, will help you to see patterns and related themes among the scores. This is especially true for the next two sets we'll be looking at, the Basic Interest Scales (BIS) and the Occupational Scales (OS).

We will wait to interpret Tony's GOT scores until we get to the OS scores. However, if you reflect on Tony's previous assessment results, from the Analysis of Life Experience Exercise, you will notice how low his Artistic score seems here in comparison with a creative emphasis there.

Basic Interest Scales

The 25 Basic Interest Scales (BIS) are organized by the GOT they relate to the strongest, as shown:

REALISTIC
Agriculture
Nature
Military Activities
Mechanical Activities

INVESTIGATIVE
Science
Mathematics
Medical Science

ARTISTIC
Music/Drama
Art
Writing
Applied Arts
Culinary Arts

SOCIAL
Teaching
Social Service
Athletics
Religious Activities
Medical Service

ENTERPRISING
Public Speaking
Law/Politics
Merchandising
Sales
Organizational Management

CONVENTIONAL
Office Services
Data Management
Computer Activities

A previous edition of the SII had 27 Basic Interest Scales, including Adventure and Domestic Arts.

Similar to the GOT scores, the average adult scores about 50 on the BIS, with most people scoring between 30 and 70. If you score higher than 50 on any of the scales, then you have responded with more consistent preference for activities related to that scale. As a result, that would be an area to look upon as a focus of your interest and to perhaps incorporate as information in your career decision making.

The opposite is true for low BIS scores. Low numerical scores mean that when compared with same- and opposite-sex members' average scores, you show a low amount of interest in that scale's activities. You can compare yourself with the average score of your same sex alone by the interpretive statement provided (Average, Moderately High, etc.).

Your results on the BIS might not be a big surprise to you. If the inventory is valid (if it measures what it claims to), it's really feeding back to you how you responded (Like, Indifferent, or Dislike) to various job titles, school subjects, activities, and so forth. It's somewhat like looking in a mirror, if you answered truthfully to the inventory items after some careful thinking. You probably already realized that you had interest in your higher-scoring scales, but you might not have realized how strong that interest was when compared with same- and opposite-sex members in the general population.

You might discover that your scores on some of the scales appear to be inconsistent with scores on related Occupational Scales (OS), to be discussed next. Perhaps you scored high on the Medical Science BIS and low on the OS for Physician. (For your information, on the BIS, Medical Science is more research oriented, and Medical Service is more social oriented.) What this inconsistency usually means is that although you have an interest in the subject matter of an occupation, you share very few other likes and dislikes with people in that occupation and thus might not enjoy the daily routine of that occupation.

Generating Career Ideas

BIS information is useful for brainstorming career (and avocational) possibilities. In fact, you might be so used to looking at an avocational interest as only a hobby that you have never tried to fit it in as a career possibility. Many adults overlook their hobbies, the things they enjoy most during their leisure time, when planning careers. Yet many other adults who do change careers bring the new career much closer to the hobby-related areas of their lives than the previous career. It's not surprising to find them much more satisfied in their work.

The BIS results do not decipher for you vocational from avocational interests. That is left up to you to determine. In other words, which do you want to try to involve in a career, which are just related to leisure, and which might be both career and leisure-related interests?

Following are Tony's BIS results. (Tony took the earlier edition of the SII that included the Adventure scale.) The top 11 of 25 scales capture all of Tony's Average and above scores.

	SCORE	RATING	INTEREST SCALE	THEME CODE
1.	(64)	High	Religious Activities	S
2.	(62)	High	Public Speaking	E
3.	(58)	Moderately High	Social Service	S
4.	(54)	Average	Law/Politics	E
5.	(54)	Average	Teaching	S
6.	(52)	Average	Writing	A
7.	(51)	Average	Music/Drama	A
8.	(48)	Average	Science	I
9.	(48)	Average	Medical Science	I
10.	(47)	Average	Nature	R
11.	(47)	Average	Adventure	R

Even though Tony had significant evidence of a social service interest from his life experience exercise, he believed at first that it would be satisfied by a management position. The interaction with staff (instructing, training, and the human relations component), he thought, would satisfy his social service interest. Yet, the Social Service scale was third highest of 25, and Religious Activities was the highest (and ranked #1 in Services in the life experience exercise).

These two scales can certainly be combined, as Tony did in his church youth group advising. They could also potentially be brought together by his becoming a member of the clergy. Tony needs to explore the areas of social service and possibly teaching (#5 on the BIS scores and a major skill cluster from the life experience exercise). When considering teaching,

Tony could look at other higher-scoring scales for ideas of what subject matter to teach: Religion (#1), Political Science (#4), Writing (#6), Music/Drama (#7), Science (#8 and #9), and Outdoor Education (#10 and #11).

Tony's interest in writing is verified by its being #6 of 25 of the BIS scores. You'll recall that three of his Top 10 (and #11) life experiences involved writing. Of the four experiences, three were in the marketing field (product business plans and commercials), and the other was more of a generally creative, human relations focus, about his relationship with his brother.

The field of law (#4 on the BIS scores) incorporates much writing, and Tony's interest from the life experience exercise (Political Science #13 and Law #15, on the Specific Content/Special Knowledge Skills) was verified. He could even specialize in environmental law (Nature #10 on the BIS scores). Writing can also be linked with Music/Drama (#7 on the BIS scores), a strong interest of Tony's. Tony pursued acting right after completing his career counseling/testing and assessment. In addition, Tony could combine his interest in writing with Science (#8 BIS), which relates to an earlier career choice Tony once had, that of a veterinarian.

Earlier, in the life experience exercise, we suggested public relations and fund-raising for Tony to consider. Two related Enterprising BIS scores were high for Tony, Public Speaking (#2) and Law/Politics (#4). Because both positions are highly persuasive (an E trait), there seems to be some support here from the two Enterprising BIS scores.

Public speaking can also be combined with Drama (#7 BIS) to support Tony's interest in Broadcasting (#1 Special Knowledge and #5 Service), specifically talk show host or news broadcaster, which includes secondary areas of writing (also involved heavily in public relations and fund-raising) and politics (news). In fact, as we're getting more familiar with Tony and his wide range of interests, you could almost picture him as a talk show host where he could pursue many topics of interest.

Science (#8) and Medical Science (#9) showed up in Tony's top BIS scores. The only prior evidence of this area from the life experience exercise was #5 and #6 Products (Health Foods and Vitamins), #7 Service (Hospital/Health Administrator), and #8 Service (Nursing Animals). It seems from Tony's results that this could be a secondary area of interest, following others that ranked higher in the life experience exercise, such as advertising/creative, public relations, fund-raising, and publication editor. Tony could focus work in these four areas in science-related products, services, or organizations.

Occupational Scales

The third set of scores reported on the SII are the Occupational Scales (OS), perhaps the scores that those taking the SII are most interested in (and perhaps the aspect that is most often misinterpreted or not interpreted at all). The OS scores compare your interests with those of people of the same and opposite sex who are happily employed in just over 100 occupations. These 200 to 300 members of an occupational group are usually members of a professional association related to their occupation. They meet the following criteria:

- Between 25 and 60 years old
- In the occupation for at least three years
- Have reported that they enjoy their jobs
- Meet some form of minimal standard of occupational performance, such as certification, licensure, or advanced degree
- Pursue their occupation with typical tasks and duties and not in some unusual way

On the SII Profile Report, both your same- and opposite-sex OS comparison scores are reported. However, as with the GOT and BIS results, your same-sex comparison scores are more likely to be good predictors for you than are scales for the other sex.

On the SII Profile Report, your score for each scale is printed in numerals for those scales normed for your sex and is also plotted graphically with an asterisk. The opposite-sex numerical score is also reported, but not graphically. The graphic display can be confusing; therefore, to make analysis of your own results easier, pull the scores out of the GOT structure and simply list them from highest to lowest as we did with the two previous sets of scores.

Someone who scores 50 on a given scale has responded to the SII items in the same way the average member of that occupation does and falls under the interpretive comment of "Similar." Following is a list of score ranges and related interpretive comments:

Score	Interpretive Comment
14 or below	Very Dissimilar
15–24	Dissimilar
25–29	Moderately Dissimilar
30–39	Mid-Range
40–44	Moderately Similar
45–54	Similar
55 or higher	Very Similar

Scores in the Moderately Similar or higher range (40 or above) on same-sex normed scales are the most useful. Usually, your Top 20 OS scores will capture all your moderately similar scores and above; if they do not, lengthen your list to include those as well.

One set of new information reported with OS scores is the one-, two-, or three-letter GOT code designation for members of that occupation. These are listed to the right of the OS names with Tony's OS scores (which follow). When a one-letter code is listed, it can at times be confusing. For example, male and female florists are described with a one-code letter: Enterprising. This is mainly because, in this case, they are business owners. Chances are that most florists have a strong Artistic side as well, but the statistical analysis done by Consulting Psychologists Press, on the subjects who were part of the Florist group tested in order to establish average comparison scores, doesn't show it as high enough to include here. Paradoxically, male and female lawyers are classified as Artistic because the lawyers tested to establish average comparison scores had this theme in common, but not other themes like Social or Enterprising. Writing is a major part of being a lawyer (as is being creative in case preparation and presentation), so you could understand the OS code of A. However, there is probably an Enterprising (persuasive) side to them as well.

Therefore, only one GOT is sometimes presented to describe an occupation even though there is usually another that plays a big part. If any of your higher-scoring OS results are coded with just one GOT, you can ask yourself, "What might that next letter be?" This approach might help your OS results make greater sense to you.

Listing the scores in order of highest to lowest helps us to see possible patterns among your higher OS scores, both by occupational title and by GOT code designation. For example, Tony's Top 20 OS scores follow:

	THEME SCORE	RATING	OCCUPATIONAL SCALE	CODE
1.	(55)	Very Similar	Guidance Counselor	S
2.	(53)	Similar	Broadcaster	A
3.	(50)	Similar	Social Worker	SA
4.	(49)	Similar	Social Science Teacher	S
5.	(48)	Similar	Minister	SA
6.	(48)	Similar	College Professor	I
7.	(48)	Similar	Advertising Executive	A
8.	(48)	Similar	Public Relations Director	A
9.	(47)	Similar	Speech Pathologist	SAI
10.	(46)	Similar	Psychologist	IA
11.	(46)	Similar	Marketing Executive	EI
12.	(45)	Similar	Recreation Leader	SE
13.	(44)	Moderately Similar	Investment Manager	ECI
14.	(43)	Moderately Similar	YMCA Director	SE
15.	(43)	Moderately Similar	Dietitian	CSE
16.	(43)	Moderately Similar	Chiropractor	I
17.	(43)	Moderately Similar	Physician	IA
18.	(42)	Moderately Similar	Lawyer	A
19.	(42)	Moderately Similar	Public Administrator	AS
20.	(41)	Moderately Similar	Elected Public Official	E

Of Tony's Top 10 OS GOT code designations, three include SA together, two show S alone, three show A alone, and three include I. In fact, nine of the Top 10 include S or A. Here we see a common situation in which one's GOT scores do not seem accurate, largely due to the fact that only a small number of the 325 best items (less than 10 percent) are used to compute these scores.

If you think your GOT scores are not accurate, you might want to try the alternative method in Figure 6.7 for calculating your GOT scores to see whether it yields results you agree with more. We use the OS GOT code designation to calculate these alternative GOT scores.

FIGURE 6.7

Verifying Tony's General Occupational Theme (GOT) Score Results Based on His Top 20 SII Occupational Scale GOT Designations

	R	I	A	S	E	C
Number of times it appears as first letter × 3	–	4×3 = 12	5×3 = 15	7×3 = 21	3×3 = 9	1×3 = 3
Number of times it appears as second letter × 2	–	1×2 = 2	5×2 = 10	2×2 = 4	2×2 = 4	1×2 = 2
Number of times it appears as third letter × 1	–	2×1 = 2	–	–	1×1 = 1	–
Total Points	0	16	25	25	14	5

Basically, we tally the number of times each letter (RIASEC) appears as a first, second, or third letter in the GOT code designations for each of your Top 20 OS scores. In Tony's case, the new results are quite different from (and fit better than) the original scores, as shown:

SII GOT Scores			Alternative GOT Scores	
55	MH	Social	25	Artistic
55	AVG	Investigative	25	Social
47	AVG	Conventional	16	Investigative
41	ML	Artistic	14	Enterprising
36	VL	Realistic	5	Conventional
33	VL	Enterprising	0	Realistic

Here Artistic jumps from fourth-highest to tied for the highest scoring GOT with Social. Investigative drops to third. Enterprising is now just two points behind Investigative, which is a jump from previously coming in last. Conventional drops, and Realistic is somewhat out of the picture. Up to this point, ASI or SAI (with E rising) seems to be a more accurate description for Tony's interests than the previous SIC (with E last). Let's move on now and take a closer look at Tony's higher OS scores and see what they might mean.

Most of the specific occupations and patterns we suggested to Tony after doing the Analysis of Life Experience Exercise are confirmed by his Top 20 OS scores.

The Advertising, Creative, or Marketing area is supported by:

- Advertising Executive   (#7)   Similar
- Marketing Executive   (#11)   Similar
- Investment Manager   (#13)   Moderately Similar

The Public Relations/Fund-Raising area is supported by

- Public Relations Director   (#8)   Similar

(There is no Fund-Raiser Occupational Scale on the SII.)

Tony's interest in Broadcasting is supported by

- Broadcaster   (#2)   Similar

The Helping Others/Social Service area is supported by

- Guidance Counselor   (#1)   Very Similar
- Social Worker   (#3)   Similar
- Minister   (#5)   Similar
- Psychologist   (#10)   Similar

There are underlying relationships to

- Social Science Teacher   (#4)   Similar
- College Professor   (#6)   Similar
- Recreation Leader   (#12)   Similar
- YMCA Director   (#14)   Moderately Similar

Tony's interest in Law/Politics is supported by

- Lawyer   (#18)   Moderately Similar
- Public Administrator   (#19)   Moderately Similar
- Elected Public Official   (#20)   Moderately Similar

In addition, the Medical/Science area was still appearing, as represented by

- Dietitian   (#15)   Moderately Similar
- Chiropractor   (#16)   Moderately Similar
- Physician   (#17)   Moderately Similar

Therefore, the major areas of advertising/marketing/creative, public relations/fund-raising, broadcasting, teaching/training, and social service suggested as a result of doing the as elsewhere life experience exercise are all supported by the fact that their related SII OS scored in the Top 20 (with most in the Similar range).

It might be beneficial to describe how we're using the term *support*. Tony's interest levels in these four areas are all similar (from Moderate to Very, though mostly in-between) to the levels of happily employed, same-sex members of those occupations. Does that mean that Tony should go into one of these occupations? Not exactly; the key word is *should*. For example, when Tony's interests are compared with those of males in more than 100 different occupations on the SII, they're similar to the interests of advertising executives, and because they like their jobs, maybe Tony would also like that job. The key word here is *maybe,* not *should.*

Tony, or anybody else, including yourself, would have to check it out, by first reading up on that particular job in a career resource book. In addition, if you are still interested in a certain occupation, you need to begin talking to persons employed in that occupation to gather more information and to begin to build your network of contacts.

Tony did some investigating of this nature for the occupation of industrial psychologist. Through reading and talking with people, Tony verified that, indeed, this occupation did incorporate many of his numerous interests. However, he also verified that he would need a second master's degree in order to qualify. Tony decided that at this point in his life he was not willing to study for a second master's degree.

So what do you do when something you think you're interested in has a low (mid-range or below) OS score? First of all, you should never make a career decision based on only one information source, including the SII. However, a low OS score in an occupation of interest to you should be considered a signal, warning you to investigate further before making a decision. Your job becomes one of trying to find out why your interests are being reported as somewhat dissimilar to same-sex members of that occupation.

In Tony's case, the only major area of interest not showing up in the Top 20 OS scores was that of publication editor. The closest related Occupational Scale is Reporter, which was in the mid-range of similarity, with a score of 37. Remember that Tony's BIS score for Writing was sixth highest of 27, yet it represented only an average amount of interest when compared with that of the same sex in the general population.

In discussions, Tony confirmed an interest in writing but mainly in the creative aspect involved with advertising/marketing campaigns. Tony expressed a lack of desire to use writing as a major occupational skill. He is not confident about his ability to write, which explains why it did not show up in the skill assessment portion of the Analysis of Life Experience Exercise. Tony once considered law school, but he changed his mind when he learned of the prominent role of writing in that occupation.

Recall that Tony ranked books, magazines, and newspapers highly (2 to 4) as products he would like to work with. Where was he coming from? Tony would like to be in a position to determine the contents of the publication but not necessarily be the one to edit (perhaps owner/publisher). With that information, we can eliminate publication editor from Tony's list of options, unless he owns the publication and works with a staff of editors to plan and organize its contents. With respect to this one general-interest area whose related OS score was lower, Tony made sense out of it and now can move on with his career decision making. When you eliminate something as a choice, be sure you know why and what you're basing that decision on.

Tony had also determined that he didn't want to pursue a social service career. As mentioned earlier, his interests in human relations, mentoring, teaching, and training could be satisfied to a large degree through a management position. He has successfully combined two major interest areas, religion and social service, through his church youth group advising. He planned to continue doing that as an avocational pursuit.

Tony was beginning to focus back on the area of advertising/marketing/creative as a primary career goal. His OS scores support this area of interest. In fact, it's not unusual to find that the SII strongly supports career options generated by the Analysis of Life Experience Exercise.

In summary, there are two ways to view the OS results. You can look at the higher-scoring, specific OS fields and consider those as options.

Or, as we've suggested all along, identify the patterns of your higher-scoring fields. In Tony's case, it's an artistic/social pattern, so it would make sense for Tony to attempt to include these types of activities in his career choice and avocational interests as well.

Other interest inventories I would recommend include the Harrington-O'Shea CDM System (self-scorable; generates scores for the six Holland GOT characteristics—quickly, accurately, and at a reasonable price), the Career Assessment Inventory Enhanced (designed to meet the needs of graduates from high school, vocational school, and two-year or four-year colleges), and the Campbell Interest and Skills Survey and the Strong Interest and Skills Confidence Inventory (both include skill-level self-assessment as an added feature with interest scores). See Appendix B: Recommended Readings: Tests and Testing Resources.

UNDERSTANDING YOUR MYERS-BRIGGS TYPE INDICATOR RESULTS

Although not specifically designed as a career assessment instrument, the Myers-Briggs Type Indicator (MBTI) has been widely applied in the career development field, helping college students and adults toward more informed career decisions. The MBTI is adapted from Carl Jung's theory of psychological type. The MBTI attempts to measure Jung's ideas about perception, judgment, and attitude in human personality, referred to as *personality type.*

Personality typing, as defined by Isabel Briggs Myers and Mary McCauley, assumes that much of our personality can be defined by dividing it into four independent preference areas, or scales: energizing, attending, deciding, and living. Within each scale we have a preference for one of two opposites that define the scale. This makes for a total of 16 different combinations, each of which defines one particular and unique personality type.

Description of the Four Preference Scales

Extroversion/Introversion (E/I) This scale measures how you are energized, where you prefer to focus your attention. People who prefer extroversion direct their energy to the outside world of people, activities, or things. They prefer to communicate more by talking than by writing and need to experience the world in order to understand it—thus a preference for action. People who prefer introversion focus more on their inner world of ideas, emotions, or impressions; they like to understand the world before experiencing it. They think about what to do before acting.

Sensing/Intuition (S/N)   This scale measures what you pay attention to and how you acquire information. Sensing indicates a preference for using your five senses to notice what is real. Two key words that describe sensing types are *realistic* and *practical*. Intuition indicates a preference for using your imagination, looking beyond your five senses to see new possibilities and ways of doing things. Thus this type values imagination and inspiration.

Thinking/Feeling (T/F)   This scale measures how you make decisions. Thinking types make decisions objectively, in a logical manner, by analyzing and weighing the evidence. The term *feeling* does not refer to feelings/emotions. Feeling types, when making decisions, consider what is important to them based on their personal value system.

Judgment/Perception (J/P)   This scale measures how you act in and relate to the outer world, your attitude, and the lifestyle you prefer. The term *judgment* does not refer to being judgmental. Those who take a judging attitude have a preference for living in a planned and organized way. They like things settled, making decisions, coming to closure, and then carrying on. Those who prefer a perceptive attitude have a preference for living in a more spontaneous and flexible manner, staying open to experience. They are confident in their ability to adapt.

MYERS-BRIGGS TYPE INDICATOR (MBTI) RELATED
SELF-ASSESSMENT TOOLS
Related Internet Site
- Keirsey Character Sorter   http://www.keirsey.com
  Keirsey Temperament Sorter II

Interpreting Individual Scale Scores

The MBTI generates two scores for each of the four bipolar scales. One score, the raw score, indicates the direction of your preference (which of the bipolar measures you prefer on each of the four scales) and is indicated by that scale's one-letter symbol.

The second score, which is numerical, shows how strong or intense your preference is. This score can be misinterpreted. Some assume that strength of preference (higher numerical score) implies excellence. This is not the case. A larger score simply means that the person, if forced to choose, is more clear about what he or she prefers.

The four levels of preference strength and intensity, corresponding numerical scores, and descriptions of MBTI examinees' reaction to each follow.

Very Clear Preference (41 or higher, or 31 for Feeling) These examinees usually agree that they hold the preferences as reported by the MBTI, as well as related attitudes and skills.

Clear Preference (21–39, or 29 for Feeling) This indicates, with reasonable probability, that the examinee holds and acts on the reported preference.

Moderate Preference (11–19) The examinee scoring at this level may still most often agree with the description of the reported preference but should be asked if he or she agrees with the interpretation.

Slight Preference (1–9) This could indicate a split within the examinee. Low scores are often a reflection of tension between the two opposite poles of the preference. It does not indicate equal excellence in, or a command of, both poles of the preference, as is the reaction of some examinees. Tony's scores on the four individual scales follow:

- Extroversion/Introversion (E/I): **E-19**, Moderate to Clear Preference

- Sensing/Intuition (S/N): **N-31**, Clear Preference

- Thinking/Feeling (T/F): **F-37**, Very Clear Preference

- Judgment/Perception (J/P): **J-23**, Clear Preference

Tony's scores reflect rather clear preferences. It's not unusual for most people who take the MBTI to have at least one scale of the four in which the direction and strength of preference are close or almost equal. However, in Tony's case the direction of his preferences is quite clear.

Thus, how you respond on the MBTI determines your preferences, and the preferred bipolar dimensions (E or I, S or N, T or F, and J or P) form your four-letter type. There are 16 possible four-letter types, for which detailed personality profiles have been assembled. There seems to be widespread agreement by those who study personality typing, as well as those who take the inventory, that these profiles closely describe the real personality of most people once the four-letter type is determined.

Understanding Your Four-Letter Type

In order to better understand your four-letter type, let's take a look at Tony's as an example. Tony's four-letter type is ENFJ—extroverted, intuitive, feeling, and judging—with all four being Clear Preferences most of the time. We could describe Tony's type as an extrovert (E), someone who is energized by what goes on around him, who prefers intuition (N), imagination, and inspiration for perceiving and acquiring information. He decides with feeling (F), based on his personal value system, and takes a judging (J), or planned and organized, attitude toward the outer world.

For an expanded description of your four-letter type, consult *Manual: A Guide to the Development and Use of the Myers-Briggs Type Indicator,* by Myers and McCauley, or *Introduction to Type,* by Myers. In addition, the *MBTI Type Booklets* are individual booklets, one for each of the 16 four-letter types.

MBTI and Career Decision Making

The Perception and Judgment Functions People are usually attracted to, and more satisfied in, jobs or careers that provide opportunities to express and use their preferences. The combination of your perception (S/N) and judgment (T/F) functions, the second and third letters of your four-letter type code, is considered to be the most important indicator with regard to career decision making. The types of preferences these two functions assess make a difference in the kind of work you will do best and enjoy the most. The more your daily work needs the kind of perception and deciding that you prefer, the greater the chance that you will experience job satisfaction.

Four combinations can be generated from these two functions:

- **ST, Sensing plus Thinking:** This person is interested in the realities of a given situation and makes decisions by logical analysis. The most satisfaction may be found in occupations where there's an analysis of facts on an impersonal level, such as applied science, business administration, banking, law enforcement, production, and construction.

- **SF, Sensing plus Feeling:** This type is interested in reality that can be observed, makes decisions with personal warmth, and is sensitive to others. Satisfaction may be found in occupations such as health care, community service, teaching, supervision, religious service, office work, and sales.

- **NF, Intuition plus Feeling:** These types also make decisions with personal warmth, but they are more interested in possibilities for projects and people than in facts. Occupations recommended for this group include behavioral science, research, literature, art and music, religious service, health care, and teaching.

- **NT, Intuition plus Thinking:** Persons of this type are also interested in possibilities but handle them by applying objective analysis and problem solving. Occupations usually satisfying to this type include physical science, research, management, computers, law, engineering, and technical work.

We've already pointed out that Tony was beginning to focus on the creative side of the advertising/marketing field, which his clear preference for Intuition supports. The creative, imaginative process in advertising matches well with Intuitive types like Tony.

Just ahead you'll see that we also recommend that Tony channel his management interest into a smaller organization (enhancing the possibility of being able to act on his values) working toward some humanitarian cause. This environment relates to Tony's very clear preference for Feeling.

Even though your major career field of interest is bound to be directly related to the kind of perception and judgment you prefer, your other preferences also play an important role.

Extroversion/Introversion This scale pertains to where you would most like to focus and use your preferred perception and judgment functions. It could help you to decide on a specific work environment or particular organization within a given field. What would your preference be? In the outer world of people and things (E) or inward, within your own private inner world of impressions or ideas (I)?

Tony is energized by his interactions with people, evidenced by his moderate to clear preference for Extroversion. This seems a good match for the usual lively work atmosphere in advertising. It is perhaps a clue to Tony that the "smaller" organization must not be too small.

Judgment/Perception This scale helps you to determine how you would like to go about your job. Would you prefer to be planning operations and, organizing activities, possibly shuting off perception as soon as you have observed enough to make a decision (J)? Or would you prefer to be more flexible and, spontaneous, able to be open to new possibilities and, allowed to suspend judgment in order to take another look and perhaps gain additional information prior to making a decision (P)?

Tony's clear preference for Judgment indicates he likes to plan, be structured in his approach, and make decisions—which will help in managing himself and others. However, the creative process such as that in advertising may need a more flexible and spontaneous approach at times. This issue was brought up with Tony, and he noted the potential conflict. Tony made it a goal to be more balanced in his approach to work and to be alert for situations that are better dealt with in a more "open to possibilities" manner.

The Career Report

One of the newer score-reporting formats for the MBTI is the Career Report, which identifies occupations most often selected by people who are the same MBTI type as you. The database used for comparing your preferences is drawn from more than 60,000 MBTI users in 208 different occupations. If you took a form of the MBTI other than the Career Report, you can ask your career counselor to order it for you from Consulting Psychologists Press. You could also get similar information from the MBTI *Manual*, Appendix D. There you will find 16 lists, representing all MBTI four-letter types, with the same 185 occupational groups listed on each, from highest to lowest by the percentage of workers in that occupation with that type.

Probably the highlight of the Career Report, as far as examinees are concerned, is that it presents two lists of occupations:

1. The 50 most popular occupations (ranked beginning with the most attractive) for your MBTI four-letter type
2. The 25 least popular occupations (with the lowest percentage) for your type

It's suggested that you look over the top 25 percent of all 208 occupational groups represented for a possible career focus—thus the reason for obtaining a list of the top 50.

This is similar to the Strong Interest Inventory (SII) Occupational Scales discussed earlier. It gives you a chance to compare your responses on the MBTI (your preferences) with those of workers in a wide variety of occupations. However, workers participating in the SII were asked whether they liked their jobs, and only those who answered positively were included. This makes the Occupational Scales somewhat more powerful, because you know you are comparing your interests with those of happily employed workers. Therefore, there is a greater chance that you will enjoy that work as well.

Only a subset of 33,000 members of the comparison groups (out of 60,000) reported on the MBTI Career Report were asked to what degree they were satisfied with their work. However, the MBTI *Manual* suggests that the impact of individuals who were not satisfied with their jobs on the rankings of the occupational samples is probably minimal.

Let's see what kind of support Tony can get from these results for the career areas he's still considering. Following are career areas that came through strongly on the Analysis of Life Experience Exercise and the SII and that are still of some interest to Tony, with related occupations from the ENFJ list, from Appendix D of the MBTI *Manual*, and their related position (highest percentage of ENFJs) on that list.

SOCIAL SERVICE RELATED

Religious:
1. Director of Religious Education
2. Specialized Protestant Minister
3. Clergy (all denominations)
4. Protestant Minister
6. Rabbi
7. Priest or Monk
20. Roman Catholic Priest
25. Religious Workers (all denominations)

Counseling:
9. Certified Psychodramatist
12. Counselor: Suicide or Crisis
14. Counselor: Runaway Youth
15. Counselor: School
23. Counselor
40. Psychologist

Teaching/Training:
8. Teacher: Health
11. Teacher: Art, Drama, or Music
39. Health Education Practitioner

ADVERTISING/MARKETING/CREATIVE

36. Marketing Professional (only related comparison group)

PUBLIC RELATIONS/FUND-RAISING

48. Public Relations Worker or Publicity Writer (only related comparison group)

BROADCASTING/ACTING

9. Certified Psychodramatist (acting combined with group counseling)
10. Actor
24. Artist or Entertainer (only related comparison groups)

You'll notice a great deal of similarity between the MBTI's listing of related occupations and the SII's higher-scoring Occupational Scales for Tony.

Information from Appendix D of the MBTI *Manual* strongly supports Tony's main career interests. His preferences show a strong similarity to those of workers in the career areas of interest to him. The career area of interest to Tony that did not appear in the Top 25 percent list is that of managers and administrators. Recall that Tony believed many of his social service, human relations, and teaching/training interests could be satisfied through a management position.

Interpreting Lower-Scoring Occupations of Choice What if an occupation of interest to you places lower down on your list (not in the top 25 percent)? For example, looking at the ENFJ list, we find clergy (all denominations) at the top with 17.79 percent of 534 workers scoring ENFJ. Now, you may think, "What's so high about 17 to 18 percent?" Remember that there are 16 possible subgroups making up each occupation's group of workers. If the workers were equally distributed among the 16 four-letter types, there would be only 6.25 percent of each type in each occupation. Therefore, you can see that 17 to 18 percent is a very high percentage representation under these circumstances.

The MBTI *Manual* states that a client should never be discouraged from entering an occupation on the basis that he or she is not the right type. No career decision should be based on any one source of information, even if it's an excellent source like the SII or the MBTI. However, it would be prudent for someone whose desired occupational choice is showing up lower on the SII Occupational Scales list or the MBTI occupational listings to investigate why this is occurring.

A first step in this investigative effort of researching a possible discrepancy between your MBTI type and a preferred occupation is to check the *Atlas of Type Tables,* by Gerald Macdaid et al. Here you'll find one page for each occupation that the MBTI reports on. On this page is a breakdown of all 16 MBTI types and their percentages of workers in that occupation. Therefore, you can immediately see how your type compares with the other 15, as far as percentage of workers in that particular occupation.

The benefit of this visual presentation is that what you thought was a lower representation of your type might have still been the fifth or sixth highest type of the 16 possible for a particular occupation. In addition, when you note which types are the highest, there might be only a one-letter (or scale) difference to your type, and it just happens to be on a scale that you scored only a slight preference on. If you change that one letter, your new type is among the highest represented for that occupation. However, if you have all clear preferences, as does Tony, switching letters would not be appropriate. What would be appropriate is to discuss with your career counselor just how that one scale might impact that particular job and its suitability for you. Three of four top-scoring scales can be a close match depending on the emphasis of that scale in the particular occupation you're considering.

Let's look at the one area that scored lower for Tony, that of managers and administrators, a broad sampling of 7,463. Looking at the appropriate page in the *Atlas of Type Tables,* we find that Tony's type, ENFJ, ranks eighth highest among the 16 types for the group of managers and administrators, with a representation of 4.92 percent. Initially, that doesn't sound like much, but a closer look produces some interesting information.

The three highest-scoring types for this occupational group, with 17.04 percent, 14.94 percent, and 10.06 percent, respectively, were ESTJ, ISTJ, and ENTJ. What do these three have in common? Yes, you get it, "T." When you think about it, a decision-making approach based more on one's personal values (F) than on objectivity (T) could create some management difficulties when the bottom line often takes priority. This was Tony's most clear preference of the four scales, so let's keep looking.

The fourth and fifth highest-scoring types, with 7.32 percent and 6.93 percent, respectively, were ESFJ and ENFP. What do you notice here? The first time "F" appears, first with S and then with N, as in Tony's type, ENFJ. So now we have reached the point where three of Tony's four scale preferences are appearing. It certainly seems worth the time to speak to Tony about his reaction to all this. How does he see his F decision-making style impeding or not impeding potential management positions? Are there any management positions that might have a better chance of fitting Tony's particular type?

Recall that some of Tony's highest values were of a religious, helping others, and ethical nature. Perhaps he could find a job in a smaller firm (less of the cold, impersonal, larger corporate atmosphere) involved directly with a cause or purpose related somehow to his highest values (such as public relations/fund-raising for a nonprofit). An additional possibility for Tony to consider is a small business of his own related to one of the areas he's interested in, such as an advertising/marketing consultancy specializing in nonprofits and related causes.

Consulting the *Atlas of Type Tables* is a good first step. If the answer is found here, so much the better. If not, then try researching the careers in published sources and by talking to people. There might be some reason, perhaps not clear up to this point, why a particular occupation scored lower for you. Therefore, careful review of career resource materials and talking with people already employed in that occupation could help identify where the discrepancy might be. If you're still interested in that occupation after careful and knowledgeable consideration, at least you've chosen it aware that the fit might not be right, rather than having unrealistic expectations.

What If You Don't Like Your MBTI Type? After your MBTI type has been identified, some aspect might not be pleasing to you. Perhaps you saw yourself in a different light and, after discussing your MBTI results with your career counselor, decided that the MBTI might be accurate. Well, you'll be glad to know that your type is not written in stone. You can develop aspects of yourself that scored lower than what you would have liked. You should discuss with your career counselor aspects of yourself that you would like to improve. Between the two of you, you should be able to come up with strategies for accomplishing that.

Other personality inventories I recommend include the Sixteen Personality Factor (16PF) Questionnaire, the Personal Career Development Profile (PCDP), and the California Psychological Inventory (CPI).

ASSESSING YOUR WORK
AND LIFE VALUES

Work Values

Your level of satisfaction on the job is directly dependent on the degree to which your work values are fulfilled. If you haven't yet completed the Work Values Satisfaction Self-Assessment in Chapter 3, whether you're currently employed or not, this would be a good time to do so. The following list of work values is somewhat condensed from the 80 involved in the self-assessment in Chapter 3:

Achievement	Physical activity
Coworkers	Prestige
Creativity	Recognition
Formal/informal dress code	Respect
Fringe benefits	Responsibility
Helping others/altruism	Routine activity
Hours	Salary
Independence	Supervisor relations
Intellectual reasoning	Surroundings/physical environment
Job security	Travel
Leadership	Upward mobility
Location/distance	Variety of duties
Personal growth	

_____

_____

_____

Add any other work-related values you can think of, and then prioritize them according to those values that are most important to you. If you've completed the self-assessment in Chapter 3, then your results here should be consistent with those.

Life Values

Following are 33 life values:

Aesthetics	Health/physical fitness
Autonomy/freedom of lifestyle	Helping others/altruism
Career	Honesty
Creativity	Intellectual growth
Education	Justice/fairness
Emotional growth/well-being	Knowledge
Family	Leisure time
Financial security	Love relationship
Friends	Morality

Nature	Religion/spirituality
Personal growth	Respect
Physical appearance	Self-awareness
Pleasure	Self-confidence
Popularity	Skill
Power	Travel
Prestige	Wisdom
Recognition	

_____   _____

_____   _____

_____   _____

Look the list over. Are there any life values that are important to you that are not on the list? If so, add these values in the space provided. The next step is to identify, in order of priority, your Top 10 life values. You'll soon realize that this is a difficult task, because they're all important values to most of us. It's hard to let go of any of these values, which the prioritizing forces you to do.

To help you zero in on your top life values, we have provided the Values in Life Questionnaire in Figure 6.8. It is adapted from James McHolland's work with the Human Potential Seminar, a structured, small-group approach designed to help participants gain greater control in their lives, as well as to increase their self-esteem. Complete the Values in Life Questionnaire by answering the questions (give them careful thought) and then noting what life values are represented by your responses. In other words, what do your responses indicate about what's important to you? By completing the Values in Life Questionnaire, you will become more focused about your most important life values and better prepared to prioritize them.

Following are Tony's Top 10 life and work values and some thoughts on how they might impact his career decision making:

LIFE VALUES	WORK VALUES
1. Religion/spirituality	1. Personal growth
2. Emotional growth/well-being	2. Achievement
3. Health/physical fitness	3. Intellectual reasoning
4. Self-awareness/confidence	4. Upward mobility

5.	Morality	5.	Salary
6.	Family	6.	Supervisor relations
7.	Honesty	7.	Creativity
8.	Career	8.	Coworkers
9.	Love relationship	9.	Helping others/altruism
10.	Financial security	10.	Leadership

When in the process of career decision making and trying to identify a field of interest, it's a good idea to take a look at your *life values* and ask, "Will this field impede in any way (directly or indirectly) the attainment of my life values?"

With respect to Tony's values in life, there's a strong ethical component (religion/spirituality, morality, and honesty). Tony needs to find an organization whose corporate mission or culture is somewhat consistent with these values in order for Tony to feel a greater possibility of his

---

FIGURE 6.8

Values in Life Questionnaire

1. Write down 2–3 decisions or choices (small or big) that you've made recently.

2. List 2–3 activities or experiences (ordinary ones are fine) that you've participated in over the past few weeks.

3. Identify 2–3 experiences or times in your life when you felt the most "alive" as a person.

4. Cite 2–3 satisfactions, achievements, or successes you've had in the last couple of weeks.

5. What 2–3 experiences or situations usually make you feel angry? (The opposite of this is your value.)

6. If you could be granted three wishes (none of which can be for additional wishes), what would yours be?

7. Happiness is: _____ .

8. If you had one week left to live, how would you spend it? Where? With whom? Doing what?

9. If you were to die in 10 years, what three things would you want people to remember you for? (or) What would you like to accomplish with your life in the next 10 years?

attaining these life values. Of course, activities outside of work can lead to the attainment of these values also (e.g., church youth group advising). However, if there's a strong values clash on the job, it could take a heavy toll on Tony's health and happiness.

If Tony is going to search for a creative job in advertising/marketing (the direction in which he is leaning), then he would fit best in an organization that operates along ethical principles. Tony also emphasizes emotional growth, self-awareness, and health/fitness as top life values. Will a potential employer place unreasonably high demands on Tony as far as hours to be worked or job-related stress, thus impacting attainment of these values? That would also be important for him to check out, because these stresses can affect two other highly ranked life values, family and love relationship.

In reviewing Tony's top-ranked *work values,* it seems that, ideally, he would like a job in which he could achieve through creative activities, resulting in personal and intellectual growth, as well as helping others (supervisor, coworkers, and clients), and eventually attain a leadership role (involving upward mobility and related salary increases).

Therefore, as Tony looks into different organizations for possible employment, this becomes more or less his checklist of the ten most important values to look for. Some are not easy to assess (e.g., supervisor/coworker relations and attaining a leadership role). However, he can make every effort during the interviewing process to check out these types of concerns. This research can uncover such things as corporate philosophy and mission, hiring, compensation and promotion trends, and related facts.

Tony can now add this value information to the other criteria he has already identified: interests, transferable/functional and specific content/special knowledge skills, and personality preferences. All of these become important areas of consideration when assessing future career possibilities.

A FINAL WORD ON SKILLS

As part of the Analysis of Life Experience Exercise, we showed you how we helped Tony to assess his transferable/functional skills, as well as to identify his preferred specific content/special knowledge skills. With regard to Tony's transferable/functional skills, he identified these from his Top 10 life experiences as the skills he thought would be essential for him to use in his next job/career.

If you did the Analysis of Life Experience Exercise for yourself, then you know how involved it is. If not, you can attempt it now. Regardless of when you have completed it, here are a few steps to add.

Review the skills in your Top 10 life experiences that you classified as essential and used to form your personal skill clusters. Ask yourself which of these you possess to a strong degree (not necessarily perfectly), and which you would like to improve in. In addition, review the skills listed earlier in this chapter (page 130) or those in *What Color Is Your Parachute?* to identify any skills that were not represented in your Top 10 life experiences that you would like to identify now as skills you want to consider using in your next job/career. Make a note of them with your other skills assessment results. Decide which of these skills you have to a strong degree and which you'd like to improve in. Review the skills list for those you do not feel you possess but would like to learn. Some can be job/career related and others can be avocationally related.

Now you're ready to classify your transferable/functional skills into three categories:

1. Skills you have to a strong degree (not necessarily perfectly)

2. Skills you have and would like to improve in

3. Skills you do not possess but would like to learn

If you're having a difficult time judging the level of skill you possess, consider talking with experts in the field in which you're hoping to apply those skills to get a better handle on your level of expertise. In addition, look for the Career Ability Placement Survey (CAPS), by Lila Knapp and Robert Knapp. It's designed to compare your abilities with entry requirements in most occupations. Also, both the *Dictionary of Occupational Titles,* published by the U.S. Department of Labor, and the *Enhanced Guide for Occupational Exploration,* by Marilyn Maze and Donald Mayall, have skill-level codes for each job description, which can aid you in judging how close your skills are to the recommended levels.

CAREER CHANGER UPDATE

★

Mac found that his people and selling skills, developed from his market research business experience, really paid off in his work as a high school counselor as well. Initially he needed to get the students to believe in him. His human relations and persuasive skills helped to accomplish that goal.

The transferability of Mac's skills is also evident in how he used his market research skills to help school administrators plan programming needs for incoming freshmen based on their eighth-grade achievement scores.

Adaptive/Self-Management Skills

There is a third category in addition to your transferable/functional and specific content/special knowledge skills, referred to as *adaptive/self-management* skills. These skills, also thought of as personal traits and qualities, describe how you adapt to and survive in your environment (home, job, etc.), as well as the style in which you use your other skills to accomplish what you set out to do.

Following is a list of 34 adaptive/self-management skills:

Accurate	Logical
Adaptable	Orderly
Adventurous	Patient
Analytical	Persuasive
Businesslike	Practical
Cheerful	Productive
Confident	Professional
Considerate	Realistic
Decisive	Responsible
Dependable	Self-starting

Ethical	Sensitive
Fair-minded	Spontaneous
Friendly	Tactful
Helpful	Thorough
Imaginative	Tolerant
Independent	Trustworthy
Intelligent	Truthful

Note the ones you believe characterize how you go about doing what you need to do, on and off the job. Add to the list any additional descriptive terms that describe your style of doing things.

What If I Didn't Complete the Analysis of Life Experience Exercise?

If you know, for whatever reason, that you're not going to complete the Analysis of Life Experience Exercise, then at least take this following minimal step. Review the skills listed earlier in this chapter (page 130) or those in *What Color Is Your Parachute?* or another suitable resource, and draw up your own list of skills you think you possess to a high degree, those you would like to improve in, and those you currently do not have but would like to learn. When you've completed this step, identify those you want to have involved in your next career and those that are more avocationally or leisure related.

After determining what skills you now have and desire to involve in your next career, prioritize them according to the ones you want to use the most. You should also identify specific content/special knowledge skills. It's quick to do, and when added to your most preferred transferable/functional skills, they will help add some focus to your career decision making. Of course, you can't decide on a career based on skills alone, so you should add the other important elements we've discussed up to now: interests, personality preferences, and life and work values.

Be creative in how you look at yourself, your skills, and your options. Those who will succeed in this belt-tightening, changing job market are the ones who are able to adapt, adjust, and change in order to stay employable. Other skills assessment instruments I recommend include the EUREKA Skills Inventory, Exploring and Developing Emotional Intelligence Skills, and the Personal Skills Map (PSM). See Appendix B: Recommended Readings: Tests and Testing Resources.

TONY FINDS HIS NICHE

It's been four years since Tony took part in the career counseling process described in this chapter. His top career goal upon leaving the counseling process was to search for a creative position in the advertising field.

Tony found it difficult getting his "foot in the door." He was able to gain some interviews but never a job offer. Feedback he received was questionable. One interviewer, when asked, reported that Tony didn't come across as if he really wanted the position, whereas Tony, who is an enthusiastic and upbeat person, felt that he had displayed that side of himself during the interview process.

Tony's gut-level feeling was that perhaps he didn't have the amount of experience these advertising firms were interested in. Tony did take a job selling advertising space in a religious publication. In doing so, he was able to remain in the advertising field, in an area related to an important part of his life—that of religion.

Tony's position in advertising space sales, as well as the two slightly related jobs that followed, fit his previous pattern of about six months to one year on a job. Obviously, he had yet to find a good fit.

A priority that continued for Tony was to find work in which he could apply his M.B.A. knowledge. One possible area, he believed, was banking and finance. Tony decided to send out 100 cover letters and resumes to banks of interest—not exactly the approach (the numbers game) that many career counselors would recommend (at least, not the only approach to be used). Yet, Tony received responses from five banks, had three interviews, and accepted the one offer that was made.

Tony's new position is that of underwriter working with small businesses in the loan process. Tony feels good about the fact that his M.B.A. has direct application. In helping out small businesses, Tony feels he is helping others (top skill and work value) though the job does not have much of a creative outlet (also a top skill and work value). He does, however, have the opportunity to fulfill these other aspects through the bank's involvement in the community. This occurs primarily in the area of fund-raising (a career choice generated during counseling) for the United Way and involvement with Boys and Girls Clubs.

Tony has been in this position now for more than two and a half years. It seems he's found some stability. When asked for his thoughts and feelings with regard to the value of his career counseling experience, he offered the following:

"It certainly helped with identifying what to look at to figure out a career path. The exercises are an important step. The identifying and prioritizing helped me gain a focus for my job search. It was a good foundation to move forward from."

CHAPTER 7

RESEARCHING YOUR CAREER GOAL

★

ON-LINE AND PUBLISHED RESOURCES

The only way for you to know whether you are lacking in education, training, or experience is by first having a clear career goal, beginning with an assessment like that in Chapter 6.

Once you have completed the assessment process, you still might not be clear about your objective. Some people are more confused than before they began because they are aware of many more possibilities than they had been considering. This is healthy confusion.

As a result, you might be considering a few different career goals. To help narrow down the possibilities, you need to do your research. The following Internet career planning sites and detailed descriptions of written career resources will help you identify valuable sources of information.

CAREER PLANNING—GENERAL INFORMATION RESOURCES

Related Internet Sites

One of the best, overall career planning sites is:

- The Riley Guide: Employment Opportunities and Job Resources on the Internet: http://www.dbm.com/ jobguide/

Other sites offering related news, articles, resources, and information:

- Career Development Manual: http://www.adm. uwaterloo.ca/infocecs/CRC/ manual-home.html/
- Career Magazine: http://www.careermag.com/
- Career Mosaic: http://www.careermosaic. com/
- Career Paradise: http://www.emory.edu/
- Career Resource Center: http://www.careers.org/
- CareerWeb: http://www.cweb.com/
- Job Options: http://www.joboptions.com/
- JobSmart: http://jobsmart.org/
- JobTrak: http://www.jobtrak.com/
- The Monster Board: http://www.monster.com/
- National Business Employment Weekly: http://www.nbew.com/
- Occupational/Labor Market Data: http://www.state.ia.us/ government/wd/noicc/
- Online Career Center: http://www.occ.com/
- Student Center: http://www.studentcenter.com/
- A Virtual Job Fair: http://www.careerexpo.com/
- Yahoo!: http://www.yahoo.com/ Go to Business & Economy, Employment.

Guide for Occupational Exploration (GOE)

The *GOE* classifies jobs into 12 Interest Areas, 66 Work Groups, and 348 Subgroups, with reference to over 12,000 specific job titles. The main idea is to identify which Work Groups you have the most interest in. You can then find specific, related job titles with *Dictionary of Occupational Titles,* or *DOT,* numbers, explained in the following section. In the front of the

GOE are instructions on how to translate your preferred interests, values, activities, school subjects, work experience, and military occupational specialties into related Work Groups.

Figure 7.1 shows the *GOE* table of contents. Beside each Interest Area title, we've provided the related Holland RIASEC theme(s) to help you identify interest areas (refer to Chapter 6).

For example, if your strongest Holland theme is Artistic, you could look at Interest Area 01: Artistic. When you look up a Work Group in the *GOE*, you'll find a general overview of jobs classified in that Work Group, some hints that can help you tell how interested you might be in those jobs, and requirements for related skills, education, or training. (Other sources of RIASEC scores include the Harrington O'Shea CDM System, the Career Assessment Inventory Enhanced, and the Self-Directed Search.)

Next, as noted, you'll find a list of specific job titles with nine-digit *DOT* numbers. The first three and last three digits are for classification purposes and are explained in the introduction of the *DOT*. The middle three digits describe the level of skill required (the lower the number, the higher the skill required) for working with data (fourth digit), people (fifth digit), and things (sixth digit) on that job. The skill levels (0 to 9) for each area are also described in the introduction to the *DOT*.

The Dictionary of Occupational Titles (DOT)

The *DOT* is organized numerically, not alphabetically. It provides (in two volumes) detailed job descriptions for over 12,000 jobs and references to over 20,000 job titles. It would be worth your time to look up related Work Groups in the *GOE*, scan the list of specific job titles, and look up in the *DOT* any jobs that sound interesting. When you look up a job in the *DOT*, scan the other jobs listed on the prior, same, or following pages. They are often closely related, and you might be interested in those as well. In addition, the latest edition of the *DOT* (1991) provides the following information with each job description: specific vocational preparation requirements, general education development (consisting of reasoning, mathematical, and language development requirements), and the physical demands involved.

If you're not clear about what's entailed, don't eliminate any possible job until you check the *DOT* description. This step does take time, but it means that you will know, with confidence, that you covered all the bases, leaving no stone unturned. That's a good feeling to have.

FIGURE 7.1

Interest Areas and Work Groups from the Guide for Occupational Exploration (GOE)

01: **Artistic (A)**
01:01 Literary Arts
01:02 Visual Arts
01:03 Performing Arts: Drama
01:04 Performing Arts: Music
01:05 Performing Arts: Dance
01:06 Craft Arts
01:07 Elemental Arts
01:08 Modeling
02: **Scientific (I)**
02:01 Physical Sciences
02:02 Life Sciences
02:03 Medical Sciences
02:04 Laboratory Technology
03: **Plants and Animals (R/S)**
03:01 Managerial Work: Plants & Animals
03:02 General Supervision: Plants & Animals
03:03 Animal Training and Service
03:04 Elemental Work: Plants/ Animals
04: **Protective (R/S)**
04:01 Safety and Law Enforcement
04:02 Security Services
05: **Mechanical (R)**
05:01 Engineering
05:02 Managerial Work: Mechanical
05:03 Engineering Technology
05:04 Air & Water Vehicle Operation
05:05 Craft Technology
05:06 Systems Operation
05:07 Quality Control
05:08 Land and Water Vehicle
05:09 Materials Control
05:10 Crafts
05:11 Equipment Operation
05:12 Elemental Work: Mechanical
06: **Mechanical (R)**
06:01 Production Technology
06:02 Production Work
06:03 Quality Control
06:04 Elemental Work: Industrial
07: **Business Detail (C)**
07:01 Administrative Detail
07:02 Mathematical Detail
07:03 Financial Detail
07:04 Oral Communications
07:05 Records Processing
07:06 Clerical Machine Operation
07:07 Clerical Handling
08: **Selling (E)**
08:01 Sales Technology
08:02 General Sales
08:03 Vending
09: **Accommodating (S)**
09:01 Hospitality Services
09:02 Barbering and Beauty Services
09:03 Passenger Services
09:04 Customer Services
09:05 Attendant Services
10: **Humanitarian (S)**
10:01 Social Services
10:02 Nursing, Therapy, & Special Teaching
10:03 Child and Adult Care
11: **Leading-Influencing (E/I or E)**
11:01 Mathematics & Statistics (E/I)
11:02 Educational & Library Services (E/I)
11:03 Social Research (E/I)
11:04 Law (E)
11:05 Business Administration
11:06 Finance (E)
11:07 Service Administration (E)
11:08 Communication (E)
11:09 Promotion (E)
11:10 Regulations Enforcement (E)
11:11 Business Management (E)
11:12 Contracts and Claims (E)
12: **Physical Performing (R)**
12:01 Sports
12:02 Physical Feats

As you review the *DOT* job descriptions, it's a good idea to keep some notes on the pros and cons of each job you're looking up. This will come in handy later as you proceed to narrow down your list of options.

Of course, you can look up any Work Group whose title alone strikes you as interesting. In addition, in the back of the *GOE* is an index that will identify the Work Group number and *DOT* number for any job title you might already have in mind. The *DOT* also has an index where job titles can be looked up to find *DOT* numbers.

The new *O*NET Dictionary of Occupational Titles*, published by JIST Works, Inc., replaces the 1991 edition of the *DOT* and provides information on about 1,200 jobs. While the *DOT* described over 12,000 jobs, many were not of great interest to most using it. O*NET job descriptions, covering close to 100 percent of the labor market, are more in-depth than those found in the *DOT*. In addition to job descriptions, it includes information on average earnings, education or training requirements, and knowledge, skills, and abilities needed.

DICTIONARY OF OCCUPATIONAL TITLES (DOT)

Related Internet Site

The new replacement for the *DOT* sponsored by the Department of Labor's Education and Training Administration Occupational Information Network (O*NET) can be found at:

http://www.doleta.gov/programs/onet/

Occupational Outlook Handbook (OOH)

Once you've looked up related jobs in the *GOE* or *DOT* and can identify those you're most interested in, then you're ready to use the *Occupational Outlook Handbook* (*OOH*) to gather information that goes beyond the *DOT* job description.

In the *OOH* you'll find 250 jobs (representing 80 percent of the workforce) described in greater detail. Categories of information include the following:

- Nature of the work (This is similar to the *DOT* description but usually a bit longer.)

- Places of employment (The more work settings of interest, the greater the chance of finding employment.)

- Training, other qualifications, and advancement (It is important to understand how one can qualify.)

- Employment outlook (The *OOH* is updated every two years, but the employment outlook information is general, for the whole country, and thus not localized for your specific area. Therefore, take note of national trends, but check out the facts where you live or might want to live.)

- Earnings and related benefits (Always note what year's edition of the *OOH* you're looking at and calculate the effect of inflation on salaries listed in older editions.)

- Work conditions (This category describes what you can expect with this type of job, but conditions vary from setting to setting.)

- Related occupations (This is another way of expanding your options and increasing your awareness of the world of work.)

After being laid off from a social work–related, nonprofit position, Victoria took her writing/editing interest to technical editing in a corporate setting. The transition was facilitated with additional coursework.

- Sources of additional information (Usually these are the related professional associations to which one can send for information.)

OCCUPATIONAL OUTLOOK HANDBOOK (OOH)
Related Internet Sites
Find the *OOH* at:
- Bureau of Labor Statistics: http://stats.bls.gov/ocohome/htm. Go to Publications.
- JobTrak: http://www.jobtrak.com
- JobWeb: http://www.jobweb.org

Let's summarize three methods for using the *GOE, DOT,* and *OOH:*

1. You have a job title in mind; consult the index of the *DOT* for a job description or the index of the *OOH* for additional information. You could also check the index of the *GOE* for the Work Group to which the job belongs, and there you'll find additional related jobs as well.

2. You can translate the Holland Occupational Themes with which you identify the most strongly into job titles by identifying the related Work Groups from the *GOE* (refer to Figure 7.1). If there are job titles that interest you and/or strike your curiosity, you can look them up in the *DOT* by using the nine-digit *DOT* number. If you desire additional information, then move on to the *OOH.*

3. If you have an interest in a general area of work and want to identify specific job titles that are categorized in it, you can look up related Work Groups (e.g., Social Services 10.01, Finance 11.06, or Communication 11.08) and find specific titles in the *GOE* and then proceed to the *DOT* and/or the *OOH.*

BEST LINKS TO OTHER CAREER SITES

Related Internet Sites

- Career Paradise: http://www.emory.edu/CAREER/
- JobHunt: On-Line Job Meta-List: http://www.job-hunt.org/
- Magellan Internet Guide: http://www.mckinley.com
- Purdue University: http://www.ups.purdue.edu Go to Services for Students, Additional Web Resources.
- Quintessential Career & Job Hunting Resource Guide: http://stetson.edu/~hansen/careers.html
- The Riley Guide: Employment Opportunities and Job Resources on the Internet: http://www.dbm.com/jobguide/
- What Color Is Your Parachute Job Hunting Online: http://www.tenspeedpress.com/parachute/front.htm

Specific Career-Focused Books

If, after reading the *OOH* information on a particular job, you're still interested in finding out more, you can check the library (or bookstore) for books focused on that particular career. Look for titles like *Careers in . . .* or *Opportunities in . . . .* The publisher of this book, VGM Career Horizons, has over 160 titles in its *Opportunities in . . .* series.

INFORMATION ON SPECIFIC CAREER FIELDS

Related Internet Sites

- America's Career InfoNet: http://www.acinet.org
  Go to Resources or Occupational Search.

- The Argus Clearinghouse: http://www.clearinghouse.net/
  Go to Business & Economy.

- Career Choices: http://www.umanitoba.ca/
  counselling/careers.html

- Career Exploration Links: http://www.uhs.berkeley.edu/
  careerlibrary/links/careerme/htm

- Career Services Major Resource Kit: http://www.udel.edu/CSC/mrk.html

- Find-O-Rama Searchable Data Base on Various Careers: http://www.review.com/career/
  find/index.cfm

- Job Web—Career Choices: http://www.jobweb.org/Catapult/
  choice.htm

- LookSmart: http://www.looksmart.com/
  Go to Business & Finance, Jobs/Careers & Work, Occupational Fields.

- The Riley Guide: Employment Opportunities & Job Resources on the Internet: http://www.dbm.com/jobguide/
  jobs.html
  Go to Resources for Specific Occupational Areas.

- Specific Career Resource Sites: http://www.stetson.edu/offices/
  career/speciali.htm

PEOPLE RESOURCES AND
INFORMATIONAL INTERVIEWING

When you've completed these steps and are still interested in increasing your knowledge about a certain career, then it's time to talk with as many people as you can who are working in that career field, in as many different work settings as you can find them in. Informational interviewing is a way of getting your more in-depth questions answered and building your network of professional contacts as well.

PART II

Preparing for the Next Steps in Your Career Change:
Strategies for Dealing with Challenges

★

CHAPTER 8

GETTING ADDITIONAL EDUCATION, TRAINING, OR EXPERIENCE

★

A key part of your research is to find out what skills are required in the type of work you're considering. In addition, what requirements are there related to education, training, or experience that one must have to be able to pursue employment in that career area? Once you have that information, you're in a better position to judge where you stand in relation to those requirements.

Even if you have determined that certain education, training, or experience is necessary, be sure to find out whether there are any exceptions to that rule. If you can identify exceptions, try to contact someone in that situation to find out everything you can about possible alternatives. Returning to school is a big time and money commitment, so you want to be absolutely sure that it's necessary in order for you to gain employment in the career area you desire.

It's not unusual for career changers, after identifying what they most want to do, to realize that they do need to acquire additional education, training, or experience. (We'll deal with the possibility of needing additional experience later.)

Seven of our ten career changers pursued further education to upgrade their skills in order to qualify to make their desired career changes:
- Ed and Patricia completed law school.
- Allen completed dental school and reports that in order to expand his dentistry practice, he has enrolled in continuing education courses to develop additional dentistry skills.
- Victoria completed a technical writing certificate program.
- Larry completed a degree program in training.
- Zephree initially started a degree program in criminal justice toward her original goal of becoming a juvenile probation officer. She is contemplating attending law school, with just one year left to her undergraduate degree program.
- Martha plans to return to school to pursue a third career, one related to her first two (teaching and restaurant owning), that of being a nutritionist and thus a bilingual one as well.

Here are some possible reasons for returning for additional education or training:

- To gain additional knowledge in a particular subject area related to your new career goal
- To complete a degree required for entry into a new career
- To prepare for a licensing or certification examination in your new career area
- To meet requirements for entrance into a graduate program necessary for your new career goal
- To stay competitive

DEALING WITH YOUR FEARS RELATED TO FURTHER EDUCATION OR TRAINING

At this point, you've determined whether or not you need additional education or training for the job you most want. Let's say you've verified that you need a college degree and haven't been in school since completing some college courses right after graduating high school. For adults who have not been in school for 15 or more years, the thought of returning to school can be anxiety producing. Some common fears of returning adult students with regard to returning to college are discussed here.

Will I Survive Academically?

Perhaps the greatest fear of returning adult students is, "Do I have the ability necessary to survive college (or other educational/training experience)?" Usually, some reality testing has to occur to help calm this fear. Just *how* hard or difficult will it be? To answer that question, first of all we will assume that you haven't gotten to this point without doing your homework. In other words, you've made a decision to pursue a new career goal based on the identification of attributes that you possess and enjoy.

If so, then the choice you've made should be somewhere in the ballpark of your abilities and skills. If not, you are at least clear on what skills you need to develop. Either way, following are some strategies that might help to lessen your fears of returning to college. (Most would apply to other related training as well.)

Speak with Instructors Visit a local college and seek out instructors in the departments in which you would be pursuing coursework. Ask them about the courses you're interested in taking, what's involved (assignments, papers, exams, etc.), what books you will be reading, and anything they can offer to help you better understand the expectations regarding student performance. You'll be able to judge your potential better based on information, rather than speculation.

Sit In on Some Classes If you happen to make a good contact with an instructor, maybe he or she will let you sit in on a class or two. Finding out how an actual class proceeds should be interesting for someone who either never has been to college or is returning after many years' absence. Visiting beginning courses in a program would be the wisest approach. This could help you avoid feeling overwhelmed by the advanced knowledge in a field you're just beginning to learn about. Taking a beginning-level course could also be a way of testing out your interest and academic ability. However, be sure to check out the strategies listed here first, before making that decision.

Ask a Friend Who Has Been in School Recently Check with your network of contacts for those who have been in, or returned to, college recently. Ask them about their experiences. Could they share with you any assignments, papers, or exams they've completed? (Again, for beginning-level courses, if possible.) Chances are that your anxieties will be lessened. You'll realize that time and effort are required for assignments and exams, but it is definitely within reach of your talents and abilities.

Nevertheless, you might still feel inadequate about certain abilities; therefore, these assignments or exams still have you worried. To help, most colleges have developmental courses in writing, reading, and mathematics. If you need help in any of these areas, you could initially avoid coursework related to it while you enroll in related developmental courses to build up your skill levels to those needed.

Study skills is another area that many returning adult college students are concerned about. There are specific workshops, tutoring, and courses offered to help college students develop appropriate study skills and thus ease the transition back to college. This could be an excellent choice for a first-time college course, especially if you have been out of school for a long period.

Visit the Returning Adult Student Office Many college campuses have an office whose staff assists returning adult students with their transition back to college. Services come in the form of individual counseling, group counseling, support groups, workshops, and the like. Their assistance can help you to become more informed about resources available to you and how to take advantage of them. If an office like this is not available to you on the campus of your school, seek out the assistance of a counselor in a counseling center or similar site. He or she can usually provide much of the same information. If someone else is designated on your campus to do so, the counselor can usually point the way.

Feeling Out of Place with Younger Students

Statistics reveal that over 50 percent of college students today are over 25. About one-third are over 30, and the level increases for graduate-level programs. Adults returning to college is a more common phenomenon than ever before. There is the opportunity to connect with all types of new people, of a variety of age groups and ethnic backgrounds.

Both Patricia (law) and Allen (dental) returned to a professional school at an age that most would think not likely—36 and 30, respectively. They survived despite the obstacles. Patricia experienced a real lack of support from her family for going to law school. Even though she would have felt much better having their encouragement, she was able to follow through. In addition, with respect to the role of support, Sandra's family tried to talk her into staying with the field of law rather than changing to become a book publisher, because they saw being a lawyer as a significant position of status for a female.

Most college instructors will tell you how happy they are to have returning adult students in their classes. The maturity level and experience they bring is refreshing and invigorating and definitely adds to the classroom experience for everyone. Often, some of the traditional-age college students lack maturity and commitment to the educational process. They are concerned only with getting through the program, grabbing their degree, and trying to gain employment. Therefore, where returning adults wonder whether they can keep up with younger students, it's quite the opposite of reality. It's the younger students who are challenged to keep up with the commitment to excellence that most returning adults value.

GETTING ADDITIONAL EDUCATION

Related Internet Sites

- America's Learning eXchange: http://www.alx/org
- Career Resource Center: http://www.careers.org/
  Go to Learning Web Sites, Learning, College and University Web Pages.
- College & University Home Pages (3,000+ schools): http://www.mit.edu/people/cdemello/univ.html
- Guide to Graduate Schools: http://www.jobtrak.com/
  Go to Students & Alumni, Resource Center, Guide to Graduate School.
- JobWeb: Colleges & Universities (identifies schools by subject area): http://www.jobweb.org/catapult/colleges.htm

- Peterson's Education &   http://www.petersons.com/
  Career Center (returning
  to school, distance learning,
  financial aid, and more):
- The Princeton Review   http://www.review.com/
  (information for under-
  graduate, graduate, medical,
  law, and business students):
- The University of Texas at   http://www.utexas.edu/
  Austin (1,000+ U.S.
  colleges/universities):
- Yahoo!:   http://www.yahoo.com/
  Go to Education, Higher
  Education, Colleges and Universities.

Getting College Credit for What You Already Know

As you prepare to enter or return to college, you'll be glad to know that there are alternative methods to the traditional classroom approach for gaining college credit, including portfolio assessment, life experience for credit, and credit by examination.

Portfolio assessment involves documenting your experiences through performance, recommendation, or both to show that you've mastered certain abilities and skills. Experiences can be drawn from employment; community service or volunteer work; independent study and reading; noncollege training, courses, or workshops; and other related accomplishments. Many traditional colleges have special credit-for-life-experience programs designed for returning adult students. A good reference to check is *Bear's Guide to Earning College Degrees Non-Traditionally*, by John Bear. It includes programs in both traditional and alternative colleges. You could also contact the Association for Experiential Education, C.U. Box 249, Boulder, CO 80309, for information on alternative education. In addition, check *Innovative Graduate Programs Directory*, published by Empire State College, and *The Adult Learner's Guide to Alternative and External Degree Programs*, by

E. J. Sullivan, published by the American Council on Education through Oryx Press.

> Zephree is finishing her undergraduate degree in criminal justice. She works full-time and is enrolled in a special program for adults that grants credit for life experience via a portfolio assessment. Programs like these help many students accomplish their desired career changes in a more timely manner.

Programs of this nature can possibly save a year, or two, of college that you would have spent in a traditional program. They also allow you to take the courses that are most important to you, because there are fewer general educational course requirements to fulfill. However, it is not an easy task. Developing a portfolio takes time and dedication. Some schools offer workshops and courses to assist in this process. If you want to get a better idea of what's involved, read *Earn College Credit for What You Know*, by Susan Simosko. For information on the process approved by the American Council on Education for gaining credit for learning outside the classroom, contact the American Council on Education, Program on Non-Collegiate Sponsored Instruction, One Dupont Circle, Washington, DC 20036.

Ask the college admissions counselors for schools where you intend to apply about earning credit through examination. Following are a few of the prominent programs in this category:

- College Level Examination Program (CLEP)
- ACT–Proficiency Examination Program (ACT–PEP)
- Defense Activity for Non-Traditional Educational Support (DANTES)
- Advanced Placement Program (APP)
- Program on Non-Sponsored Instruction (PONSI)

IF MORE EXPERIENCE IS NECESSARY

Perhaps, as a result of your research into the career you're most interested in, you discovered it wasn't in having college coursework or a specific degree where you fell short. Rather, you were able to identify the need for experience, using certain skills, maybe in a particular work environment. In this situation, there are a few possibilities to check out for gaining necessary experience.

Volunteering

Don't think you have to work a lot of hours to be welcomed as a volunteer. Volunteering is experiencing a new wave of popularity. Volunteers are often welcomed even if only available for a few hours a week. This could be an excellent way to check out your career area of interest while polishing skills and gaining meaningful experience (as well as increasing your network of contacts). There's usually an office on college campuses that serves as a resource center for volunteer activities, both on campus and in the surrounding area.

Internship

Both profit and nonprofit organizations offer the opportunity for you to gain work experience in exchange for your services at a lower rate of pay, usually for a year or two. If this type of opportunity fits for you, then it could be most worthwhile for both parties—if you can afford to do it. Perhaps a current job could be worked on a more flexible schedule, or reduced hours, thus making an internship opportunity more of a possibility. Consult the *National Directory of Internships,* published annually by the National Society for Experiential Education, or Peterson's *Internships,* published by Peterson's Guides.

VOLUNTEERING AND INTERNSHIP
Related Internet Sites

- Action Without Borders   http://www.idealist.org
  (Nonprofit Websites, volunteer
  information):
- Find Your Future (search for   http://www.4work.com/
  internships/volunteer work):
- JobTrak: http://www.jobtrak.com/
  Go to Students & Alumni, Jobs
  and Internships.
- The Peace Corp: http://www.peacecorps.gov/
- Student Center Where Do   http://www.aboutwork.com/
  I Go from Here?:   jobs3/

CAREER CHANGER UPDATE

★

Zephree gained her current position as a legal advocate as a result of the work she accomplished as a volunteer for the same organization. Not only did she gain valuable experience as a sexual assault and violence victims' advocate, but it led to a terrific job offer as well.

Temporary Work

The temporary-work market has experienced huge growth, with an estimated 2.2 million workers employed on a temporary basis in 1997 (1 million more than in 1990). With downsizing, many companies still experience the same amount of work to get done, or more. Rather than hiring new employees, they've turned to either calling back those they cut (if they're still available) or, more likely, making use of temporary services (referred to as contingent workers—any job for which there is no explicit or implicit contract for long-term employment). In this way, the employer saves on the costs of benefits (usually not provided for temporary help), especially health insurance. Yet it still helps employees who otherwise could be out of a job. However, it's not unusual, these days, for agencies who place temporary employees to offer group insurance for their workers.

Having spread across most job fields (including white-collar areas such as accounting, legal, marketing, human resources, information systems, and administrative functions), temporary work is likely to be available in an area related to your career interests. One-third of all new jobs created today will be filled by temporary workers. This can provide you with the opportunity to increase your skills and gain the type of work experience in which you're interested and perhaps even attain a full-time position at the location where you're temping.

Part-Time Work

Another avenue to consider for gaining needed additional experience is part-time work, which would probably pay more than an internship. Its applicability for you really depends on the type of experience you're looking for and how that's possibly attained. The appealing aspect of gaining experience through part-time work is that you can continue with your full-time job or college coursework.

All four of the approaches presented here (volunteering, internships, temporary work, and part-time work) might offer a chance for you to gain the experience you need for the career area you're interested in. They can help you in further checking out the career field and work environment and developing some meaningful professional contacts, as well as guiding your decision making and leading to the attainment of your career goals.

CHAPTER 9
PRACTICAL CONCERNS: TIME AND MONEY

★

In this chapter we focus on the challenge of finding the time and money you will need for your career change. Being organized about your time can be the difference between success and failure. You can enhance the accomplishment of your goals when you are organized about your time and can plan, more effectively, to complete the goals you set out to accomplish.

TAKING CONTROL OF YOUR TIME

Each of us has his or her own way of dealing with the subject of time management. For some of us, our current time-management techniques are sufficient—we're on top of the tasks we need to complete. However, others need tips on spending time effectively.

How Do You Spend It?

Before you can exercise effective time-management techniques, you need to recognize how you currently spend your time. This can be easily done by simply sitting down and thinking about what and when you do what you do, as well as by keeping a log of the activities you take part in, including those related to work, family, social, and leisure aspects of your life. You might find you have more free time than you thought (or time you can make available by sacrificing less important activities, like watching television).

Both Ed and Patricia attended law school part-time, at night, for four years while working full-time in jobs related to the law to some extent (criminal law clerk and law librarian, respectively).

Develop a Weekly Schedule

The next step is to develop a schedule for each day of the week, indicating time that is already committed. This could include your work schedule or course schedule. Be sure to add in the time for commuting back and forth.

Next, block off those days and times when something regular occurs: family dinners on weekends, bowling night, exercise time, time alone for yourself, or organization meetings. Keep in mind that none of this is written in stone. You'll need to remain flexible about scheduling activities. You might decide as your goals become clearer that cutbacks are needed in some areas, as far as time demands. However, it's wise to always have some time scheduled (even if less than usual) with those people of greatest importance to you, as well as some time alone for yourself.

Once you have figured out how you spend your time in a typical week, you're more clear about what time is available for the new tasks you are encountering: college (or other related training) or job searching while still employed. If you are unemployed, you could be spending 40 to 80 hours a week on your search, whereas if employed full time, you could be spending 15 to 25 hours per week.

Set Your Goals

Here's what we suggest you do next: Every Sunday, sit down with your weekly schedule and figure out what you want to get done that following week. If you're back in school, what work needs to be accomplished in terms of readings, papers, and so on? If you're job searching, what contacts need to be initiated, which need to be followed up on, and what readings, and other related tasks might you complete?

Then estimate the time needed to accomplish each goal. Next, plug these goals into the time slots available on your schedule. This is where your juggling skills might come into play. In addition, if time is tight, you'll need to set priorities and let go of some activities in favor of your educational/training or job search goals.

As you develop your plans on Sunday for the upcoming week, write out each day's goals and the allotted times to work on them. Carry these daily schedules, or To Do lists, with you every day for easy reference. This will prevent the feeling of all your intended goals spinning around in your head. Write it all down, carry it with you for easy reference, and save yourself one big headache.

Stay Flexible

You'll need to remain flexible with regard to your weekly schedule. It's not unusual for circumstances to change, thereby creating the need to revise your schedule. In fact, it's not unusual to make small revisions each day on your goals if they took more time or less time to accomplish than anticipated or if other legitimate priorities came up.

So don't consider your goals as being carved in stone. However, you'll know better than anyone else how you are really doing with respect to your goals. Are you making excuses or procrastinating? Or are you doing everything within your power to accomplish your goals and reach for the success that you have decided you want for yourself?

FINDING THE TIME FOR EDUCATION, TRAINING, OR EXPERIENCE

With work and family responsibilities, it's no surprise that finding time to return to college is a concern. This issue can be approached from a couple of different directions.

First of all, delivery methods for offering college credits have changed over the years. Classes no longer take place only in the traditional classroom. Options now exist for learning in the home, the workplace, university/college satellite branches, and community-based sites (libraries, park districts, community centers, etc.) via correspondence (see John Bear's *College Degrees by Mail* and Frey's *College Degrees You Can Earn from Home*), audiocassette, videotape, television, on-line services, and related approaches. These are referred to as *distance education* options, meaning that living and learning take place away from the central campus. Some traditional colleges have one or more of these types of programs (though most are found at alternative schools), as well as evening, weekend, and summer intensive programs. Contact the following organizations for further distance education information: National Distance Learning Center (NDLC), Owensboro Community College, Owensboro, KY 42301; and United States Distance Learning Association (USDLA), Box 5106, Livermore, CA 94583.

In addition, the National University Continuing Education Association (NUCEA) in conjunction with Peterson's Guides has published two books related to long-distance learning. The one dealing with correspondence programs is *The Independent Study Catalog,* and the other, which focuses on various electronic media and formats, is *The Electronic University: A Guide to Distance Learning.*

DISTANCE LEARNING AND ON-LINE COLLEGE EDUCATION
Related Internet Sites
- Peterson's Education and Career Center: http://www.petersons.com/
- Western Governors University: http://www.westgov.org/smart/vu/vul.html

---

Second, planning is important. Once your career goal is clearly established and related education/training requirements are identified, it's important to plan out your college program in a manner that is sensible for you, pertaining to your current ability and skill levels and what you can handle with regard to your other responsibilities. Figure two hours of study time for every hour of class time, for starters. This will probably lessen as you go. Counselors and faculty can assist you with this step. If you have never applied solid time management techniques to accomplish your goals, this would be a good time to start.

The demands on your time when you're returning to school are very similar to time demands for carrying on a job search or starting your own business. It's important to communicate with your significant others what your plans are and what the related demands on your time will be. Being organized about your time will also help ensure that your studies don't interfere with your current work situation. In fact, it's probably a good idea, if feasible, to inform your supervisor about your educational plans and what you hope to accomplish. Your employer may even be willing to help pay for it, though it usually has to relate to your current job.

JOB SEARCHING WHILE EMPLOYED

When you first read the words "Job Searching While Employed," your initial reaction might be, "Impossible!" You might think that the standard business hours of 9 A.M. to 5 P.M. are the only times one can job search. Therefore, since you're working full-time, it can't be done. This is not at all the case, as the following guidelines explain.

Stay Employed

Don't quit your job, if at all possible. Unfortunately, there is still a negative stereotype attached to unemployed applicants by many prospective employers, as unfair as it might seem. However, with the vast number of downsizings, layoffs, early retirements, and the like, there's more understanding these days toward people who are unemployed.

In general, employers' reaction, though somewhat less so now than in the past, to applicants who are unemployed is similar to the common response when you first applied for credit. No one would give you credit unless you already had it, which makes getting your first credit card difficult. In the job search scenario, employers are unwilling at times to hire the unemployed, so you cannot get a job unless you already have one. However, if you have some type of special training that employers are looking for, they may weigh that as more important than your unemployment status.

Though that sounds a bit insane, if it's the reality out there, then it's important to be aware of it and to hang on to your current job. If the job becomes unbearable and it would be a serious mistake to stay on—for reasons related to stress, for example—then try to find temporary or interim work.

Making Contacts

As you identify people you want to talk with, either those you already know or people whom others in your network refer you to, you'll want to write them a letter stating your interest in the career area. The letter adds that as a potential career changer, you would appreciate talking with them about their experiences. The letter is followed up with a call within a week or ten days.

The call should happen during the day. If you have some privacy in your current position and can manage to complete some calls during the day, fine. However, if you're in a position in which that's just not possible, you might be able to get some calling done on a coffee or lunch break, from a phone booth if necessary. If you want to contact people in a management position, chances are that they get in before 9 a.m., and you might catch them then. The purpose of the call is to set up a mutually convenient meeting time.

These informational meetings will also need to be strategically planned around work. We suggest early breakfast or lunch meetings (or early weekday evenings and even possibly Saturdays, if they prefer). You could offer to treat as a way of thanking your contact for taking the time to meet with you. The cost can be kept manageable by selecting appropriate types of eating establishments.

Interviewing for Hire

When it comes to job interviews, some delicate timing issues arise. These meetings are a priority, and you could consider using personal or vacation days for them.

The potential new employer wants to see you for a first or follow-up interview. How do you handle it?

Well, if it's a first interview, try to do it at the interviewer's convenience. If it's a follow-up interview, on the other hand, it's fine for you to try to schedule it at a convenient time for you. You might be hesitant to ask for a day and time that is most convenient for you and that may be different from what was offered, but keep in mind that if a prospective employer is interested in you, he or she will understand your situation and try to be flexible. Let the interviewer know that your first responsibility is with your current employer. Any employer worth working for will respect and even be encouraged by your sense of professionalism and responsibility.

FINDING MONEY FOR EDUCATION
OR TRAINING

A number of variables determine how much money you'll need to finance your education. These include whether the school you're considering is public or private, offers two-year or four-year programs, or is in your state or out of state. You should know that there's no age restriction on financial aid from the federal government. Also, the less money you have, the more loans and grants are possible. Finally, community colleges or less expensive state universities can be good options for you.

Some alternative college programs can be expensive but, due to their accelerated pace, are twice as fast to complete as traditional private college programs. Therefore, the cost at alternative colleges could actually be less. In addition, when compared with the cost of traditional state colleges, after adding travel, parking, and athletic and recreation fees not usually part of alternative programs, they might not be that much more.

Sources of funding your return to college include the following:

- **Student loans**
  State loans:
  All 50 states have financial aid programs that award need-based grants. When you fill out the Free Application for Student Aid (FAFSA) form, required by all colleges, you automatically apply for state aid in many states. Many private colleges and some state schools are currently using the PROFILE form, which is released by the College Scholarship Service (CSS).

  Federal loans:
  Stafford Student Loans—relatively low-interest loans guaranteed and subsidized by the federal government
  Perkin Loans—loans made by colleges with money provided by the federal government; the interest rate is usually lower than for the Stafford Student Loans

- **Fellowships**
- **Employer reimbursement**
- **Loans from banks, friends, or relatives**

It's a good idea, as soon as you know what schools you'll be choosing from, to read the financial aid section of their catalogs and then to contact the financial aid offices and follow through on applying for aid. We suggest that you apply to more than one school, because each school will have its own restrictions or policies on awarding student aid.

Processing of financial aid applications usually takes four to six weeks, so you can see the importance of being organized. Often, applicants receive money from a combination of aid programs, most of which are determined based on need and must be maintained with certain grade point averages and credit hour completion rates. Check with the schools you're interested in for possible differences.

If you're currently working full-time, chances are that you won't qualify for aid on a need basis (even though you might really need it). However, there are still federal and state-sponsored loans that do not depend on need and usually do not have to be paid back till you stop attending college. These programs are offered in conjunction with banks and have relatively low interest rates, so check around.

Be sure to check with your employer to find out whether a program exists to help reimburse you for your college expenses. Usually, if a program exists, your employer will expect that your coursework relate to your job (some firms might apply this more liberally than others) and that certain grades be achieved. If your employer does offer this benefit, find out whether you can attend private or public colleges and if there's a certain dollar amount you have to spend per year.

In addition, check with the financial aid office to see if any in-house scholarships are available that might relate to you (e.g., returning adult students, women, minorities). These can be highly competitive but are worth investigating. Also, if you belong to any professional organizations, there might be scholarships available for members.

Other sources for possible financing of college costs include the following:

- Religious, civic, fraternal, or service organizations (Chamber of Commerce, Rotary, Elks, Kiwanis, American Legion, B'nai B'rith)

- Special-interest groups related to women, religion, or ethnic background

- Personal loans from family or friends, with interest included that is less than that for a personal bank loan

If all else fails, a home equity loan is a possibility to consider, as is a loan from an insurance policy. Both usually have interest rates that are lower than those for personal bank loans.

Because three of our career changers are former servicemen, they funded their return for education through the GI Bill, a federal program designed for that purpose:
- Allen for dental school
- Larry for a degree in training
- Mac for his master's in counseling

If it's possible for you to start your coursework at a community college before moving on to a four-year college, you might consider doing so. This alternative will be less expensive and allows you to get started with your studies as well. You might also check into the feasibility of on-the-job training for accomplishing the goals you have in mind. Check Appendix B, "Recommended Readings," for books on the subject of Financial Aid for Additional Education and Training.

FINANCIAL AID FOR EDUCATION

Related Internet Sites

- College Money Matters: http://www.signet.com/collegemoney
- FastWeb Scholarship Search   http://www.fastweb.com
  (more than 275,000
  scholarships):
- Financial Aid for Graduate   http://www.jobtrak.com/
  Students: Go to Students & Alumni,
  Resource Center, Guide to
  Graduate School, Financing Your
  College Degree.
- Peterson's Education &   http://www.petersons.com/
  Career Center:
- The Princeton Review: http://www.review.com
  Go to Site Search and Search
  for Financial Aid.

- U.S. Department of   http://www.ed.gov/offices/OPE
  Education (financial aid
  information):
- Yahoo!:   http://www.yahoo.com/
                           Go to Business & Economy,
                           Companies, Education,
                           Financial Aid.

FINANCING YOUR JOB SEARCH

Obviously, your employment status will determine a great deal about how you will finance your career change. If you're employed, you have a paycheck coming in, but it will make your job search longer, perhaps an average of six to eight months (if you devote 15 to 25 hours a week to your search). This can vary depending on the field you're pursuing employment in and your level of motivation, as well as the job search techniques used. If you are unemployed and devote 40 to 60 hours a week to your job search, you can probably cut the length of time in half, to about three to four months, on average. Of course, the downside is no income.

Back to the Budget

If you are unemployed, the issue becomes much larger than financing just your job search—it becomes one of survival as well. Probably the best first step to take is to get a handle on whatever sources of money you have and then take a look at your living expenses as well as job search costs.

Start the budget process by identifying your sources of cash. Possible sources include the following:

- Savings

- Securities, mutal funds

- Loans from sources such as home equity, insurance policies, and retirement/401(k) plans

- Unemployment compensation

- Severance
- Loans from friends and relatives
- Sale of personal items (camera, stereo, second TV, second car, etc.)

Once you've calculated your available cash, you need to do the same for your living expenses. (We'll worry about specific job search costs a bit later.) As you begin to review your expenses, ask yourself where you can cut back. Areas for possible cutbacks include new clothes (unless you need some for your job search), food (eating in and out), utilities, entertainment, and even housing, if it becomes necessary. A few suggestions follow:

- Don't sell your house unless absolutely necessary. With rising costs, you might never be able to afford one again.
- Don't let go of any insurance on your home, car, or health.
- Payment of larger debts might be negotiable. Talk with your creditors and perhaps make arrangements to pay only the interest owed for a short time.
- It might be tempting to run up credit card bills. Resist this, unless it's absolutely necessary, perhaps using credit for job search expenses rather than actual life expenses (food, shelter, transportation).

Need Additional Cash?

Even with tightening up, your expenses might still be more than you have available to you. If you tapped out all your sources, you might be able to find an interim, temporary, or part-time job. If you can afford it, we suggest part-time (up to 30 hours per week) in order to give you more daytime hours for your job search. If you are squeezed for dollars, this might be the best alternative. It will take a load off your mind, and you'll be able to more fully concentrate on your job search. You'll feel more confident and increase your chances of accepting the best possible offer, rather than jumping at the first decent offer.

Let's look at the possibilities related to interim or part-time work.

Temporary Work As described in the previous chapter (with regard to the need for additional experience), temporary work has grown tremendously and is now a means of employment in many career areas. Temporary work provides an excellent opportunity for generating additional needed cash. You could seek temporary work related to your career field, if possible, or work in an area in which you have employable skills (e.g., desktop publishing) but that is not necessarily related to your career goal.

Part-Time Work   You might be able to find part-time work in your career field, but at a lower level. Alternatively, part-time work in an unrelated field often requires little skill or experience and is easier to find. Part-time work in your own field has the same advantages as listed for temporary work. In addition, if your last full-time job doesn't generate a good reference for you, the temporary or part-time job might.

Even if your part-time or temporary job is unrelated to your career goals, it can still serve a purpose by stopping the gap between jobs or ending the loss of income. Perhaps it's not something you're crazy about doing, but if the situation warrants it, you should be ready to face reality.

Whatever interim job you take, temporary or part-time (related or unrelated to your career goals), try your best to have some flexibility in daytime hours for your job search. Certain jobs fall more naturally into this category: bar and restaurant work, cab driving, and retail sales. So you're asking, "How does it look to potential employers that you're working at a lower-level position with reduced responsibility and wages?" Let's rephrase the question to, "How does it look to a potential employer that under an extremely tight job market, in order to meet your expenses, you were responsible enough to find work, be employed, and continue your job search, even if that work is at a lower level?"

Most employers are likely to be understanding and respectful, as long as what you describe as a tight job market is true for your career field. Try to market yourself so that they can see that you have the knowledge and skills they're looking for.

If all else fails, there's always the alternative of public aid to help you get through this temporary period of unemployment. If you have misgivings or consider this a handout, be sure to do all you can in your job search efforts to shorten your unemployment period, and accept what your government is offering to you to help you get back on your feet. If you've worked hard in your prior jobs, you deserve some help.

YOUR JOB SEARCH EXPENSES

In your career change, you must get out there and talk to as many people as you can in the job you're targeting for yourself, in as many different work settings as you can find them, in order to build your network of contacts and gain desired employment. However, this approach does not come without its expenses. Here are some of the more common expenses that you can expect to encounter, using primarily the networking approach to job searching:

- Appropriate clothing
- Professional organization memberships
- Professional meetings, seminars, workshops
- Professional and trade publications
- Informational interview meals
- Office equipment or access to it
- Transportation

These costs can add up, so you'll want to budget them with your other expenses. Only you are in a position to judge how that might be done. However, if you're having a hard time on your own, even with these suggestions, you might want to consult with a financial advisor to come up with a sound financial plan. Inquire at your bank; perhaps they can provide this assistance.

WHEN CHANGING CAREERS MEANS
A CUT IN SALARY

As you proceed in pursuing your career change, you might experience a reduction in pay. With this possibility in mind, you need to know just how low you're willing (and able) to go, so that you are in a position to respond appropriately. Otherwise, the danger exists that you will accept a salary offer that makes your minimally acceptable lifestyle difficult to attain, resulting in dissatisfaction with your new position.

In making his career change, Larry knew he'd be taking an initial salary cut; he just didn't know exactly how much—or how much he could afford. So he sat down with his wife, and they figured out what a bare-bones budget would look like. In other words, just how low could they go, knowing that there was the potential of future salary increases in such a position. This way he would know how to respond to forthcoming salary offers.

The salary he was offered was a few thousand short of Larry's bottom line (remember, he was responsible for a wife and three children), but making the career change was important to Larry. He accepted the position and made up the difference with a loan from his insurance policy that carried a low rate of interest.

As a result of good financial planning, Larry could proceed confidently, even though the new salary was a tough cut. He knew that his family's bills would be paid, even if things would be tight for a while. His research on salaries for the position he accepted with this particular firm indicated that he could expect significant raises in a reasonable amount of time. Thus, Larry and his family would be able to regain their standard of living and possibly surpass it in the not-too-distant future.

If a salary cut is necessary to get started in a new career, you'll be much more willing to face that reality if you know in your heart that the increased satisfaction of the new position (and perhaps increased family time as well), compared with your former position, will make it worthwhile.

If you discover that your desired career change means a reduction in pay and would leave you below your minimally acceptable income level, then some additional thinking on your part is necessary. First, ask yourself, "As a result of my research on myself and careers, is this career goal still my first choice?" If you answer yes, then the next step is to figure out how to raise your income level to what you identified as minimally acceptable. Consider the following questions:

1. How big is the gap between your minimally acceptable salary level and the salary of the new position?

2. How long can you expect that gap to exist? Based on your research, if all goes well in the new position, when might you expect a raise, and about how much of one?

3. What can you negotiate with new employers as far as the following:
   - Use of a company car
   - Six-month salary review
   - Opportunities for advancement

4. Will your new job help you to develop the skills needed, or do you already have enough, to possibly have your own part-time consulting practice on the side? This can be done in a large variety of fields: accounting, public relations, training, marketing, graphic arts, personnel, and others. This will make it a bit easier to accept the lower-than-desired salary in the full-time job.

Look at the Brighter Side

A lower salary is tough to accept, both psychologically and monetarily. However, consider that you've done your homework and you're sure this is the career goal you want to attain. We operate from the philosophical point of view that if we're doing what we like the most, it's usually what we're best at. This leads to success, which in turn leads, in most cases, to some form of financial prosperity as well.

Moreover, your research on your career goal, as well as conversations with your potential employer, might indicate that this financial crisis will not last long. Perhaps you're confident that over time, within reason, your salary will become more acceptable and, sooner than you realized, even surpass your former salary. Keep in mind as well that many adults who change to more satisfying careers claim they never regretted making the change, despite lower salaries.

Also, a most important factor is that you need to have respect for this new position—that is, you need to feel that it is in itself a respectable job. By respect, we mean there's a good match with your higher-ranked life and work values. Therefore, what you consider to be most important is involved either directly or indirectly with this new position, thus making it respectable to you and for you. This, too, will help in accepting a lower-than-desired starting salary. Finally, assuming you do find greater satisfaction in your new position, you'll probably also experience greater physical and mental health, which in many ways is more valuable than anything.

CHAPTER 10
Strategies for Dealing with
a Tight Job Market

★

Staying Abreast of the Trends

In this chapter we will first discuss how economic, societal, demographic, and technological trends affect the job market and highlight some general and specific occupational forecasts. Then we'll suggest strategies for how you can best prepare yourself to deal effectively with these trends and forecasts, thereby increasing your chances for success. We'll also discuss strategies for changing your career within your present place of employment, developing your networking skills, researching employers in the library, and job searching long-distance.

Economic Trends

Unemployment Decreases, But Skills Gap Remains   The widespread corporate restructuring in the early 1990s, which led to relocation of industries, downturns in specific industries, some industry and plant shutdowns, and related layoffs and firings, has now subsided. In fact, some downsized workers have been rehired by former employers as temporary workers.

Unemployment is at a 25-year low, yet one problem remains: many of the available jobs require high levels of education and skills. Many unemployed people lack the necessary skills to function in an emerging postindustrial high-tech society. Estimates are that up to 75 percent of unemployed people lack basic skills and thus need remedial training prior to job skills training.

JOB MARKET TRENDS/EMPLOYMENT STATISTICS
Related Internet Sites

- America's Career InfoNet: http://www.acinet.org/
                                      Go to Trends.
- 1990 Census Lookup   http://venus.census.gov/
  (demographic information):   cdrom/lookup
- NOICC Home Page   http://www.state.ia.us/government/
  (labor market information):   wd/noicc/
- Industry Book: http://www.studentcenter.com/
                                      where/industry/industry.htm
- The Riley Guide: http://www.dbm.com/jobguide/
  Employment Opportunities   trends.html
  & Job Resources on   Go to Labor Market
  the Internet: Information State by State.
- U.S. Bureau of Labor   http://www.bls.gov/
  Statistics (BLS):   Go to Surveys & Programs,
                                      Employment Projections.
- U.S. BLS Data Home Page: http://stats.bls.gov:80/datahome.htm
- U.S. Industrial Outlook: http://www.ita.doc.gov/industry/
                                      otea/usio/usio95.html

Small Business Growth   Another result of the vast restructuring of corporate America is the growth of small businesses. Many displaced mid-level managers (and even those who survived downsizings but feel insecure about their future) have opted to start their own businesses. The leaner corporations now outsource much of their work formerly completed in-house, which helps lead the way for successful small businesses.

Since 1970, an estimated 66 percent of new jobs have been with companies of 100 or fewer employees. In the future, up to 75 percent of new jobs will be with companies of 20 or fewer employees. It is estimated that 11.5 million people will be self-employed by the year 2005, a 15 percent increase from 1992 and twice what it was in 1970.

A Global Economy   As most of us realize, the economy of the present and the future is global. Foreign trade is increasing, especially with companies doing business in Asia and Europe, yet the United States is experiencing a huge trade deficit. Our imports are ahead of our exports, which means more money is going out than is coming in. This leads to a decrease in jobs as a result of buying the goods of others, not our own.

If less money is coming in (both from sales inside and outside the United States), it will keep businesses from expanding, thus hurting job growth here. Also hurting job growth is unprecedented debt, on three levels: national, corporate, and personal. The global economy has also eliminated geographic boundaries of business activities, resulting in some jobs being transported overseas.

Decline of Major Cities in the Northeast and North Central United States   A result of current economic trends finds old urban centers of the Northeast and North Central regions, mainly manufacturing and related service industries, experiencing decline and high levels of unemployment. Growth is currently found in suburban and semi-rural areas of cities located in the Southwest, West, Southeast, and Northwest (and a few cities in the East). Population as well as wealth and economic activity will continue to shift into these areas, based on

---

CAREER CHANGER UPDATE

✴

On the positive side, Ed hopes to take advantage of the passing of NAFTA (the North American Free Trade Agreement). A bilingual lawyer with strong sales skills, he believes corporations interested in setting up business in Mexico will be eager to hire someone with his background.

high-tech communication and service industries that require an edu-cated labor force.

Societal Trends

Societal trends include those that reflect current interests, values, and habits of society at large.

The Environment   More and more Americans are becoming envi-ronmentally aware and concerned. This strong emphasis on environmen-tal issues impacts many sectors of our economy, including government agencies, manufacturing, engineering consulting firms, and waste han-dling and recycling businesses. This, in turn, affects environmental con-servation–related careers in such areas as chemistry, biology, geology, engineering, computer science, finance, law, and even fund-raising.

Health and Fitness   In addition to increased environmental awareness, Americans are more health and fitness conscious today. This push to be slim, trim, and healthy is creating jobs in areas such as health clubs; fitness equipment; clothing; exercise physiology and athletic training; physical therapy; recreation-related activities and equipment; food content, packaging, and design; restaurant and fast-food menus; dietary supplements; and more.

Aging of the Population   The aging population means that there are more retirees with more leisure time and other needs related to housing, health care, fitness, shopping, senior care, travel, recreation, and entertainment. With an estimated 4.3 million people over the age of 85 by the year 2000 (5.7 million by 2010), a trend that is growing is that of assisted living. This independent housing approach provides resi-dents access to help with daily living activities such as meals, laundry, and bathing, and with social activities as well, without subjecting them to the loss of privacy common to many traditional nursing homes.

More Singles   More people are electing to delay or forgo mar-riage, and more divorced individuals are joining their ranks. This results in more discretionary income to spend on themselves, perhaps much like those who do marry but have no children, as described next.

Double Incomes, No Children   Also added to groups with increased spending options are people who do marry but wait longer to have children or choose not to have children. We see much of this discretionary spending taking place in leisure and entertainment areas such as health clubs, travel, movies, restaurants, cultural events and activities, TVs, VCRs, and stereos.

Baby Boomers and Their Children By the year 2005, more than 76 million baby boomers (born between 1946 and 1964) will be between 41 and 59 years of age, and their children will be growing up. This development has already had and will continue to have ramifications for child care, education, clothes, toys/games, and furniture, among other things. Baby boomers themselves will have certain needs, ranging from help with health-related concerns (e.g., bad backs) to advice on future retirement (e.g., financial planning).

Schools in Crisis Another societal trend is the crisis of our public school systems. For a variety of reasons—poor management, lack of funding, high dropout rates, lack of solid family structure and parental guidance—students are coming out of the elementary and secondary public school system without the skills necessary for the jobs available today and in the near future.

Employers find themselves needing to provide basic skills (reading, writing, and math) instruction in order to get their employees in position to learn from training for a particular job. A bright spot on the education front is the community colleges: they seem more in tune with current labor market needs in providing a range of business and vocational training related to those needs.

Demographics

Most of the data in this section comes from the November 1997 issue of the *Monthly Labor Review* and the Winter 1997–98 *Occupational Outlook Quarterly,* both published by the U.S. Department of Labor. These and other related resources are listed in Appendix A.

Women During the period from 1996 to 2006, about one-half (49.6 percent) of labor force entrants will be women, compared with 44.5 percent in 1986 and 42 percent in 1979. By the year 2006, 70.6 million women will represent 47.4 percent of the workforce, 61.4 percent of all adult women, and 69.5 percent of women between the ages of 25 and 54.

Women are now the main breadwinners for 20 percent of the nation's families. Sixty-six percent of married women with children are now in the labor market. In 27 percent of households, the wife makes 80 percent of the husband's salary. There are now 26 million two-income, baby-boomer households.

African-Americans, Hispanics, and Asians By the year 2006, African-Americans, Hispanics, Asians, and other minorities will represent 28.7 percent of the workforce, up from 25.1 percent in 1996. They will also represent 38.9 percent of new labor-force entrants between 1996 and 2006. Also, by the year 2006, women and minorities will together make up about 62.5 percent of the U.S. workforce.

We can also expect by the year 2006 a workforce of 148.9 million workers (compared with 133.9 million in 1996), with an additional 2.1 million African-Americans, 4.6 million Hispanics, and 2.3 million Asian-Americans. These statistics predict the following minority representation in the workforce by 2006: 17.2 million (11.6 percent) African-Americans (a 13.8 percent increase), 17.4 million (11.7 percent) Hispanics (a 36.2 percent increase), and 8 million (5.4 percent) Asian-Americans (a 41 percent increase, including Native Americans, Alaskan Natives, and Pacific Islanders). The white, non-Hispanic workforce representation will be 108.2 million (72.7 percent, a 7.2 percent increase).

Aging of the Population By 2006, there will be 63.6 million Americans (28.7 percent) over the age of 55. In addition, 15.2 percent of the population will be over 65, more than twice the percentage in 1940. Between 1996 and 2006, the number of older adults will grow twice as fast as the labor force as a whole. The largest group of workers will be those between the ages of 35 and 44 (35.5 million, 23.8 percent), followed by those between 45 and 54 (35.2 million, 23.6 percent). About one of every three persons (29 percent) will be over age 50 by the year 2006, with workers having an average age of 40.6, compared with 1996's average age of 38.2.

Only 17.2 percent of the population will be in the 16–24 age group by the year 2006 (known as the "birth dearth"). This figure is down from 18.9 percent in 1986 and 22.9 percent in 1976. As a result, fewer young people are filling entry-level jobs, leaving a shortage of workers for these jobs.

Because of this, older workers are being pursued by employers, and not just for entry-level positions. Their strong work ethic and special skills are highly valued by employers. Even after downsizing, companies still need workers. They might tap into those they had let go (if they're still available) or keep retirees active (most on a part-time basis).

DEMOGRAPHIC STATISTICS
Related Internet Site
• U.S. Census Bureau: http://venus.census.gov/cdrom/lookup

Technology

The emerging high-tech and service society will require highly specialized and skilled workers who are prepared to make job and career changes. One can't be too specialized, however, or risk becoming obsolete. Advances in computers, robotics, fiber optics, biotechnology, and genetic engineering have generated new businesses and shut down others. If not retrained, workers in declining industries fall into lower-paying, unskilled service jobs. The emphasis on high-tech machinery and computers is a challenge for employers and employees alike. Technology has allowed an increasing number of workers to work at home. It's estimated that by 2005, 15 to 25 million jobs will be performed partially or entirely at home.

Forecasting Occupational Trends

The Shortcomings   Occupational forecasts for the future can be helpful but must not be taken too seriously, for a variety of reasons. By "too seriously," we mean planning your career decisions based on future trends alone. Keep in mind that in forecasts of occupational trends, frequently the statistical applications used assume that there will be a steady rate of growth, which may not be the case. At times, these forecasts represent "best guesses" of what might be. The forecasting has no way to accurately account for unanticipated events such as the following:

• Shifts in population
• Political decisions regarding international crises and domestic economic failures
• Technological advances
• Economic cycles of prosperity and recession

In addition, the forecasts are usually presented on a national basis and are not localized to your particular geographic area. For example, if paralegal work is identified as a fast-growing occupation, it could still represent a very tight job market in your area. And the opposite could be true as well. Forecasts related to the agriculture, forestry, and fishing industries have been declining for years, yet there is some growth in the agricultural services industry, which includes landscape and horticultural services. Therefore, this one aspect of an overall declining industry is generally still strong and might be so in your geographic area as well.

We suggest that you contact the professional associations related to your career interests. They might have projections for their particular field on a geographic basis. In other words, they might be able to tell you where in the United States the demand is highest for the career you're interested in.

The *Occupational Outlook Handbook* also gives some general job outlook information, though only on a national basis and somewhat briefly. For a more in-depth occupational outlook including fastest-growing areas in a particular career field, best bets in that career, and future trends, read *Jobs '98,* by Kathryn Petras and Ross Petras.

Keeping these potential shortcomings in mind, let's examine some major forecasted industry and occupational trends.

General Occupational Trends   Overall, there will be more jobs in knowledge-based industries and fewer in production-based industries. By the year 2005, an 80/20 percentage breakdown is predicted. Service industries now employ three times the number that are in manufacturing, construction, and mining industries. These service industries include health care, business services (advertising, marketing, accounting, public relations, computer and data processing, etc.), retail, wholesale trade, food, transportation, communication, education, and finance.

Two-thirds of all workers currently provide a service rather than produce a material good, reflecting a wide range of services and related pay, from fast food to managerial, legal, communications, and computer.

Specific Occupational Trends   Let's take a look at two specific sets of occupational forecasts for 1996–2006 from the *Occupational Outlook Quarterly,* Winter 1997–98. Figure 10.1 shows occupations with the fastest projected growth, and Figure 10.2 shows occupations that will have the largest numerical increases. More than half of the fastest-

FIGURE 10.1

Fastest-Growing Occupations, Projected for 1996–2006

	(PERCENTAGE GROWTH)
Database Administrators, Computer Support Specialists, and all other Computer Scientists	118%
Computer Engineers	109
Systems Analysts	103
Personal and Home Care Aides	85
Physical and Corrective Therapy Assistants and Aides	79
Home Health Aides	76
Medical Assistants	74
Desktop Publishing Specialists	74
Physical Therapists	71
Occupational Therapy Assistants and Aides	69
Paralegals	68
Occupational Therapists	66
Teachers, Special Education	59
Human Service Workers	55
Data Processing Equipment Repairers	52
Medical Records Technicians	51
Speech-Language Pathologists and Audiologists	51
Dental Hygienists	48
Amusement and Recreation Attendants	48
Physician Assistants	47
Respiratory Therapists	46
Adjustment Clerks	46
Engineering, Science, and Computer Systems Managers	45
Emergency Medical Technicians	45
Manicurists	45
Bill and Account Collectors	42
Residential Counselors	41
Instructors and Coaches, Sports and Physical Training	41
Dental Assistants	38
Securities and Financial Services Sales Workers	38

FIGURE 10.2

Occupations with the Largest Numerical Increases, Projected for 1996–2006

	(NUMBERS IN THOUSANDS)
Cashiers	530
Systems Analysts	520
General Managers and Top Executives	467
Registered Nurses	411
Salespersons, Retail	408
Truck Drivers, Light and Heavy	404
Home Health Aides	378
Teacher Aides and Educational Assistants	370
Nursing Aides, Orderlies, and Attendants	333
Receptionists and Information Clerks	318
Teachers, Secondary Schools	312
Child Care Workers	299
Clerical Supervisors and Managers	262
Database Administrators, Computer Support Specialists, and all other Computer Scientists	249
Marketing and Sales Worker Supervisors	246
Maintenance Repairers, General Utility	246
Food Counter, Fountain, and Related Workers	243
Teachers, Special Education	241
Computer Engineers	235
Food Preparation Workers	234
Hand Packers and Packagers	222
Guards	221
General Office Clerks	215
Waiters and Waitresses	206
Social Workers	188
Adjustment Clerks	183
Cooks, Short Order and Fast Food	174
Personal and Home Care Aides	171
Food Service and Lodging Managers	168
Medical Assistants	166

growing occupations for the period are in health services. Other major occupational categories represented include computer technology and personal services. In addition, one-third of the fastest-growing occupations are professional and technical occupations that require substantial postsecondary education (a bachelor's degree or more).

The 30 occupations with the largest numerical increases are estimated to account for more than half of the total employment growth of the 500 jobs for which projections were developed for the period of 1996–2006. Among the occupational groups represented are retail, health services, education/social services, office/clerical, and computer technology.

Health services, business services, social services, and engineering, management, and related services are expected to account for almost one of every two jobs added to the economy during the 1996–2006 period. More specifically, occupations appearing on both lists, showing both the fastest (percentages) and largest (numbers) growth include: home health aides, personal and home care aides, medical assistants, adjustment clerks, special education teachers, computer engineers, systems analysts, and database administrators/computer support specialists/computer scientists. Note that some of these occupations with high replacement needs also have low average incomes (e.g., home health aides and personal care aides).

It doesn't take long to see that the "hot" careers today center around health care, retail sales, and high-tech occupations. Remember that these represent the highlights of occupation trends forecasted and are in no way meant to be complete (especially with regard to geographic areas).

So what do you do if the career you're thinking of isn't on these Top 30 lists? Don't give up. Do the research; find out the status of your career choice via published and people resources. If you can identify a geographic region where you would have a better chance for such a career, then consider whether you are willing to relocate. Additional suggestions follow on how to best prepare yourself for the occupational trends that lie ahead.

Preparing Yourself for the Future Job Market

Skills, Skills, Skills! It is vital to develop new specific content/special knowledge skills that are responsive to a changing job market. For example, a writer having difficulty finding a suitable position might do

some research and discover that he or she would be much more competitive in today's high-tech, service-oriented job market with desktop publishing skills. The key here is *flexibility:* accepting new ways of doing
things and attempting to acquire the new skills being required of your
profession.

Considering that most career areas are highly competitive, adapting
the following strategies can enhance the possibility of your success in
being competitive in today's job market:

- Identify what you most want to do, your purpose or mission in
  life. What contribution would you like to make to society
  through your work? Complete a thorough self-assessment
  process involving the identification of your interests, skills,
  values, and personality traits.

- Combine your self-assessment results with job market demand
  and demographic information to identify career fields of interest
  to you.

- Develop an expertise; become the best you can in the career you
  most want. Learn new specific content/special knowledge skills
  in order to stay up-to-date and be more competitive in your
  career field of choice.

- Become computer literate to the extent necessary for your career
  area of choice and learn a second language if it's appropriate to
  do so.

- Learn how to effectively job search, emphasizing a networking
  approach. Research employers and target small and medium-
  sized growth companies that are adapting to new information
  technologies.

- Maintain flexibility in how you see yourself and your career;
  strive to be adaptable to change, which includes considering the
  possibility of relocating to a geographic area where positions in
  your preferred career may be more available. Develop a global
  perspective, especially in management, marketing, and finance.

With regard to the last suggestion, maintaining flexibility and striving to be adaptable, William Bridges points out the changing nature of
work and jobs in his book *Job Shift.* He predicts that many of us will

truly become contingent workers with little job security. He refers to the nature of careers as becoming *composite careers,* in which one can become involved in a variety of roles, such as starting a business, becoming a consultant or an independent contractor, or doing freelance work, part-time work, or piecework at home.

Because of the possibility of taking assignments and projects from different organizations as we perform in any number of these career roles, Bridges states that the process of managing one's time will become much like that of a self-employed person. He stresses that we must learn to manage our own careers, as if we're in business for ourselves. And, in fact, while juggling these various career roles, many of us will be in business for ourselves.

Bridges further discusses this viewpoint in his book *Creating You and Co.: Learn to Think Like the CEO of Your Own Career* and is echoed by Farren, Hakim, and Harkness in the suggestion of developing an entrepreneurial mind-set with respect to our own careers (see Appendix A for specific titles).

With regard to personal development, we recommend striving for a healthy level of self-esteem, becoming as adept as possible at oral and written communication, and developing your interpersonal skills. Work at strengthening personal attributes such as enthusiasm, dedication, and innovation. If you work on these types of goals, you will be making yourself attractive to potential employers and thus more competitive for today's job market. Now we turn to an often neglected option, that of changing careers with the same employer.

CAREER CHANGER UPDATE

★

Victoria decided to leave the struggling auto parts franchise industry and use her knowledge gained from dealing with the print industry (in a prior position she oversaw printing of all material her office generated) to search for a position that she felt had better potential: a print buyer.

RESEARCHING AN INTERNAL CAREER CHANGE

Rather than searching elsewhere or waiting around for someone to offer you a promotion, consider initiating an internal campaign to seek a change with your present employer. For an internal campaign, you will still need to set an objective, prepare a presentation, and establish contact with those who can help you reach your goal, just as you would if you were changing employers. However, it's easier to conduct an internal campaign, because the information and contacts you need are more readily available to you.

Basic Steps for an Internal Campaign

Richard Germann and Peter Arnold outline some suggestions for an internal career change campaign:

1. All communication, oral and written, should be positive. Focus on your strengths and accomplishments.
2. Have a realistic objective that benefits both you and your company.
3. Timing is important. Always move from a position of strength. Don't undertake an internal campaign if you're behind in your work or have other related problems. Do your best to correct the situation, and then proceed.
4. Stay with your campaign through to its resolution. Pursue the negotiation process if and when it comes about.

As with any decision, the better the information you have, the better your position for making a sound decision. Therefore, in order to set a meaningful and realistic objective, you need to do some research:

1. Become very familiar with what your company does, its goals, and its methods for reaching them. This could be available in the company's brochures, public relations materials, or annual report, as well as from other employees.
2. Get familiar with the organizational structure, formal and informal, and reporting lines. Develop an organizational chart.

3. Identify key people related to your objective, and learn about their professional and avocational interests in order to make it easier to talk with them.

4. Find information about formal and informal policies and procedures for seeking an internal change.

5. Broaden your scope of knowledge about developments in business, labor, economics, and related areas by reading newspapers and newsmagazines. These are time-consuming activities, but they can provide you with insights into current trends which in the end could more than make up for the one to two hours a day that you invest in them.

6. Stay abreast of what's happening in your industry or professional field by joining professional organizations, reading their publications, and attending workshops and conferences. This is also a valuable source of insight into the latest developments in your specific career field, as well as of potentially helpful contacts.

This general and career-specific information will enable you to better assess your situation and plan your future goals, including whether you should undertake an internal campaign in the first place and, if you do, what your objective might be.

Internal Campaign Objectives

Figure 10.3 will help you use the information you gathered from the Work Values Satisfaction Self-Assessment exercise in Chapter 3 to set objectives for yourself. Possibilities are listed on the Internal Campaign Objective Analysis Chart. To the left of each objective possibility are the corresponding work value categories, with space to the right of each value category to record your average satisfaction and satisfaction percentage scores from the Work Values Satisfaction Self-Assessment.

In other words, if you pick one or more of the possible objectives, the work value categories to the left marked with an X are affected. Those marked with a question mark (?) might also be affected, but it would depend on the specific circumstances in your individual situation. You'll notice a line through the work value category A, "Company/ Organization." If you have considerable dissatisfaction with the company/

FIGURE 10.3

Internal Campaign Objective Analysis Chart

WORK VALUE CATEGORIES	A. COMPANY/ORGANIZATION (/)	B. WORK ENVIRONMENT (/)	C. SUPERVISOR RELATIONS (/)	D. THE JOB ITSELF (/)	E. REWARDS/BENEFITS (/)	F. PROFESSIONAL GROWTH OPPORTUNITIES (/)	G. PERSONAL DEVELOPMENT GOALS (/)	INTERNAL CAMPAIGN OBJECTIVES
			?	X		?	?	1. Revised job description
			?		X	?		2. New job title
				X	?	X	?	3. Increase in responsibility/authority
		?	?	X		?	?	4. Transfer to different department
					X			5. Salary increase
		?	?	?	X	?	?	6. Promotion
		?	?	X	?	?	?	7. Newly created position

organization you're currently with, then an internal campaign is most likely not a viable goal for you.

If you know that certain work values are not in doubt and will be positively impacted by a certain objective in your current employment situation, then write in an X over the related question mark. Circle those X's and question marks that interest you and apply to your situation, thus signifying potential objectives and goals for you to pursue in an internal campaign. In addition, if you decide not to seek a change within your current employment setting, but rather to look externally, this analysis chart can help you focus on goals and objectives for that search as well.

Steps to Take in an Internal Campaign

First, prepare a positive, strongly written presentation in letter form about why your employer should accept your objective and how the organization will benefit from it. For a detailed description of how to prepare the presentation letter, consult Germann and Arnold (see Appendix A).

If you address your letter to someone senior to your current supervisor, consider the following suggestions:

- Ask for your supervisor's permission to make your presentation to the decision maker.

- Send a copy of your presentation letter to your supervisor.

- If you expect a negative reaction from your supervisor to your request, address the presentation letter to both the decision maker and your supervisor simultaneously. This will make it difficult for your supervisor to obstruct your presentation.

If you're having difficulty with your current supervisor, it's best to first try to resolve that situation before pursuing your internal campaign. It could take one or two months of concentrated effort to remove this obstacle, if it's possible at all.

A few days after you send the letter, call to request a meeting with the decision maker. At this meeting, different reactions are possible. If you sense there's some interest in your proposal, you might be able to negotiate a compromise, or the decision maker might agree right up front. In any case, you don't need to reach a final decision yet; arrange for a follow-up meeting. This will give you time to think things over.

If you get a negative response, ask for the reasons why. There are at least two possibilities:

1. You need to do something before resubmitting your proposal at a later date.
2. You will not be able to accomplish your career goals with your current employer and therefore need to make a change.

Even the second outcome is positive; at least you know where you stand and now can proceed accordingly. If all in-house options fail or you've chosen not to try them, then the next step would be to prepare for an external job search. It is helpful at this point to talk with people who are working in positions like those you're interested in, in as many different work settings as they may be found. This process, known as networking, is the focus of the following section.

NETWORKING

There's nothing complicated about networking, although many are confused by it, misuse it, or fear it. Networking is simply the development of mutually beneficial relationships. The key word here is *mutually*. Both you and your contacts will benefit from your networking efforts, as this section explains.

The Purpose of Networking

The purpose of networking is the exchange of information, advice, and referrals, via the informational interview process, to assist in attaining your goal of changing careers. As competition becomes fierce in some fields and there are fewer qualified candidates available in other fields, both employers and career changers rely on networking—the former to identify qualified candidates and the latter to communicate professional and personal skills to employers. Employers hire those they like personally and professionally. The informational interview, the vehicle for networking, gives them an opportunity to informally get acquainted with potential candidates.

The Formal and Informal Job Market

The jobs listed in newspapers, trade journals, and employment offices, which constitute the formal job market, represent only about 25 percent of the total jobs available at any given time. The ads in the newspapers tend to be either low-end or high-end jobs in terms of skills. Want ads work for some career fields better than others; you'll need to find out what works best in your field of interest. Most jobs, therefore, are part of the informal job market. They are not advertised or listed at agencies.

Because of this structure, you must rely on yourself to make sense of the whole process and identify available jobs. During your job search, divide your time up according to the percentage of time a particular job search method works. For a general example, take networking (informal job market) versus ads and agencies (formal job market). Because approximately 75 percent of the jobs are found via the informal job market through networking, that's where you should spend 75 percent of your time. However, people still get jobs via the formal job market, so you should spend the other 25 percent of your time there.

Employers Prefer Networking

This might come as a surprise, but employers would rather use informal networks also. They know that if they advertise a position, they could be overwhelmed with resumes, phone calls, and visits. They have a need—a position to fill—and they want the quickest way to find a qualified applicant. Many can't afford to hire through an employment agency, which may charge 15 to 25 percent of the position's annual salary as a fee. In addition, most would rather go with a known quantity (via networking with friends, family, or business associates) than an unknown quantity (an applicant responding to an ad). Unknown applicants represent a greater risk in terms of time, money, and training to employers.

The Challenge of Networking

Be honest during an informational interview—just request information; don't ask for a job. However, the networking process is indeed a good way to find a job. This sometimes seems like a contradiction. As a career changer, you probably do have many questions and could use the information. Even when you're experienced (or further along in the career planning process), there's always more to learn. Nonetheless, at this point your main objective is to get that targeted job.

The dilemma is that if you say you just want information and it becomes clear you actually want a job, you are likely to ruin your new contact. So, how can you be honest without ruining your chance of gaining that new contact? We suggest that you be specific about what type of information you want. Let your contact know, from your initial request for an informational interview and thereafter, that you're interested in the following or similar areas:

- Advice on opportunities in that particular field
- Strategies for gaining employment
- Feedback on how realistic your career goals are as you research your ideal job

This approach is straightforward about your intentions. You're seeking more than general information at this point; you have decided on a career field, and it's acceptable to say so. However, whether asking in writing or on the phone, be sure to state that you do not expect a job to be offered or referred to during the proposed interview. This helps put the potential interviewee at ease and removes pressure because of certain expectations they think you have. If, during the course of your informational interview, something in terms of a possible job comes up, great—but don't expect it.

In regard to finding the people with the power to hire, don't go after them unless your contacts lead the way. Attempt to reach them via contacts and networking your way up. Hiring professionals are usually the busiest, and they don't usually have a lot of time for networking. Therefore, they'll be more inclined to make time if you're a known quantity with a mutually known contact person.

Although some experts will tell you not to waste your time with people who do not have the power to hire, we believe they are mistaken. People not in a direct hiring position nevertheless could have insights about the career field, companies, or a particular organization. Also, many will have contacts that lead to persons with the power to hire. You will never find out unless you take the time to check it out.

What People Fear the Most About Networking

Many mature and capable adults fear picking up the phone and calling someone they don't know, even when the name is given to them by a mutual contact. After all, they wonder, who would want to talk to them? That's not a complicated question to answer. Those who have 15 to 20 minutes to spare and like their jobs will usually talk with you in an informational interview. If you get turned down, it's likely that they're just too busy or simply don't like their job and don't want to talk about it. In this case, try not to take it personally. Ask whether they can recommend someone else for you to talk with, thereby continuing to build your network.

If you're hesitant about this process, start with people you know and those they refer you to. It's easier with that intermediary contact person.

Your Goal: GET HIRED

It's best to be candid with yourself about the long-range, overall goal of networking—to get hired. The networking process—GET HIRED—can be described as follows:

- **G**enerate meaningful career options.

- **E**mpower yourself.

- **T**ell everyone you know.

- **H**onesty

- **I**nformation

- **R**eferrals

- **E**xchange

- **D**evelop

Generate Meaningful Career Options   Most career planning experts advocate, as a first step in the process, the establishment of a meaningful career goal. By establishing a goal that relates to your major interests, skills, values, and personality traits, you give your career change a meaningful focus and direction. Because the job market reality is out there, and you'll have to deal with it when your search is under way, it helps to be focused. If you're not focused, at least generally, in a direction that has personal meaning for you, you'll end up being scattered in approaching your job search and will increase the possibility of gaining a job you are not satisfied with. It's a matter of doing your homework (on yourself) and research (on related careers).

Empower Yourself   Take control of your job search. Learn how to tap into the informal job market via the networking process. Networking involves connecting and interacting with other individuals who can be helpful to you during your job search. Perhaps you can be helpful to them as well, presently or in the future.

Some people think they need to be aggressive to be successful at networking. This is not so. What is needed is the ability to establish warm, productive human relationships. You need to be purposeful, not aggressive. In addition, it helps to be patient and persistent to give the process a chance to work for you. Your attitude and how you handle yourself is of utmost importance. You will need to be honest, sincere, and enthusiastic and to dress appropriately as you seek career information, advice, and referrals from your network of contacts.

So now you might be saying, "All this networking stuff is fine and dandy, but what's a shy person supposed to do?" Networking might sound overwhelming or even unattainable for someone who is shy. However, even shy people can be successful at networking; they just have to work harder at it. You can practice networking with people you already know and feel comfortable with (family, friends, coworkers). You can call these practice informational interviews. Pick three or four people whom you know well and ask them if they would be willing to take part in your practice interview.

Then set up a time and a place—on the job, at home, at a restaurant—wherever you're most comfortable, for starters. Make a list of questions you would like your interviewee to answer about his or her job. Some examples follow:

- How did you get started in this career field? What are the best ways to look for a job in this field?
- What are the education or training requirements for your job?
- Describe a typical day on your job. What activities do you participate in? What skills are most important?
- What do you consider to be the benefits or highlights of your job?
- What challenges (problems) are you faced with?
- How's the future outlook in this career field?

These are just meant to get you started. Of course, feel free to add other questions you think are important to ask.

INFORMATIONAL INTERVIEWING

Related Internet Sites
- http://danenet.wicip.org/jets/jet-9407-p.html
  (three-page overview)
- http://www.studentcenter.com/inside/bea/bea.htm
  (read actual interviews)

After a number of practice informational interviews, you should feel more comfortable branching out to talk with individuals working in jobs you're interested in.

Richard Bolles also has a suggestion to help shy people overcome their hesitancy in networking. He suggests you pick an interest, something you're enthusiastic about, and find someone else who shares that interest. For some, just finding someone else who shares an interest is challenging enough, but it is well worth the effort. It's a way to get yourself moving, to refuse to fall victim to your shyness.

When one of your contacts offers you a referral to someone, send the person an approach letter. Your letter should be typed and have a businesslike appearance. You might even create your own letterhead using word processing software and a high-quality printer, or have it created at a print shop. Include your name, address, and phone number.

Your approach letter should include the following content:

- Who referred you to the person you're addressing

- Who you are, your current employment situation, what specific information you want, and how much time you need (15 to 20 minutes)

- Why you picked this person to speak to and how you hope he or she can help you

- When you'll call to set up an appointment (a specific day, within one week)

Your approach letter could also have some information about the person's employer that you have found as part of your research. You might even add some ideas related to the career field that you've been thinking about and would like the person's opinion on. This says something about your interest and commitment level and might lead your referral to be more inclined to respond positively. You need to make yourself sound worth meeting. An example of an approach letter is shown in Figure 10.4.

No resume is sent, just the approach letter. When you tell your referral what you would like to discuss, also assure the person that you are not looking for a job or expecting a job to come as a result of your informational interview. It is acceptable, however, to take your resume along to the interview itself to get feedback on it and perhaps to leave it with your contact person on your way out, if you feel the situation is right for doing so. If you feel you established good rapport and received good information, then the situation could be right for asking your referral to take a look at your resume for possible suggestions. You could either leave one with the person or mention that you'll incorporate his or her

FIGURE 10.4

Approach Letter Example

Donna Long
850 Ridge Avenue
Evanston, IL 60202
(847) 555-1212

April 13, 1999
Pamela Morris, Director
Midwest Center for Better Nutrition
1000 N. Michigan Avenue
Chicago, IL 60601

Dear Ms. Morris,

In a recent conversation, a mutual friend, Bob Grant, suggested that I contact you. Bob felt you could be of some assistance to me. Having now worked in the human resource field for six years, mainly in the benefits area, I'm looking to expand on my experience by researching new possibilities.

I'm especially interested in transferring my human resource experience to a nutrition-related nonprofit setting. I've always had an interest in nutrition and hoped, at some point, to involve it in my career. The nonprofit field interests me as well, for its challenges as well as rewards.

Currently, I'm seeking the advice and information of accomplished professionals, such as yourself, in nutrition-related nonprofit organizations, with regard to:

- the nature of work in nonprofits in general and in the Midwest Center for Better Nutrition more specifically
- what you believe the future holds for human resource professionals in nonprofits
- how to best expand my network of contacts and identify additional, related nonprofit organizations
- job search strategies

Let me assure you that I don't expect a job offer or even a referral to a possible job. I would like to focus on the topics listed above, as well as any others you think would be worthwhile to cover. I'm sure the knowledge you've gained from your experience in this field could benefit me.

I'd like to request 20 minutes of your time to accomplish the goals I've outlined in this letter. I'll call you next Wednesday in the hope that we can arrange a mutually convenient meeting time. Thank you very much for your consideration.

Sincerely,

Donna Long

suggestions and send a revised copy in case he or she hears of something that might be of interest to you.

Be sure to call your referral person on the date you state in your approach letter. Be prepared prior to your call. Have a copy of the letter in front of you, along with your calendar (remember, be organized). Jot down any key points you want to state, but keep the conversation brief, just a few minutes. You want to try for a friendly exchange with the goal of establishing rapport. Once you're connected, ask whether the person had a chance to read your letter. Be ready to suggest possible appointment times. Don't explain on the phone what is written in the letter, unless the person hasn't read it yet and asks you to summarize its contents. Try not to conduct the interview on the phone. You'll need face-to-face contact to gain the best possible rapport with regard to establishing a new contact.

Sometimes you may be dealing with a secretary or receptionist on the phone, and you'll want to treat this person in a professional manner as well. The secretary will most likely ask who you are and the purpose of your call. You can then state your name and note that the party you're calling is expecting your call. (Remember, in your approach letter you stated specifically what day you'd be calling.)

If the person you're calling isn't available, you have a choice of leaving a message or calling back. If you leave a message, you might not get a return call. On the other hand, you don't want to call back too many times and risk alienating yourself. Two possible solutions are to ask for a good time to call back or to call when the secretary is not likely to be around (before or after regular business hours or during lunch).

Remember, in the scenario we're depicting here, you were referred by a mutual contact person. This should enhance the likelihood of achieving your goal. As you get more experienced with the process, you can also try contacting people "cold" (without the mutual contact person). That's when more of the potential problems might arise. Either way, with or without the mutual contact person, try not to take it personally if your calls are not returned. It's difficult for you to know why your call is not returned, and it's a terrible energy drain to worry about it. You'd be better off channeling the energy in a more productive direction.

A variety of scenarios and interactions are possible between you and a secretary or the person you're trying to reach. If you're interested in sample scripts for responding to these various situations, ranging from "I'm busy" to "Let me connect you to personnel," consult *Information Interviewing,* by Martha Stoodley.

As you get more familiar with the networking process, you'll soon realize the importance of being organized. Keep an index card file on each contact, including each one's name, address, and phone number; who referred you to the person (and his or her name, address, and phone number); a record of all contacts made by phone, in writing, or in person; and your next steps related to each contact. File the cards alphabetically or chronologically using a master calendar.

Tell Everyone You Know What Your Goal Is and What You Need That's right, "everyone," assuming of course that they are positive relationships. Did you know that each adult has an average of 250 to 300 contacts? Therefore, each new contact you meet leads to another 250 to 300 people. It is estimated that each of us is only six or seven steps away from reaching anyone else in the world. Start with those you're closest to: family, friends, and relatives. Also include past and present employers, past and present coworkers, classmates, teachers/ professors, and members of organizations you belong to. Then check your personal phone book and your Christmas and Hanukkah card lists for some you might have forgotten.

CAREER CHANGER UPDATE

★

Some members of Victoria's network surprised her by offering jobs she never would've considered herself. Others saw her applying her skills in ways she hadn't thought of. It was an eye-opening experience for her: as she decided not to be too focused in her current job search, her career options expanded.

Next, identify everyone you know whose business is to know others. This includes a wide range of people: bankers, lawyers, doctors, accountants, etc.

There it is—your army of helpers, all with hundreds of their own contacts. Notwithstanding Victoria's experience, in order to help your army help you, you'll need to tell them, as specifically as possible, what you need. The only way to do this is to have a focused field of interest. When you do, you can reach each of your contacts and say something like the following (let's call it your 30-second introduction):

"Hello, Bob, this is Donna Long. The reason I'm calling today is that I'm considering a career change. I'd like to take my human resource experience to a different setting, preferably one related to nutrition, which is a big interest of mine, perhaps in a nonprofit organization. I'm not sure if you can help directly, but I thought maybe you'd know someone who'd be willing to sit down and talk with me for 20 minutes. I'd like to find out more about the nature of working in such a setting and suggestions on how to conduct my job search. You can assure any potential contacts of yours that I'm not expecting a job offer or referrals to job offers. I'm sincerely interested in gaining as much information as possible. Would you know of someone who might be helpful?"

Bob might or might not be of assistance, but if you call everyone you know, you'll be surprised at how fast you get results. In this case of human resources in a nutrition-related nonprofit organization, good contacts to start with would be your doctor, health maintenance organization, or nutrition-related store.

CAREER CHANGER UPDATE

★

Zephree learned of the volunteer position, where she helped sexual assault and violence victims, through a related professional organization's publication.

Once you have a firm handle on your target career, you can join a professional association. Student memberships are usually available at lower rates. To identify associations related to the fields of interest to you, consult the *Encyclopedia of Associations,* published by Gale Research. Once you join, participating on committees and related activities will afford you a better opportunity to demonstrate your abilities and skills and become known to others. Other benefits of association membership typically include the following:

- Membership directories are a source of additional contacts.

- Publications will keep you up-to-date with events and developments in the field and possibly job listings as well.

- Career information is available, such as job descriptions and, information on graduate programs and professional licensing/ certification.

- Associations publish lists of employers in the field.

- Conferences/conventions/workshops are offered on a national, state, or local level.

- Annual national conventions often have a placement service that brings together employers and job candidates from all over the country.

Larry knew that a major professional training organization was holding a national conference in his area. Even though the cost was high, and it was at a time when he had himself on a tight budget in general, Larry requested access to the exhibit area—the best place to network and meet potential employers.

He was able to negotiate a discounted fee. Once there, Larry visited with numerous vendors of the type of equipment he has worked with. Upon his return, he contacted three people he had met whose companies were located in his area. They all became potential employers.

Vincent took advantage of a three-day workshop offered, at a modest fee, by a national bookseller association on starting one's own business. The information gained was most helpful to him as he readied himself for opening his specialty bookstore.

CAREER CHANGER UPDATE

☆

Vincent has continued to take advantage of membership in professional organizations and related networking approaches. Through an independent booksellers' organization he has shared, with other bookstore owners, in-store appearance talent, with everyone benefiting. In addition, in order to be able to offer an ongoing schedule of in-store appearances, Vincent regularly networks with publishers and authors.

Allen has become an active leader in dentistry professional associations and values being able to play a significant role in the future of dentistry.

Thus, the experiences of both Vincent and Allen are examples of how professional association memberships not only are a valuable source of information and contacts during a career change but also can enhance one's professional business practice afterward.

PROFESSIONAL ASSOCIATIONS
Related Internet Sites
- Career Resource Homepage: http://www.eng.rpi.edu/dept/cdc/ homepage.html/
- IPL Associations on the Net (AON):   http://www.ipl.org/ref/AON/
- JobWeb: Visiting Professional Associations: http://www.jobweb.org/catapult/ assoc.htm
- Scholarly Societies Project (lists 1,129 organizations):   http://www.lib.uwaterloo.ca/ society/
- Yahoo!:   http://www.yahoo.com/ Go to Business & Economy, Organizations, Professional.

Trade publications (magazines, journals, or newsletters) in your field of interest can also contain information for generating possible contacts. A useful directory that some might overlook is the Yellow Pages. You can use this resource to identify related organizations and companies that can lead to new contacts as you build your network. Local newspapers and business magazines are also excellent sources to consult on a regular basis. They will keep you up-to-date with business news, activities, and events in your area and names of people you might be interested in meeting.

Another method for generating contacts is through field experience from school, an internship, a temporary or part-time job, or volunteer work. Not only will you get more familiar with the career field and related organizations, but you'll be able to continue to build your network of contacts as well.

Notice that we have moved from your first level of contacts (friends, family, service providers) to situations that involve more difficult contact making and situations in which you do not have the benefit of a mutually known intermediary person. You'll find that as you work with your first level of contacts and gain experience with the networking and informational interviewing process, you'll feel capable of taking steps to reach out and contact people on your own. This is sometimes referred to as *cold contacts.*

We believe that cold contacts are a good idea, preventing your relying too heavily on referrals. You can always say to someone, "As a result of researching my ideal job, your company was mentioned as a place to contact." Then you can proceed with your 30-second introduction and ask whether you can schedule an informational interview. However, if you're still on the shy side, you might want to stay with the referral approach until you're more comfortable making cold calls.

IDENTIFYING CONTACTS WHO SHARE SIMILAR INTERESTS

Related Internet Sites

Identify newsgroups or mailing lists related to your interests. These are essentially discussion groups centered around the field of interest in which you'd like to make contacts. To search by keyword, try:

- Alta Vista Search: http://www.altavista.digital.com/
- CareerCity Job Databases: http://www.careercity.com/

- Career Resource
  Home Page: http://www.eng.rpi.edu/dept/cdc/
                                newsgrps.html/
- Deja News: http://www.dejanews.com/
- Excite Home: http://www.excite.com/
- The Internet Sleuth: http://www.isleuth.com/
- Liszt (the Mailing List   http://www.liszt.com/
  Directory):
- Search.Com: http://www.search.com

Other sources for groups related to your interests include:

- Action Without Borders   http://www.idealist.org/
  (links to 7,500 nonprofit
  resources):
- Publicly Accessible Mailing   http://www.NeoSoft.com/internet/
  List (contact by interest   paml/
  field):

Honesty   Be sincere and honest in all your dealings with contacts. You know that an important part of any good relationship is being honest with yourself and others. Don't deceive others by saying you need information when you're really trying to get a job interview. In the initial stages of the career planning process, it's fairly easy to state the type of information you're seeking about a career area of interest. There's a lot to explore with someone already working in the field.

If you're at the point of looking for a job, just be more specific about the type of information you need. Using networking and informational interviewing as a ploy for a job and not for information, advice, or referral will appear insincere and untrustworthy. Others will recognize that you're trying to use them for your personal gain. You will not gain, and you'll probably hurt the chance of others who follow who are genuinely seeking information.

Information   Your stage in the career planning process will determine what kind and how much information you need. Even in the advanced stages, there's still more to learn. You must communicate your purpose, do the related research, and have questions prepared. Here are some guidelines to keep in mind for carrying out your informational interview and networking efforts.

1. **Develop a positive relationship:** Establish rapport by asking the interviewee about his or her background. Take a genuine interest in the person. Use tact and diplomacy; don't be pushy or overly assertive.

2. **Obtain information:** Do your research and have your questions ready. Try not to be sidetracked with taking notes. Use note taking for specific information only (names of people, organizations, etc.) and summarize responses afterward. Ask for the person's reaction to your idea and plans. Are you making sense? Toward the end, if it feels right (and you have one ready), get feedback on your resume.

3. **Continue building your network:** Add to your network of contacts by asking for a referral at the end of your interview.

4. **Show your appreciation:** Let your interviewee know how he or she has helped you at the conclusion of your interview, as well as afterward with a thank-you note.

5. **Keep your contacts informed:** Let your interviewees know that you'll keep them informed of your progress. This step has two purposes: they'll appreciate knowing that they played a role in your success, and you'll want them to remember who you are. You never know what might come up on the very day your note or call comes in.

6. **Be flexible about who you'll talk with:** If you're unable to talk with the person you targeted, be prepared and willing to talk to someone else (if an alternative is not offered, you could make such a request).

7. **Don't interview just a few people:** Do as many informational interviews as possible, with as many different people as you can who are doing the job you're interested in, in as many different types of work settings as you can find them. This is the only way to get the clear and complete picture of your ideal job.

8. **Research the field first:** Never go on an informational interview without at least reading up on the basics of that particular job. Your questions reflect what you know. Don't waste your contacts' time by asking questions that they know you can read about in a book.

Larry followed a particular manufacturer for a few years by the ads it ran in the newspaper for training positions. He used library resources to further research this particular company. Once he was able to identify the person he wanted to interview with, he contacted that person and arranged an appointment for an informational interview.

The interview went well. Larry and his interviewee hit it off and began a professional friendship. Larry received far more information than he had contemplated, including job descriptions, desired skills and experience for new hires, and even an organizational chart.

Larry was eventually hired by the very same company for an entry-level training position, once he completed the additional education that was required.

Referrals   The three major purposes of networking and informational interviewing are to gain information, advice, and additional referrals related to your career area of interest. Whenever an informational interview has gone well, in your estimation, you should ask your interviewee if he or she knows anyone else who would be beneficial for you to speak with. However, it's important not to *expect* a referral. Allow your interview to progress at its own natural pace. If, by the end of the interview, you sense that rapport has been developed, then chances are that your interviewee will offer a referral upon your request. If he or she does, consider it something very personal and special. Appreciate it as a gift; it's not owed or expected, but an individual might respond to your request.

Exchange   Offering your help, in any way possible, to your interviewee is symbolic of the exchange factor of the informational interview/networking process. Your interviewee might thank you for your offer but have no request of you at that time. He or she might get back to you in the future, however, if the occasion arises. In the meantime, if you think the person is competent and people you know could benefit from his or her services, then you might consider making referrals of new clients to that contact.

Develop   Developing yourself, increasing your skills, is another goal of the networking approach to job searching. The informational interviewing process affords you an opportunity to develop your communication skills, as well as your ability at establishing rapport and positive interpersonal relationships. As a result, your self-confidence and self-esteem are certain to increase. However, to benefit you have to be willing to risk.

In addition to interpersonal and communication skills, you will have the opportunity to further develop your job search skills. You'll become more familiar with a variety of job search techniques (in addition to networking), get feedback on improving your resume, enhance your interviewing skills (even if you are the one doing the interviewing), and gain invaluable insight and advice pertaining to your career field of interest.

Keep your network active by staying in touch, even while employed. It will help you stay abreast of the latest developments. Also, relating with others who have similar interests enriches your life. Finally, there's no telling when you'll be job searching next and need a solid network of contacts.

Let's assume you've contacted the person you were referred to and held a successful informational interview. You need to send two thank-you letters within two days. One is to the person who referred you to the interviewee, simply letting him or her know the informational interview took place and went well, and the other to the person you interviewed.

The thank-you note to the person you interviewed should accomplish the following:

- Confirm how he or she was of help to you (be specific).
- Reinforce the person's knowledge and expertise.
- Be positive about your strengths and demonstrate a grasp of the topics discussed.
- Thank the person for any additional referrals and state approximately when you'll contact the new referrals. The person will want to pass the word along to the new contact. State that you'll let him or her know about the results.

RESEARCHING EMPLOYERS*

Gathering available information about an organization or an employer will help you throughout the career change process. For example: Your

*Contributed by Mary Jane Hilburger, Associate University Librarian, Northeastern Illinois University.

cover letter can be individualized for the specific employer. Your resume might emphasize skills and experience in the corporation's line of business. During an interview, you can show knowledge, interest, and enthusiasm about specific events that pertain to the company. As a prospective employee, you can choose to accept a job offer knowing the actual strengths and weaknesses of the organization.

Gather Useful Information

Information that can always be useful includes the following subjects.

The Organization's History and Age   Significant events, founders of the organization, major changes that have occurred, and patterns of growth reveal the corporate culture and can give you an indication of what kind of company it is to work for.

Products and Services   Long-established products or services, new ones, and proposed or developing ones reveal the direction the organization is heading. Find information about the organization's industry or providers of similar services or products. Find out the strength or weakness of the industry as a whole. Uncover strategies and goals by examining products or services.

Financial Information   Examine the financial condition of the organization. Gather information on sales, profits, costs, liabilities, and assets for profit-making corporations by looking at financial statements and balance sheets. Look at the annual budget and annual reports for nonprofit organizations.

Personnel Issues   Find out about benefits and training available to employees, staff morale, and employee satisfaction. Find out about salaries. Find out if the workforce is unionized and the history of labor negotiations.

Divisions, Subsidiaries (in For-Profit Companies), and Branches (in Nonprofit Organizations)   Chart the patterns of growth, the various divisions of the organization, and locations of the divisions. Find out about the physical condition of the organization's buildings.

Management Style and Reputation   Gather information on the corporate culture and decision-making processes, and obtain an organization chart, if possible. Find out how the business handles public relations during a crisis to judge its reputation.

Information like that suggested in this section can be retrieved from company publications, through libraries, or increasingly on the Internet.

EMPLOYER/COMPANY INFORMATION

Related Internet Sites

- EDGAR Database (financial-oriented-company database): http://www.sec.gov/edgarhp.htm
- Hoover's Online! (fee based): http://www.hoovers.com/
- How to Research a Company: http://www.studentcenter.com/where/feet/feet.htm/
- Identify Companies by Your Interests: http://www.studentcenter.com/where/company/company.htm/
- Infoseek: http://guide-p.infoseek.com/
  Go to Business, Company Profiles.
- JobWeb: http://www.jobweb.org/
  Go to Employment Information, Employer Profiles.
- LookSmart: http://www.looksmart.com/
  Go to Business and Finance, Companies and Industries.
- Mansfield University: http://www.mnsfld.edu/depts/lib/mu-biz.html
- Net Locator—Jump to Search Results: http://nln.com/ad.htm
  Go to Business, Public Company Information.
- Searchable Company Database: http://www.companylink.com/companylookup.cfm
- Searchable Company Database: http://www.studentcenter.com/where/company/company.htm
- Thomas Register of American Manufacturers: http://www.thomasregister.com
- Yahoo!: http://www.yahoo.com/
  Go to Business & Economy, Companies, Directories.

Three of our career changers benefited from their library research. Before his informational interview, Larry did a search of periodicals in the library and came up with four or five articles about the company he was interested in. That might not sound like many, but they provided Larry with names of people in the organization, the corporate philosophy, and help in further understanding the company in general. This allowed him to ask more informed questions during the informational interview.

Martha regularly does library research to keep up-to-date on products related to her restaurant business. Vincent even used library circulation data in researching which books were most often taken out in the subject areas in which he intended to start his specialty bookstore, the fields of history and mystery.

Questions to Answer About the Company

Use the following series of questions about your target organization to structure your search, then consult the sources mentioned at libraries or other information centers. Ask for help from a reference librarian if you need suggestions on how to begin or continue.

Is the Employer For-Profit or Nonprofit? If it is a for-profit corporation, is it public, private, or a subsidiary or division?

Public corporations have raised funds to establish, operate, or expand their business by selling stocks, or equity, in their company. They sell their stock on stock exchanges: the New York Stock Exchange, the American Stock Exchange, some regional stock exchanges, or the NASDAQ computerized trading system for over-the-counter (and usually smaller) corporations. Publicly owned corporations must file reports with the U.S. Securities and Exchange Commission (SEC) and must make their financial standing available to their stockholders and prospective stockholders. Many libraries have sources that provide access to this financial information also. Because of this, it is easier to get information on a public corporation than on other kinds of organizations.

Private corporations do not sell stocks on stock exchanges and do not have to report their financial status to the SEC. Private companies usually are smaller than public companies, but sometimes large private companies remain private to avoid revealing sensitive and highly valuable information to their competitors.

Subsidiaries and divisions of companies are owned by a parent company. Finding information about them can be difficult, because information is combined with all other subsidiaries or divisions of the parent company. Subsidiaries have their own officers and boards of directors, while divisions are an organizational unit of the firm. The parent company can be either public or private.

Check directories of businesses as a first step. Traditional print business directories give short factual information such as the address, telephone, Telex, and fax numbers; products and Standard Industrial Classification (SIC) codes; annual sales; number of employees; stock exchange (if public) on which company shares are traded; and names of top executives. Because currency is essential, try to use only the current year's print edition. Directories are also available on the Internet and generally carry more recent information than print directories. Several of the most useful are the following:

- *Ward's Business Directory of U.S. Private and Public Companies.* Gale Research, Inc. Annual.
  Provides information on 200,000 companies and identifies them as public, private, subsidiary, or division. It includes ranks by sales within industries so that chief competitors can be identified. A fee-based Internet version may be available at your library as Information Access Corporation's Business & Company Profile Database.

- *The Directory of Corporate Affiliations.* National Register Publishing Co. Annual.
  Provides information on who owns whom for U.S. subsidiaries, divisions, and affiliates. A parent company list is the main list, which provides a hierarchical order for all the "children" for both public and private corporations. It provides headquarters addresses and names of executives and, if available, sales and employee numbers for each.

- *Standard & Poor's Register of Corporations, Directors, and Executives.* Standard & Poor's Corp. Annual.
  Lists over 55,000 public and private corporations. Its second volume includes biographical information on executives, and its

third volume contains indexes by industry, geographic location, and ultimate parent. An electronic version is available on CD-ROM and on the Internet; check to see if your library subscribes.

- *The Million Dollar Directory: America's Leading Public and Private Companies*. Dun & Bradstreet Information Services. Annual.
  This directory includes 160,000 public and private companies with a net worth of over $500,000, a sales volume of over $25 million, and 250 or more employees. An electronic version is available on CD-ROM and on the Internet; check to see if your library subscribes.

- *Thomas Register of American Manufacturers*. Thomas Publishing Co. Annual.
  This source emphasizes the products that 150,000 public and private companies produce. The 26-volume set resembles the telephone Yellow Pages. A free Internet version is available at http://www.thomasregister.com.

- *Dun's Business Identification Service*. Dun & Bradstreet Information Services. Semiannual. Microfiche.
  This microfiche set provides listings of more than 10 million U.S. business establishments, both public and private. Because of the expense of a subscription, only the largest business libraries can afford to own this.

- *CorpTech Database of 45,000 High Tech Companies*.
  A membership service, this database tracks high-technology industries and provides free access to selected items. http://www.corptech.com.

Is the Corporation Public?   After you have looked at directories to identify the corporation and you have determined that it is public, you can gather a significant amount of information from its disclosure reports. Because publicly held corporations sell stock to the public, they must disclose financial information on a regular basis. This is available to the job seeker in a variety of forms. Copies of the reports are also often available at the company's home page or from its public relations office. Large libraries may maintain a microfiche copy.

The federal Securities and Exchange Commission (SEC) requires corporations to file 10-K annual reports electronically. These are available at the SEC's EDGAR database at http://www.sec.gov. Additional reports, called 8-K reports, must also be filed if the company is experiencing significant financial changes. These reports include financial statements; discuss and analyze the financial condition of the company; and disclose its subsidiaries, the properties it owns, the extent of its foreign operations, whether its sales are dependent on a few large customers, and ownership of major blocks of company stock.

A print annual report is sent to stockholders and prospective stockholders shortly after the company's fiscal year ends. An electronic version is usually available at the company's home page. Annual reports depict the company to its best advantage and can have public relations purposes, but they also offer useful information for the job seeker. They contain financial and management information interspersed with expensive photographs and graphics. They include an income statement of the company's financial activities in the last year, a balance sheet showing the company's total value or net worth, and an auditor's report certifying that the data was reported using Generally Accepted Accounting Principles (GAAP). The annual report also contains the letter to stockholders (sometimes called the president's letter) as well as a management discussion of the past year's activities and possible future directions of the company. It will identify specific products and how successful they are and sometimes break down a company's statistics by line of business, called segment. It might also identify the location of the company's facilities. Management organization, strategies, and plans for the future are often included as well.

The following sources reprint information from the filings to the SEC and from annual reports, as well as provide additional information:

- *Moody's Manuals.* Moody's Investors Service. Annual. Summarize 400,000 corporations' and institutions' financial status and provide a brief company history, information on any mergers, name changes, business lines and products, location of plants and properties, and the status and rating of investment safety of the company's bonds. There are seven manuals in the series, arranged by type of corporation. An electronic version is available on CD-ROM and on the Internet; check to see if your library subscribes.

- *Standard & Poor's Corporation Records.* Standard & Poor's Corp. Annual.
  Lists corporations alphabetically and includes a company history and financial statements and balance sheets. It provides information similar to that in *Moody's Manuals.* An electronic version is available on CD-ROM and on the Internet; check to see if your library subscribes.

- *Compact D/SEC.* Disclosure, Inc.
  This company disc business service extracts information from the SEC filings and reformats it onto one disc for over 12,000 actively traded public corporations. It includes the full text of the president's letter and management discussion from the annual report. Many large libraries subscribe to this service.

In addition, because public corporations sell stock, many investment advisory services track their status. Using a service such as the following, you can evaluate the strength of the stock on the market, one measure of the strength of the corporation:

- *Value Line Investment and Expanded Service.* Value Line, Inc. Weekly business service.
  Follows the movements of more than 3,800 stocks. Arranged by industry, it measures, evaluates, and recommends specific stocks. It identifies high-growth companies and describes the well-being of the industry as a whole.

Is the Corporation Private? Most companies in the United States are not public. If you have determined from business directories that the company is private, you might have a hard time gathering additional information. The company may have a website, but financial data and annual reports will not be available. See the related listings for finding Internet resources. If information is not available about the specific company, gather information about the industry as a whole.

Periodicals and business newspapers are the most likely source for additional information. Use periodical indexes to locate citations to specific articles. Look up the company name or the industry to identify citations. These sources are easiest to use in their electronic form, which often will include the full text of the article. The most useful indexes follow:

- *ABI/Inform.* University Microforms Inc.
  Available in an electronic database version only, this index to over 800 periodicals provides useful abstracts (summaries) of the articles.
- *Business & Company Profiles.* Information Access Corporation.
  Indexes industry trade journals, regional business magazines, and popular business journals.
- *Business Periodicals Abstracts.* H. W. Wilson Co.
  Available in print and an on-line database version, this source indexes 350 general, scholarly, and business periodicals and trade journals.
- *Wall Street Journal Index.* University Microfilms Inc.
  An index to the *Wall Street Journal* business newspaper.

Most libraries carry business magazines to which these indexes and databases refer. Bear in mind that most of the publications are national in coverage and will only report on very large local corporations. When you find an article on or related to your target company, you can use it to make a favorable impression. Realize that most staff in the company will be aware of the coverage, especially if it is very positive or very negative. Some of the noteworthy publications are the following:

- *Barron's National Business and Financial Weekly.*
  This newspaper emphasizes companies and their market conditions that affect the values of stocks, bonds, options, and other investments.
- *Business Week.*
  A weekly with many extensive articles on nationally famous companies. It carries many special issues on industries, executive salaries, and top public and private companies.
- *Forbes.*
  A general biweekly that celebrates the free enterprise system and carries articles on company activities, industry developments, and economic trends. It has a November issue listing the 200 best small companies.
- *Fortune.*
  A semi-monthly magazine that carries lengthy articles on national companies. An April issue identifies the

Fortune 500, and an August issue identifies the *Fortune* International 500.

- *Inc.*
  This monthly magazine covers small, entrepreneurial companies. It is useful because small firms are currently doing the most hiring.

- *Nation's Business.*
  This monthly reports on business activities, companies, and prominent businesspeople.

- *New York Times.*
  This daily New York City newspaper has a useful business section.

- *Wall Street Journal.*
  This business newspaper, published on weekdays, has a focus on finance, industry, and business. Its occasional feature articles on executive recruitment are useful.

There are thousands of additional magazines and newspapers that carry articles on companies that might provide job prospects. Almost all companies belong to an industry association that publishes a trade journal. Such journals provide the most recent articles on trends and new products in the industry. By reading the trade journals, you can keep informed of events in the entire field. Ask at your library about what journal subscriptions it holds and how they might be of help to you. The *Encyclopedia of Associations* will identify what associations are relevant.

Is the Corporation a Subsidiary or Division?   A parent company might own the company in which you are interested. Finding information on the "children" of conglomerate public companies can be just as difficult as finding information on private companies. Be sure to look for information under the parent's name in the sources listed for either public or private companies.

Is There a Company History?   Company histories can reveal what kind of work environment exists at a company and any corporate legends and culture the company has. By referring to such information at an interview, you can give a favorable impression. Look on the Internet for the company's home page for its version of the business's history. The following sources might contain information:

- *The International Directory of Company Histories.* St. James
  Press, 1998.
  Arranged by industry, this directory profiles more than 3,000
  major public and private companies worldwide that have U.S.
  sales. Each profile has an excellent and detailed description of its
  founding to its present state of activities.
- *Hoover's Handbook of American Business 1998.* Edited by Gary
  Hoover, Alto Campbell, and Patrick J. Spain. Hoover's Business
  Press, 1998.
  Profiles of 500 major U.S. companies, including lists of compa-
  nies creating the most jobs and eliminating the most jobs over
  the past ten years. http://www.hoovers.com/.

What Is the Status of the Industry as a Whole?   Finding out
about the industry as a whole and associations that serve the corporation will give you insight into the opportunities and the business climate. It might help you assess the strengths or weaknesses, even if you
cannot locate information about a specific company. There are associations and directories for every industry. Locating and reading the trade
journals for the industry is helpful. The following sources are of particular additional interest:

- *Moody's Industry Review.* Moody's Investors Service. Looseleaf.
  This service provides comparative statistics for major competitors and includes net income, profit margin, assets and returns
  on assets and capital, and composite stock price movements for
  the industry.
- *Standard & Poor's Industry Surveys.* Standard & Poor's Corp.
  Quarterly.
  In narrative form, this source describes and analyzes major
  industries in the United States and evaluates their status. Some
  financial statistics are included for the leading companies.

What Occupational and Salary Information Is Available?   Consult the following sources:

- *American Almanac of Jobs and Salaries.* Avon.
  This reference describes jobs in federal and state governments,
  the arts, sciences, technology, business, service industries, and
  the professions, along with salary ranges.

- *American Salaries and Wage Survey.* 4th ed. Gale Research, Inc. Annual.
  This compilation of occupations and their corresponding salaries from over 300 federal, state, and trade associations ranges from national coverage to local city coverage. It is useful in estimating the level of salaries of an occupation.

- *America's Career InfoNet.*
  Provides information on occupations and salaries. http://www.acinet.org/.

- *Area Wage Surveys.* U.S. Bureau of Labor Statistics. Annual.
  This annual for 70 metropolitan areas includes occupations in the clerical, professional, custodial work, and materials movement and maintenance areas and provides hourly and weekly earnings. Comparison of wages between cities is possible.

- *Dictionary of Occupational Titles.* U.S. Department of Labor, Employment and Training Administration. (See *Occupational Outlook Handbook.*)

- *Dun's Employment Opportunities Directory/The Career Guide.* Dun & Bradstreet Information Services. Annual.
  Identifies employment opportunities for public, private, and nonprofit organizations with more than 1,000 employees. It also lists educational requirements and available company benefits and training opportunities.

- *Occupational Compensation Survey.* U.S. Bureau of Labor Statistics. Annual.
  Describes the level and distribution of occupational pay for many metropolitan areas and provides weekly and hourly earnings for professional, administrative, technical, clerical, maintenance and toolroom, materials movement, and custodial occupations.

- *Occupational Outlook Handbook (OOH).* U.S. Department of Labor, Bureau of Labor Statistics. Biennial. http://stats.bls.gov/ocohome.htm.
  The *OOH* has job information on 250 jobs, representing 80 percent of the workforce, and the *Dictionary of Occupational Titles* (*DOT*) has 12,000 job descriptions with references to over 20,000 job titles.

SALARY INFORMATION

Related Internet Sites

- America's Career InfoNet: http://www.acinet.org/
                                 Go to Resources or Occupational
                                 Search.
- Compensation & Benefits   http://www.mcs.net/~glanger/ala/
  Report: ala.html
- JobSmart (Salary Surveys):   http://jobsmart.org/
- Yahoo!:   http://www.yahoo.com/
                                 Go to Business & Economy,
                                 Employment, Salary Information.

Check the *Occupational*   http://stats.bls.gov/
Outlook Handbook: http://www.jobweb.org/

What Biographical Information Is Available?   Through some standard references, you can identify the key people in a company and gather background information about them. In an interview, knowing something about the chief executive is very impressive. *Standard & Poor's Register* and the *Million Dollar Directory,* both listed previously, give brief background information. Also try the following:

- *Biography and Genealogy Master Index.* Gale Research, Inc.
  Comprehensive index to current and retrospective biographical dictionaries and Who's Whos. It is available on CD-ROM or the Internet; check to see if your library subscribes.

- *D&B Reference Book of Corporate Managements.* Dun & Bradstreet, Inc. Annual.
  This book covers 200,000 presidents, officers, and managers of 12,000 service companies and provides data on present business connections and present and former business positions.

- *Who's Who in Business and Finance.* Marquis Who's Who/Macmillan Directory Division. Biennial.
  For this directory, North American and international business professionals who are of current business reference interest

submit biographical data, which is reviewed and formed into a short sketch. *Who's Who in America,* another Marquis publication, offers broader and more general coverage for North America.

Is the Entity a Small, Local, or Regional Corporation? There are many more small, for-profit companies in the United States than any other kind of company. They can range from a partnership employing five people to very large regional private companies. Gathering information on them is difficult. Sometimes all that will be available are listings in the telephone book or an industrial or service directory. As noted previously, when locating information about a specific company is not possible, gathering information about its industry can be a useful alternative. Asking for additional suggestions from a reference librarian is recommended. The following sources are some possibilities:

- *Annual state industrial directories and state service directories.*
  Every state has a manufacturer's directory that lists public, private, and very small firms; their locations, products, and staff; and sometimes the computers the company uses. Most libraries own the print directory for their state. Larger states will also have a services directory, which lists similar types of information for companies that sell some kind of service. Often they are available electronically.

- *Local newspapers and regional business periodicals.*
  Often local newspapers will cover a high-profile company in the area or provide useful information about a small company. On-line databases, such as Newspaper Abstracts or Business & Company Profiles, available through large libraries index many of the major local papers, or your library might clip articles for a newspaper file of local interest.

- *Telephone book Yellow Pages.*
  The Yellow Pages contains advertisements for producers, sellers, and services available in a local area. You can also find locations and phone numbers of competitors to your organization. An Internet version is available at http://s15.bigyellow.com/.

Is the Employer International?   Many companies do business throughout the world. In many cases, a well-known company is a subsidiary of a foreign company. The SEC requires some foreign parent companies that sell stock in the United States to file reports using a 20-F form—one good source of information—but many other companies do not have to register. Using periodical indexes to identify pertinent articles will uncover useful information also. Finally, there are many directories listing worldwide companies, including the following:

- *Directory of American Firms Operating in Foreign Countries.* 13th ed. World Trade Academy Press, 1994.
  Lists companies operating in foreign countries and includes officers. Volumes 2 and 3 list the company by country and give local addresses and the products the facility produces.

- *Hoover's Handbook of World Business.* Edited by Patrick J. Spain and James R. Talbot. The Reference Press, 1995–1996.
  Profiles 227 public, private, and state-owned corporations overseas, 100 European and 40 Japanese companies, as well as companies in more than 30 other countries.

- *International Organizations.* Gale Research, Inc. Annual.
  Over 9,000 international nonprofit organizations and associations can be located using geographic, key word, and executive indexes. This source formerly was included in the *Encyclopedia of Associations.*

- *Principal International Businesses.* Dun & Bradstreet International. Annual.
  More than 55,000 leading companies and their subsidiaries are listed and arranged by country. Includes approximate sales, number of employees, and whether the company imports or exports.

- *World Business Directory.* Gale Research, Inc. Biennial.
  Lists more than 140,000 businesses involved in international trade for 190 countries. Volumes 1 to 3 are arranged by country; volume 4 includes product data, industry data, financial and employment data, and indexes.

INTERNATIONAL CAREER RESOURCES

Related Internet Sites

- Career Mosaic:
  http://www.careermosaic.com
  Go to International Gateway.
- Council on International
  Educational Exchange
  (CIEE):
  http://www.ciee.org/work/
  index.htm
- DePaul University:
  http://www.depaul.edu/~educate/
  student/internat_resource.html
- International Career and
  Employment Network
  (ICEN) (job search resources):
  http://spider.ucs.indiana.edu/
  ~intlcent/icen/
- International Resources:
  http://www.t-bird.edu/IRFRM.htm
- JobWeb:
  http://www.jobweb.org/global/
  global.htm
  or
  http://www.jobweb.org/catapult/
  interntl.htm
- Links to International
  Resources on the Internet:
  http://www.duke.edu/
  %7elpmaskel/intl_hrefs.html
- Purdue University:
  International Job Listings:
  http://www.ups.purdue.edu/
  Student/internal.htm
- Purdue University:
  International Resources/
  References:
  http://www.ups.purdue.edu/
  Student/picc
- The Riley Guide:
  http://www.dbm.com/jobguide
  Go to Resources for International
  Job Opportunities.

Is the Employer a Nonprofit Organization?   There are more than 300,000 employers in the United States that are nonprofit. They include government agencies at the federal, state, and local levels. Within education, there are nonprofit private schools and public schools offering higher, secondary, and elementary education. There are also social service agencies at the national, state, and local levels. Health-related organizations likewise often are nonprofit. Finding information about all of these is difficult, but information is available.

If the organization is a government agency or a tax-supported agency, ask a reference librarian if there is a handbook to the city or if the agency has a website. Federal, state, and local governments publish information that describes and summarizes the activities of each department within the government. Other suggested sources:

- *Local governments.*
  Many local governments have websites describing activities of each department of the government. Libraries often have a newspaper clipping file on local government and can also direct you to relevant local websites.

- *State blue books.*
  Available from all state governments, these books summarize activities of each state department. Ask at your library for your state's version or go to the state's home page on the Internet.

- *U.S. Organization Manual.* Government Printing Office. Annual. Summarizes the activities of each federal agency. Of particular interest is the Office of Personnel Management, which recruits civil service positions throughout all agencies and maintains federal job information centers in major cities. Using this guide to research a specific agency will be useful. You can access government agencies' home pages from http://www.access.gpo.gov/su_docs/index.html.

If the organization is a school, consult directories of schools available at every library. Peterson's Guides, Barron's, and Lovejoy's are some of the publishers that produce such directories. Ask for help in how to locate sources you need.

NONPROFIT ORGANIZATIONS
Related Internet Sites
- Action Without Borders   http://www.idealist.org/
  (nonprofit websites):
- Find Your Future: http://www.4work.com/
- Good Works (directory of   http://www.essential.org/
  social change organizations):   goodworks/about.html/

- Internet Non-Profit Center: http://www.nonprofits.org/
- Nonprofit Resources   http://www.clark.net/pub/pwalker/
  Catalogue: General_Nonprofit_Resources/

If the organization is a social service agency or a health organization, again specific directories are available. Check at your library for the subject "social service—directories," "community health services—directories," or "health facilities—directories." Ask a reference librarian to help you find them. Also check to see if there are newspaper articles on the organization. In addition, many such organizations must file a report annually with a statewide regulatory agency. While these reports usually are not published, they are available for inspection at the agency. Look for the state agency that regulates corporations; often it is the Secretary of State.

As you can see, gathering information about a prospective employer will involve serious research in a library and will require a commitment of time and sometimes money. Libraries offer many directories, handbooks, indexes, and histories that contain information on organizations. To help narrow your search, asking for suggestions from a reference librarian is a worthwhile strategy. With time and energy, researchers can weave together small amounts of information from a variety of sources to produce a tapestry of information on a particular organization and enhance their chances of employment.

CAREER CHANGER UPDATE

★

Recently, as Larry began his new job search he realized he was struggling to get focused—that is, to know what he really wanted. He reports that a day in the library (a place with which he was very familiar but hadn't visited lately) researching positions, salaries, and employers helped to turn things around—afterward he felt back on track.

JOB SEARCHING LONG-DISTANCE AND RELOCATION

In today's tight job market, relocating becomes a strategy that you can employ in your job search to gain an advantage in obtaining the type of work you're most interested in. How does one go about job searching long-distance?

Know Your Career Goal and City of Choice

The first task in job searching long-distance may be obvious—identifying geographically where you want to live—yet many people might not be sure. You need to be specific about what city or town you wish to reside in. If you just pick a general area within a state, your search will be unfocused and less effective. The same applies to your career goal. You need to be focused in order to increase the possibility of success.

If you're interested in more than one city, rather than trying to carry out more than one long-distance job search, which decreases your chances for success, prioritize the cities in order of preference and begin with the most highly ranked choice. Give the process four to six months, and at that point you can decide whether to redirect your energies to your next city of choice.

There are a couple of ways to approach identifying your city of choice. You, or you and a significant other, might have a particular city in mind based on factors other than your career goals. Or you might know that there are better possibilities in a particular city of getting the type of job you're seeking.

Now, with electronic job searching, once you know your career goal and city or cities of preference, you can access information from numerous databases to determine which companies in your desired geographic location(s) have related positions. If you select the kind of job you want, the size and type of company or organization for which you'd like to work, location desired, and other related information, the databases can generate a list by searching for the criteria you highlighted. The employers cited can then be contacted directly.

Since there are more than 600 databases on 500 systems, consulting an electronic research service bureau can save you time and money. One such bureau is Pro/File Research in Flourtown, Pennsylvania. For further information check under "Electronic Job Searching" in Appendix B.

Networking Long-Distance

If you're already taking advantage of computer database services to identify employers, that's great. In addition to that approach, the following suggestions for networking long-distance are offered, assuming you've identified the city where you want to pursue your career goal. You will begin to network through the use of published and people resources.

- Subscribe to local papers and related business/industry publications. Pay particular attention to news of companies that are expanding.

- If you can get someone to send you a phone book (Yellow Pages), that would be helpful. Your local public library might have one, or you can inquire there about publications that have similar information.

- Contact officers of the Chamber of Commerce to ask for information related to the city as a place to live and any information about career fields you're interested in.

- Identify and contact civic leaders (Rotary, Kiwanis, Elks, etc.) or government officeholders.

- Check for alumni of colleges you attended who live in that area.

- Ask members of your network if they know someone in your target city.

- Identify and contact officers (on a state or local level) of professional associations related to your career goal.

- Contact religious leaders (you don't necessarily have to be of the same denomination).

- Contact education leaders for information or suggestions of others to reach, such as a university placement director. Even though they're geared for helping their own graduates find jobs, they might be willing to share a name or two with you. They probably wouldn't consider you as competition for their main clientele, unless you are looking for an entry-level position.

- Contact officers of major companies for any information they might be willing to share.

- Use Internet sites, such as the following, to identify related companies, professional associations, job ads, and more.

JOB SEARCHING LONG-DISTANCE
Related Internet Sites
Newspapers
- Career Path (read more than   http://www.careerpath.com
  35 major city newspapers'
  employment ads on-line,
  including *Atlanta Journal-Constitution,
  Boston Globe, Chicago Tribune,
  Denver Post, Los Angeles Times,
  New York Times, San Jose Mercury
  News,* and the *Washington Post*):
- National Business   http://www.nbew.com/
  Employment Weekly:

Professional Associations
     See listing on page 239.

Government Employment

Federal
- Fed World—The U.S.   http://www.fedworld.gov/
  Government Bulletin Board: Go to Federal Job
       Announcement Search.
- Federal Jobs Digest: http://www.jobsfed.com/
- Federal Jobs Opportunity Board: ftp://fjob.mail.opm.gov
- FRS Federal Jobs Central: http://www.fedjobs.com/
- JobWeb (has federal   http://www.jobweb.org/Search/
  job listings):   jobs
       Search for "federal" and "job."
- The Resume Place (new federal   http://www.resume-place.com/
  government format):
- The U.S. Office of   http://www.usajobs.opm.gov
  Personnel Management:

State
- America's Job Bank   http://www.ajb.dni.us/
  (maintained by the Department

of Labor, U.S. Employment
Service, linking more than 2,000
State Employment Service
Offices in the United States):

Sites with National Job Ads

- CareerCity Job Databases: http://www.careercity.com/
- Career Resources @   http://www.jobbankusa.com/
  JobBank USA:
- GoodWorks (social change   http://www.essential.org/
  organizations):   goodworks/about.html
- HEART/Career Connections: http://www.career.com/
- Internet Career Connection: http://www.iccweb.com/
- NationJob Online Jobs   http://www.nationjob.com/
  Database:
- World Wide Job Seekers: http://www.cban.com/

Using names of common contacts or mutual friends whenever possible will help increase your positive response rate.

For these initial contacts, use the telephone or E-mail when requesting printed material, and letters when addressing specific individuals for information or referrals to help develop your network. Start this process at least two months before making an exploratory visit to your target city. This time is to allow for responses and follow-up correspondence. Your follow-up letter serves to thank the contact for any information and to state your desire to set up an informational interview for the period you'll be visiting. Let the person know that you'd like to call for an appointment when you visit. Also, state that you're not expecting a job from your visit, just a chance to ask questions.

Once your preliminary research and initial letter campaign are well under way, it's time to consider when you will visit your target city. Using vacation time is a wise approach to take and perhaps your only one, if you are presently employed. Try to schedule at least one visit of at least two, and ideally three, weeks in your target city.

Upon your visit, you can treat this job search as you would a search where you now reside, pursuing informational interviews with your contacts. However, your effort is compressed into a shorter time. With little additional time available, leave your sight-seeing until after settling the employment question. You'll need to be focused, stay focused, and work hard at your networking and job search efforts.

CAREER CHANGER UPDATE

✶

Patricia, who was willing to relocate, used the Internet in two ways during her recent job searching efforts, to identify firms with jobs of interest to her:

On Yahoo! (http://www.yahoo.com/) she went to Business & Economy, and then Careers. There she found a variety of databases, did a keyword search, and found ads for lawyer positions in California, where she most wanted to end up in order to be closer to her aging parents.

The National Law Journal site also had job listings. She identified one of interest in New Jersey.

An alternative approach is to stay open with regard to geographic location and be willing to investigate opportunities wherever they may present themselves. One aid for identifying employers and positions may be available through your professional association membership.

Some associations provide their members an on-line job bulletin board listing related job openings across the nation. This may involve a modest fee (higher for nonmembers) but allows you to job search nationally from the comfort of your home, using your computer.

Another service that may be provided through your professional association is membership with a resume database firm, such as Job Bank USA in McLean, Virginia. Employers use these to identify candidates for job openings. Check with your professional association with regard to these and other related job search services.

Relocation Resources

Choosing a City　A community's growth and decline trends should be considered as part of your criteria. Perhaps the Chamber of Commerce or a related office can send you some information. In addition, consult *Places Rated Almanac: Your Guide to Finding the Best Places to Live in North America,* by Richard Boyer and David Savageau. This publication provides information for over 300 major cities on cost of living, housing, job opportunities, education facilities, climate, health care, environment, safety, transportation, the arts, recreation, and economics and provides rankings. These aspects sum up the areas to assess when you're considering relocation.

Zephree actually visited the city of interest to her and job searched there. Upon finding a job opening in a county pre-adult probation program, she applied, with the intention of moving to this city. When she returned home, she wondered why they would ever give that job to someone not yet living there. Worried about this possibility, especially because she felt she hadn't made clear to them her willingness to relocate, Zephree packed her bags and moved there.

She immediately visited the personnel office where she had her interview and let the person know that she, indeed, had moved to that city. Impressed by her desire and action, management hired her within a week. This is perhaps not the approach we'd recommend, but it was a risk, in this case, worth taking.

Handling Expenses   Major costs involved in relocation include housing, travel, child care, closing costs of old and new home, increase in mortgage payment or apartment rent, temporary living expenses, moving expenses, and a possible increase in the overall cost of living. The expenses you incur in a work-related move that's at least 50 miles farther from your old address than your last job was may be deductible. Check with your tax advisor.

Long-Distance Research   As already mentioned, most research can take place in the library. In addition, two publishers—Bob Adams and Surrey Books—have series that identify employers and organizations (*Job Bank Guides* and *How to Get a Job in . . .* , respectively) in specific cities or states, including the following:

- Atlanta
- Boston
- Chicago
- Dallas/Fort Worth
- Denver
- Detroit
- Florida
- Houston
- Los Angeles
- Minneapolis

- New York
- Ohio
- Philadelphia
- Phoenix
- Portland

- St. Louis
- San Diego
- San Francisco
- Seattle
- Washington, DC

RELOCATION

Related Internet Sites

- The Canadian Guide to   http://infoweb.magi.com/~issi/
  Working & Living Overseas
  (anywhere):
- Cost of Living: http://www.studentcenter.com/
                               region/region.htm
- JobWeb: http://www.jobweb.org/
                               Go to Career Services, Planning
                               Relocation Resources.
- Relocation Salary Calculator: http://www.homefair.com/home
- USA CityLink Home Page: http://www.usacitylink.com/

Relocating Counseling Service   Cendant Mobility provides information on housing and schools in any community, as well as spouse career counseling. The company's address is 40 Apple Ridge Road, Danbury, CT 06810. Regardless of what sources you use to research your target cities, you can evaluate them in a similar manner to that used in making a career choice. Establish and rank your particular criteria for assessing a target city and try to narrow your list down to the top two or three communities. Then, as suggested earlier, begin the long-distance job search process with your top choice target city.

PART III

*Strategies for Groups with Special Challenges
in the Workplace*

✯

CHAPTER 11

WOMEN AT WORK

★

WOMEN IN THE WORKFORCE: THE NUMBERS KEEP GROWING

The Statistics

Although the rate of growth for women in the labor force is expected to slow, it will still increase at a faster rate than that for men. In the period 1996–2006, about half of labor force entrants (49.6 percent) will be women, compared with 42 percent in 1979 and 44.5 percent in 1986. In addition, by the year 2006, there will be 70.6 million women in the workforce, representing 47.4 percent of the total.

Women are also the major breadwinners in 20 percent of U.S. families. Sixty-six percent of women who are married with children are working, compared with 62 percent in 1985, 57 percent in 1980, and 47 percent in 1975.

What Do These Numbers Mean?

Women are a growing force in the workplace and must be recognized. Yet, certain challenges still face women on the job. This chapter reports on these challenges and offers suggestions on how to most effectively deal with them. On the brighter side, things are beginning to change for the better—we'll highlight where.

CORPORATE CULTURE

The corporate/business culture is an important aspect to assess as women decide on which organizations they wish to work for. So, how can you check out the particular culture of an organization, particularly related to how women are treated? First, during your visits or research via informational interviews, company literature, or library resources, try to examine the following aspects: attitudes or "vibes," whether teamwork is noticeable, how employee contributions are recognized, and any related history of decision making, including the hiring and promotion of women.

If you discover a business culture that offers an atmosphere in which men and women work together and are encouraged and rewarded for their contributions and achievements rather than being caught up in vicious, unproductive office politics, then you have found what can be considered a successful culture. Essentially, you want a good match between your values and those of the organization. In the meantime, what can women do to enhance their image and power in corporate America?

Enhancing Women's Image and Power in Business

Janet Hauter offers the following suggestions.

Develop Positive, Healthy Business Relationships   There's no better way than the networking process to build and enhance your career. Obviously, networking doesn't end with acquiring a job. A whole new focus takes place with beginning a new job, both within your organization specifically and in your career field more generally.

Women have come to realize the vitality of the "old boy network" to advance in their careers. Thus, we find that women are increasingly creating formal networks of their own. Professional relationships developed throughout one's career need to be nurtured and maintained by sharing information and offering support. Check in your geographic area for career-related women's networking groups.

Find a Mentor   More and more large organizations are establishing formal mentoring programs as a means of speeding up the learning process for new employees. It shortens the time it takes for them to be productive and helps them to understand the big picture. The more powerful your mentor, the clearer the path to promotion. In the absence of a formal mentoring program, you might be able to identify a potential mentor in your organization. Work at establishing positive relationships with everyone possible, and perhaps a mentoring relationship will develop. It helps make life easier to have a helping hand reaching out to offer assistance and advice.

Control Information   Through your networking and research, stay up-to-date in your field. Many people believe that information equals power. Even if you're not all that concerned about moving up, power can help to secure where you are as well.

Control Resources   If you're responsible for a budget, then be responsible in your operation from it. Those higher up will find it difficult to promote anyone who isn't.

Tap Hidden Pockets of Power   Via your networking efforts, you will be able to establish positive, professional relationships with a variety of people, those in recognizable power positions and those not so recognizable (by title). If your goal is to move up, then these would be important people to establish positive relations with.

Protect the Power You Have   Don't abuse others by using coercion or other negative power moves (e.g., making staff do your personal chores).

Discrimination

Carol Kleiman describes discrimination as a practice that effectively keeps qualified women from rising to the top job, no matter what their education, experience, or years with the company. According to Kathryn Petras and Ross Petras, women are likely to be found in corporate staff rather than line functions; they tend to be placed in positions in corporate communications, human resources, finance, legal, marketing research, public relations, and systems departments. Yet to make it into senior management, it's usually necessary to have line experience in core areas like marketing, production, and sales. Suggestions to overcome such obstacles include the following:

- Identify what experience is needed to reach your goal.
- Plan ways to get that experience.
- Ask for the type of projects and assignments you'll need.
- Seek out corporations that offer women lateral experience or those that place women in line positions.

As corporations change, becoming more flexible organizations, they'll offer cross-functional training to more of their executives.

Wages and Other Benefits In general, research has shown that the more women employed in a particular occupation, the lower the pay. Most low-pay, low-status white-collar jobs are held by women in disproportionate numbers. Nearly 75 percent of working women are employed in traditionally female, low-wage jobs. One reason for this is that many employers have long viewed women as secondary earners whose families do not depend on their income. The number of working mothers who are the sole source of support for their families has steadily increased, as has the rate of working mothers who live in poverty. Women in general earn about 67 percent of men's earnings in similar employment.

In addition, access to health insurance and other benefits is often blocked as well. Those working in traditionally female occupations have the highest uninsured rate. Sixty-two percent of minimum-wage earners are women, and one-half of all women workers earning $5 an hour or less are without health insurance. Also, over 15 million women of child-bearing age in the United States have no public or private medical coverage. One in eight births in the United States each year is not covered by any health plan. The average cost of having a baby is now $4,300.

The best suggestion for women with regard to salary and related benefits is to do the research. Know what you deserve to be paid with your particular set of skills and experience. Then prepare yourself to negotiate, as well as you can, to obtain the fairest salary possible. It's simply more difficult to do without the information. You'll be left guessing whether you're being treated fairly. With the right information, you'll be able to plant your feet solidly, stand tall, and ask for what you know you deserve.

The Glass Ceiling   Basically, the term *glass ceiling* refers to women's difficulty in getting promoted beyond a certain point. Women have made gains. They make up 41 percent of all management positions, but less than 5 percent of top executive jobs belong to women. In fact, that percentage decreases to less than 3 percent when viewing women's representation in *Fortune* 500 companies' senior management positions, with 105 having no women corporate officers at all.

The June 1995 issue of *Career Opportunity News* reported that the Glass Ceiling Commission, a government-sponsored research group that interviewed *Fortune* 500 CEOs and managers throughout the United States, identified three levels of anticipated barriers to the advancement of women and minorities:

- **Societal barriers:** The current education system and the stereotyping on the basis of race, gender, or ethnicity have restricted the supply of qualified women and minorities.

- **Internal structural barriers:** Many women and minorities are isolated from jobs on a career track to management as a result of recruitment policies and corporate culture.

- **Governmental barriers:** As a result of a lack of monitoring and enforcement of employment requirements and laws, as well as limitations of data collection practices used to identify problems, women and minorities have been limited in their career track advancement.

The Glass Ceiling Commission also reported that workers seemed to be clustered in industries on the basis of gender more than race. Service industries, for example, employ 75 percent of all women now working. Among the most equitable is the insurance business, where the proportion of women and men as managers is equal, and the worst is represented by the utilities industry, where less than 20 percent of managers are female.

What additional areas, to that of insurance, seem to offer the best choice for women interested in top-level management positions? According to Petras and Petras, other financial services industries, such as banking and brokerage, are more likely to offer women senior management positions. In addition, high-tech jobs tend to be gender blind, because the key to success is learning how to use technology. The pay gap here is also less, with women earning 82.7 percent of male salaries.

Executive women (1,251) surveyed in Catalyst's *Women in Corporate Leadership: Progress and Prospects* responded in the following percentages as to what prevents women from advancing to corporate leadership roles:

- Male stereotyping and preconceptions (53 percent)
- Lack of significant general management or line experience (50 percent)
- Exclusion from informal networks (50 percent)
- Inhospitable corporate culture (37 percent)
- Women not in pipeline long enough (31 percent)

The best bet suggested by Petras and Petras is in information systems with financial services firms or pharmaceutical companies, whereas tough barriers still exist in manufacturing and retail. In addition, we suggest that women identify corporations that sponsor corporate training for female mid-level managers for higher-level positions.

The bottom line is that companies cannot afford to eliminate what will soon be one-half of the workforce from top-level management positions and expect to keep up with their competition. The good news is that businesses are now beginning to allow more local control and promotion of teamwork to ensure their place in a changing and more competitive marketplace. Those that can adjust and adapt to change will have opportunities. Diversity is more welcomed, and management styles are becoming more cooperative (an acknowledged strength of women).

How can women increase their odds of gaining upper-management positions? Here are some suggestions for success:

- Develop a management style with which male managers are comfortable. Unfortunately, for women in business, success often depends on how well they fit into a male-dominated corporate culture.

- Think positively about what you can do; seek out difficult or challenging assignments; consider striving to exceed performance expectations.

- Finally, as previously mentioned, try to attract strong and influential mentors.

For additional insights into how some of our nation's most successful women executives overcame barriers and the strategies they used, check Debra J. Swiss, *Women Breaking Through: Overcoming the Final Ten Obstacles at Work.*

Up Is Not the Only Way   With many career advancements stalled in layers of middle management, making a lateral move might be viable for both women and men. A lateral move could be used on one job as a springboard to another. Because downsizing has eliminated many positions for which the "ladder" used to be climbed, expanding oneself laterally offers greater variety and perhaps necessary experience to be competitive for those fewer, higher-level positions. It might not yield more money, but it could cure your burnout, broaden your experience, and boost your marketability both within and outside your company.

Some companies are making provisions within their newer structures for lateral moves for their employees after seeing how it helps employee motivation and productivity. The ability to transfer to a different department might become the new nonmonetary reward for excellent performance. Both women and men need to rethink the nature of traditional career paths and examine how they're defining success.

OWNING A BUSINESS

Many women are turning to owning a business as the path of choice for career advancement. The National Foundation for Women Business Owners currently estimates that 36 percent (nearly 8 million) of all businesses are owned by women, and this figure is predicted to rise to 50 percent by the year 2005. One of every four (18.5 million) U.S. workers is now employed by a woman-owned business. This represents more Americans than those employed by all *Fortune* 500 companies combined. Female-owned businesses generate more than $2 trillion in sales a year.

Organizations you might want to contact and some useful directories follow:

- **American Society of Women Entrepreneurs**, 2121 Precinct Road, Suite 240, Hurst, TX 76054.
  Promotes women entrepreneurs pursuing business opportunities in America and abroad through legislative action, education, and resources of interest to women business owners.

- **Catalyst National Network of Career Resource Centers**, 120 Wall Street, New York, NY 10005.
  Promotes changes for women in the workplace and researches and publishes findings on women's issues and career information.

- **National Association of Female Executives**, 135 W. 50th Street, 16th Floor, New York, NY 10020.
  Offers programs for women-owned businesses and operates a venture capital fund for small businesses.

- **National Association of Women Business Owners**, 1100 Wayne Avenue, Suite 830, Silver Spring, MD 20910.
  Promotes the economic, social, and political power of women entrepreneurs through the creation of innovative change in business culture, building alliances, and transforming public policy.

- *A Directory of Non-Traditional Training and Employment Programs Serving Women,* Washington, DC: U.S. Department of Labor, Women's Bureau.
  Lists programs that offer apprenticeships.

- *Women Directors of Top 1,000 Corporations,* Washington, DC: National Women's Economic Alliance Foundation.

See additional resources for women listed at the end of Chapter 12.

WOMEN IN BUSINESS
Related Internet Sites
- Business of Women: http://www.web-search.com/women.html

- SBA Women's Business Ownership Homepage (check Outside Resources Hotlist at the bottom): http://www.sbaonline.gov/womeninbusiness/

SEXUAL HARASSMENT

Joyce Lain Kennedy describes sexual harassment as including unwelcomed sexual advances, requests for sexual favors, or other conduct of a sexual nature, verbal or physical. Actions can be described as sexual harassment when the aggressor's conduct unreasonably interferes with a worker's job performance or creates an intimidating, hostile, threatening, or offensive working environment.

What Can Be Done About It?

Sexual harassment can keep women out of certain jobs and from advancing in the ones they have. As bad as sexual harassment is, what might be even worse is figuring out what to do about it. Even though studies show that 45 to 85 percent of women have experienced some form of sexual harassment, only about 3 percent ever complain or file a complaint.

Filing a complaint could make things rough on the job. If we take the view of the work environment as being a people environment, it's easy to recognize the importance of maintaining good rapport with those you work with and report to. Women are reluctant to complain for fear of being branded a troublemaker, becoming a victim of an unpleasant work situation, or future employers' being reluctant to hire them.

In addition, some women are reluctant to leave a job, especially when they need the salary or lack the confidence to find another. As Richard Bolles suggests, if you think you can survive the ordeal in good shape (perhaps the harasser is disliked by many others), then seek the advice of a lawyer and consider filing a complaint.

As a beginning step, when you are harassed sexually on the job, tell the perpetrator in a cool, calm manner that the specific behavior (name it) bothers you and to please not repeat it. It's important to let it be known from the start that a particular behavior is disturbing to you and you want to see it ended. This will perhaps detour the aggressor from acting in such a way again and might save you the ordeal of filing a complaint. Kennedy offers some other suggestions about what to do if confronted with sexual harassment on the job:

- Don't ignore the situation; seek advice from coworkers and friends.

- Keep a log or diary noting incidents. Be sure to store it in a safe (locked) place. You will need this type of information if you decide to file a complaint with the company or a government agency.

- Carry a small microcassette (concealed) recorder to document evidence.

- Take advantage of your company's internal complaint procedures. Unfortunately, harm to you and others might never end otherwise.

- Send the offender, by certified mail, a letter outlining and stating incidents.

Will the Future Be Better?

There is some good news. As a result of the October 1991 Hill/Thomas hearings, there's been a raised consciousness across the United States with regard to sexual harassment. Many companies have developed explicit, printed policies for dealing with sexual harassment. With the increasing number of women entering the workforce, a company that doesn't establish clear and effective policies in this area can leave itself open to expensive lawsuits and a negative reputation as an employer.

It is now the responsibility of every company owner and top management to create a workplace atmosphere where women can feel safe to file complaints if they feel mistreated. In researching companies, women can attempt to ascertain the company's policies toward sexual harassment.

BALANCING WORK AND FAMILY

More Choices

There are various options from which women can choose in pursuing work and family goals. Many positive gains have been made by women (societal, career, and family related), but these changes make decision making more confusing.

Increased Responsibility

Women (particularly those in their late twenties, thirties, and early forties) find themselves caring for both young children and aging parents while pursuing a career and holding together a marriage as well. Many women believe they have to forgo educational opportunities or postpone taking the steps necessary to advance on the job.

A real problem is the lack of high-quality affordable child care and the ever-increasing need for elder care.

Child and Elder Care   It is estimated that about 40 percent of the workforce is involved with providing care for both their children and elders. As reported earlier, many mothers have lower wages and can't afford either of these alone, much less both (especially single mothers). Family care-giving roles for mothers can bring about periods of interrupted income and, thus, disrupt careers. Twenty-five percent of mothers of preschool children who are not in the paid workforce say they would work if access to safe and affordable child care existed. It's estimated that 25 percent of a low-income working mother's earnings go to child care.

What's needed is a more comprehensive plan for subsidizing and regulating child care and elder care. With more women entering the workforce and the aging of the population, eventually these types of programs will come about. In the meantime, we all need to push for it.

CHILD CARE
Related Internet Site
- Yahoo!:   http://www.yahoo.com/
                                  Go to Business & Economy,
                                  Companies, Children, Child Care.

There Is Hope At least for the time being, more and more companies are offering flexible hours, job sharing, and part-time work options (some with benefits), and sometimes provisions for child care as well, to help support mothers in the workplace. These benefits have as an overall goal the balance between a good career and family life for employees. Employers' motivation is either one of benevolence or the reality that highly skilled employees are getting harder to find, and soon half of all potential employees will be women. Therefore, they do what they can to attract the most qualified women to work for them. Yet the vast majority of companies are not yet progressive enough to incorporate these improvements. Because of this and hard economic times, a tight job market, and a desire to be with their children, many women are dropping out of the workforce to be full-time mothers.

DISPLACED HOMEMAKERS

Traditionally, the term *displaced homemakers* applied to women at mid-life whose children had grown up (or nearly so) and because of widowhood or divorce suddenly found that they could no longer continue in the role of homemaker. With the increase in divorce, women are often forced even earlier than mid-life to seek employment. Many women also decide to do so voluntarily, because they want the challenge and stimulation of a career.

Some major concerns of these career beginners or reentries are as follows:

- Can I find a job?
- Will I be able to succeed in the workplace?
- Can I both work and care for children well?
- Will I be able to support myself and the children?
- If I need further education or training, can I afford it?

Skill identification is a crucial part of the self-assessment process for this group. Homemakers often underestimate their skills, which usually include, for example, finance, time management, organization and planning, communication, negotiation/mediation, training, public relations, leadership, and administration/management.

Some good resources for helping women in the transition from home to the workforce are as follows:

- **American Business Women's Association,** 9100 Ward Parkway, P.O. Box 8728, Kansas City, MO 64114.

- **Women Work! The National Network for Women Employed,** 1625 K Street NW, Suite 300, Washington, DC 20006.

WOMEN'S RESOURCES

Related Internet Sites

- FeMiNa—Web Search for Women: http://www.femina.com/

- IGC: WomansNet: http://www.igc.apc.org/womensnet/
- Search Directory for Women: http://www.w.wwwomen.com/

- The Smart Network: http://women.com/
- Women's Resources on the Web: http://www.women-online.com/women/

- Workplace Strategies: http://www.advancingwomen.com/workplace.phtml

- Yahoo!:   http://www.yahoo.com/
  Go to Business & Economy, Employment, Women in the Workplace@.

CHAPTER 12

MINORITIES

★

AFRICAN-AMERICANS, HISPANICS, AND ASIAN-AMERICANS: INCREASING DIVERSITY IN THE WORKPLACE

The Statistics

By the year 2006, African-Americans, Hispanics, and Asian-Americans will represent about 27.3 percent of the workforce, up from 24.6 percent in 1996. Close to 40 percent (38.9 percent) of new workforce entrants between 1996 and 2006 will be members of a minority.

MINORITY REPRESENTATION IN THE WORKFORCE
Related Internet Site
- U.S. Bureau of Labor Statistics (BLS):   http://www.bls.gov/

The Facts Behind the Numbers

The U.S. workforce is growing in diversity. Companies are responding to shifting demographics and a shortage of highly skilled labor by actively recruiting minority workers and setting up programs to help encourage minority advancement.

Yet the percentage of minority workers who have reached management positions is still low. According to the Equal Employment Opportunity Commission (EEOC), as reported by Kathryn Petras and Ross Petras, in 1990 only 5.9 percent of all managers in the United States were African-Americans, and only 3 percent of these were in corporate management.

Richard Bolles reports that minorities are making advances in the workforce. For example, the number of African-Americans with incomes of $50,000 or more doubled between 1982 and 1987. However, much more still needs to be accomplished, as indicated by the following facts:

- One-third of the nation's 30.2 million African-Americans live in poverty.
- African-American unemployment is twice that of the rest of the nation.
- The median income of African-American families is half that of white families.

WHAT'S IT LIKE TO BE A MINORITY?

The Label

Just being identified as a minority can have a negative impact. Some minorities wonder if they're perceived as equals by nonminorities. This in turn can cause distrust on both sides of the equation. When you add all this to the experience of possibly biased career-related testing, counseling, and placement practices, as well as workplace discrimination, you can understand how the stress can bring about a lack of self-confidence and confidence in the system among minority workers, job seekers, and career changers.

The Role of Values

Considering a history that includes the enslavement of Africans and African-Americans, disenfranchisement, discrimination, and poverty, it is not surprising that many minorities have come to value family, sharing, communication, and interdependence. This can make it tough to adjust to a workforce that reflects the values of independent thinking, autonomy, and competitiveness.

The Pressure Is On

Unfortunately, many of the majority harbor doubts about minorities and have formulated or inherited certain stereotypes often based in ignorance and fear. Examples are that minorities are lazy, unmotivated, untrustworthy, and less intelligent. Therefore, if a minority person gets the right kind of training and effectively competes for and gains a professional career position, Miguela Rivera believes there's even greater pressure to perform on the job than what is usually demanded of non-minorities. In other words, we all need to develop the skills to succeed in our career, but Rivera asserts that minorities have to do even better to dispel the doubts.

In the workplace, we need to know how to handle ourselves professionally, communicate effectively, develop positive interpersonal relations, become skillful at interoffice politics, develop expertise in our field, and basically know what and why we're doing what we're doing. Research has shown that minorities survive by overachieving, blending in, and avoiding the spotlight. Those who question, stand apart, or speak out run the risk of being further labeled as rebels, malcontents, or radicals.

Often minorities can feel torn between two worlds—their culture and that of corporate America. They can feel pulled in both directions and end up not really feeling part of either. Corporate America is also responsible for helping to eliminate stereotyped thinking and bias among its employees through multicultural education initiatives. We'll discuss ways this can be accomplished later, but first, we'll take a closer look at the problem of discrimination.

DISCRIMINATION

The Law

Title VII of the Civil Rights Act of 1964 prohibits discrimination in hiring, promotion, compensation, and other conditions of employment based on race, color, creed, gender, pregnancy, or national origin.

The Challenge

The challenge is knowing how to recognize discrimination when it's occurring and how to handle it. Cydney Shields and Leslie Shields suggest going with your gut feeling, for starters, then looking for disparities in treatment, wages, assignments of jobs, and the like. Yet you still might have difficulty distinguishing rational opposition from racism or sexism. In many situations, you must listen carefully to what people are saying and try to understand what they're objecting to. If they sound irrational, then you're probably dealing with prejudice, which literally means contempt without facts. However, if the objections seem rational, you need to be able to identify possible underlying fears and attempt to take action to allay such fears. In addition, there may be specific actions you can take regarding how you're going about your job that might help to remedy the situation.

Decision Time

If you do feel you're being discriminated against, you could deal with it by persevering and attempting to dispel fears through your actions. This is a slower approach, perhaps, but it can work. If the discrimination continues, then you're in a position to decide whether to proceed through the channels set up within the company (starting with your supervisor) for filing a complaint.

One tough aspect of deciding whether to file a complaint is determining whether it's worth the possible grief it might bring. You certainly could be risking retaliation or even losing your job. Judge your situation of discrimination on the basis of its seriousness and its effect on you. If there's a strong pattern of bias, fighting it might be advisable. However, ask yourself these questions first:

- Is it worth paying attention to?
- Can you do anything about it?
- Is it affecting your performance or place in the organization?
- Are you using this claim of discrimination as an excuse for not achieving your goals?

You need to decide whether the benefits of fighting back outweigh the potential costs. Know the consequences before taking action.

Suggested Steps to Take

Here are steps to follow and questions to answer if you think you've been discriminated against (been terminated, been passed over for a promotion, received an unusual work assignment, etc.):

1. Stay calm; don't overreact; maintain your dignity and professionalism.
2. Find out what happened (e.g., if fired):
   - Was a whole section or organization let go?
   - Was your immediate supervisor fired also?
   - Does the action seem to be the result of poor business conditions, slumping company sales, or loss of a contract?
3. If you were fired as a result of normal changes in business and the marketplace (and it's imperative that you objectively find out), then pack your bags and move on.
4. If you were the only one fired, ask for the reason. Were any less senior or less competent staff retained? If so, you may have been a victim of discrimination.

With regard to not receiving a promotion:

1. Are you qualified in terms of education, technical expertise, communication skills, and leadership ability?
2. Had you been passed over before?
3. Did someone more qualified or with more seniority get the job?
4. Take a good look at yourself and answer the following questions:

- Are you adequately prepared?
- Has your performance been consistently good?
- Have you followed through on assignments?
- Have you been a team player?

5. Have any past difficulties between you and the company been documented in writing?

Once these questions have been answered, you're in a better position to judge whether you have a case of discrimination. Let's say you do have a case. What's next?

Proving discrimination can be both difficult and upsetting. You might be stigmatized and labeled a troublemaker. Even if you gain the promotion, what will it be like for you back on the job? Your enemies can make life miserable for you and eventually drive you out anyway. Maybe so, but at least you're doing something about it. If more people follow your example, it's bound to help decrease discrimination in the future, especially at your workplace. Ignoring it will not make it go away.

If you believe you have a case and want to proceed, take the following steps:

1. Go to management, starting with your immediate supervisor. Tell them how you feel and give specific reasons. Be able to show your qualifications, and state that you think the decision to fire or not to promote you was based on racial or cultural bias.

2. Talk with your company's Equal Employment Opportunity officer or a branch office of the EEOC (check the Yellow Pages under U.S. Government).

3. Seek the advice of a lawyer and decide whether to sue. Most cases are settled out of court but can still take 6 to 18 months before being finalized.

The best protection in cases of dismissal for poor performance is good record keeping, especially copies of performance evaluations. At annual reviews or evaluation time, make sure to get a written copy of your report (including a summary of conversations). Make sure it's accurate and challenge anything that's not. Ask what you can do to improve and be more qualified for promotion (have this summarized in writing also). In this way, you've got it all in writing. This precaution can support your case or circumvent it to begin with.

CORPORATE AMERICA RESPONDS

It's in Their Best Interest

With shifting demographics showing a continuous increase of minorities in our population, companies want workers that reflect their customers. Recruitment of minorities is one goal of their establishing programs to address cultural diversity, in order to attract, train, and retain minority workers. However, even with such programs, individuals still have their own biases and might view minorities as an unknown quantity and perhaps as being somewhat threatening—that's where education efforts come into play.

Caucus Groups

Some companies have formed caucus groups in which minority workers meet to share problems and advice, as well as to offer suggestions to management on minority issues. These, however, will work only if management is serious, listens to the suggestions, and responds when appropriate.

Mentoring

It's easy for minorities in the workforce to become isolated, especially if they are among the first to be integrating a particular department or business. Some businesses have established mentoring programs to help new hires learn the ropes and have a better chance to advance their careers. If none exists officially in your workplace, seek out others who can help you understand the expectations and realities of the work environment. It's also helpful if your mentor can put you in touch with the informal network that can help you attain recognition and advancement. Formal company titles might not tell you exactly where the power is.

Diversity Management

A growing trend among corporations is to have a position or office designated as diversity management to coordinate multicultural training. With the workforce becoming increasingly ethnically and racially diverse, management needs to learn how to work and manage groups with a wide range of backgrounds. The goals of diversity management programs include the following:

- Dispel false assumptions based on ethnic group or gender

- Enhance communication

- Work out misunderstandings that arise

- Lead to the elimination of racist and sexist discrimination

This new direction in management has led to a need for cultural diversity managers. To qualify, one generally needs a background consisting of human resources experience and an advanced degree in an area such as sociology or organization development.

NETWORKING: ONE KEY TO AVOIDING RACIAL DISCRIMINATION

Networking is perhaps the best-known way to neutralize or circumvent prejudice and discrimination in the workplace for yourself. You will rarely, and probably never knowingly, be referred to someone who is likely to discriminate against persons like yourself. However, don't operate in exclusively minority networks. Tap into nonminority networks as well, using any or all of the following approaches:

- Volunteering

- Community activities

- Attending career-related workshops and seminars

- Informational interviews

- Connecting with nonminorities you know from school, work, and similar places

Don't wait for others; reach out to them. In addition, try not to let the fact that a handful of nonminorities have an attitude problem mean that you develop one as well.

Welcoming Minorities

Look for companies that offer specific programs and recruitment drives for minority workers. A good source is the annual February issue of *Black Enterprise* covering the best places for African-Americans to work. Also, check the resources that follow, which include associations, directories, and periodicals.

Minority Trade and Professional Associations

- **Association of African American Women Business Owners,** c/o Brenda Alford, P.O. Box 13858, Silver Spring, MD 20911.

- **Hispanic Alliance for Career Enhancement,** 200 S. Michigan Avenue, Suite 1210, Chicago, IL 60604.

- **Latin Business Association,** 5400 E. Olympic Boulevard, Suite 130, Los Angeles, CA 90022.

- **National Association of African American Chambers of Commerce,** 750 St. Paul Place, Suite 1920, Dallas, TX 75201.

- **National Association of Negro Business and Professional Women's Clubs Inc.,** 1806 New Hampshire Avenue NW, Washington, DC 20009.

- **National Center for American Indian Enterprise Development,** 1200 New Hampshire Avenue NW, Suite 445, Mesa, AZ 85236.

- **National Hispana Leadership Institute,** 1901 N. Moore, Suite 206, Arlington, VA 22209.

- **National Hispanic Business Group,** 730 Fifth Avenue, New York, NY 10549.

- **National Network of Hispanic Women,** 12021 Wilshire Boulevard, Los Angeles, CA 90025.

- **Native American Indian Chamber of Commerce,** P.O. Box 27626, Tucson, AZ 85726.

- **U.S. Hispanic Chamber of Commerce,** 1030 15th Street NW, Suite 206, Washington, DC 20005.

- **U.S. Pan Asian American Chamber of Commerce,** 1329 18th Street NW, Washington, DC 20036.

Resources to Organizations

- *Asian-American Information Directory*

- *Black American Information Directory*

- *Guide to Black Organizations*

- *Guide to Hispanic Organizations,* Public Affairs Department, Philip Morris Ltd., 120 Park Avenue, New York, NY 10017.

- *Hispanic-American Information Directory,* Gale Research, Inc., 645 Griswold Street, Detroit, MI 48226.

- *Minority Organizations: A National Directory,* 5th ed., 1997, E. Oakes, ed. Chicago, IL: Ferguson Publishing.

Minority Business Periodicals

- *Black Careers,* P.O. Box 8214, Philadelphia, PA 19101.

- *The Black Collegian,* Black Collegian Services, Inc., 140 Carondelet Street, New Orleans, LA 70130. http://www.blackcollegian.com.

- *Black Enterprise,* Subscription Service Center, P.O. Box 3011, Harlan, IA 51593. http://www.blackenterprise.com.

- *Equal Opportunity,* Equal Opportunity Publications, 1160 East Jericho Turnpike, Suite 200, Huntington, NY 11743.

- *Minority Business Entrepreneur,* 3528 Torrence Boulevard, Suite 101, Torrence, CA 90503.

MINORITIES RESOURCES
Related Internet Sites

For All Minorities

- Career and Job Resources for Minorities:

  http://www.stetson.edu/~Rhansen/diversity-resources/
  Go to General Diversity Resources.

- JobWeb:

  http://www.jobweb.org/hr/minorities.htm

For African-Americans

- The Black Collegian Job Assistance Selection Service (JASS):

  http://www.black-collegian.com/jobsg.html

For Hispanics

- Saludos Web: Careers, Employment, and Culture:

  http://www.saludos.com/

CHAPTER 13
PEOPLE OVER AGE 50

★

THE POPULATION IS AGING

The Statistics

For the period 1996–2006, people whose age is 45 to 64 are expected to generate the highest growth. By 2006, 28.7 percent of the population, nearly one of every three people, will be over age 55 (compared with 26.3 percent of the population in 1996), representing 15.4 percent of the labor force (compared with 11.9 percent of the labor force in 1996).

By the year 2006, 15.2 percent (33.6 million) of the population will be over the age of 65, twice the number in 1940. Between 1996 and 2006, the number of older workers will grow twice as fast as the labor force as a whole. Thirty-six percent of those over 55 will still be working by 2006 (compared with 30 percent in 1996). Workers will have an average age of 40.6 in 2006, compared with 1996's average of 38.2.

REPRESENTATION IN THE WORKFORCE OF PEOPLE OVER AGE 50
Related Internet Site
• U.S. Bureau of Labor Statistics (BLS):   http://www.bls.gov/

The Reality

Two major trends today are the aging of the population and the skills gap. Potential labor market entrants do not have the higher-level skills that most available jobs require. This can be an incentive for the older workers who want to continue employment or resume it after an absence from the workforce. Yet they might have some barriers in their way, the biggest being age discrimination.

Dispelling Myths

Older adults interested in remaining in or returning to the workforce must fight the impression some people have that age is linked with decreasing capability for work and training. Studies have shown that chronological age has nothing to do with one's functional capacity.

Intellectual capacity does not begin to diminish until well into the seventies, if at all. Age does not affect speed, attentiveness to detail, stamina, or accuracy. Older workers have fewer accidents and fewer sick days than younger workers. They still have the ability to learn new things, and their basic personality stays the same. Research has also shown that workers over age 50 have a stronger work ethic, higher productivity, less alcoholism and drug use, more patience, longer tenures, more willingness to learn, and better attitudes than their younger associates. The fact is that most workers over age 65 today are vigorous, healthy, mentally alert, and still young in outlook.

REASONS WHY OLDER ADULTS CHOOSE TO STAY IN THE WORKFORCE

Many Still Need the Money

Many older workers have been victims of downsizings, encouraged to take early retirement (or were let go) while lower-paid, younger workers took over their responsibilities. The fact is that many still need the money to pay bills or care for a loved one who is ill. Many need to supplement their Social Security income. (There are limits on earnings in addition to Social Security; call the Social Security Administration if you have questions.)

Other Reasons

Some choose to work because it's good for their mental and physical health. Others do it so as not to be around their spouse all day. Yet others choose to work so they can be with their spouse all day, working together. It all depends on the individuals involved and the nature of their relationships.

CHOICES FOR THE OLDER WORKER

If an older worker can afford to do so financially, the following choices for how to stay in or return to the workforce are possible.

Work Part-Time

Working part-time enables one to spend more time on leisure pursuits and hobbies. Samuel Ray states that the number of part-time jobs has increased 21 percent since 1980. Twenty percent of women and 6 percent of men are working, by choice, in permanent part-time jobs. Twenty percent of the part-time jobs require a college degree.

Employers are becoming more flexible in both offering part-time jobs and hiring older adults, in an effort to lessen the skills gap mentioned earlier. The types of jobs that offer the best possibilities for part-time work are those that can be independently completed or are project oriented. The skills looked for the most include writing and computer programming. We'll discuss further the skills employers are most interested in.

The organizations in which you would most likely find part-time work include the following:

- High-growth, high-tech companies in the earlier stages of growth, when there's more opportunity

- Nonprofit organizations, such as libraries, museums, universities, and human services organizations

- Small businesses, which are less bogged down in bureaucratic hiring policies and need experienced workers

- Federal, state, and local government

Few *Fortune* 500 companies are recruiting; they're still downsizing. However, some have found themselves short-staffed. Therefore, possibilities might exist as a consultant or contractor. In general, though, older workers are recommended to seek out newer, smaller businesses. They're hiring more, and they offer better access to the person doing the hiring. Many low-pressure, low-paying part-time jobs exist as well, in fast food, retail, day care, and other areas. These might not sound appealing, but they might serve as a good option for the older worker without the experience or skills required by other part-time jobs.

Self-Employment

Self-employment usually involves work as a consultant or subcontractor providing services to companies and even your former employers, but now you're setting your own fees and hours. A couple of key references to check are *Starting a Mini-Business: A Guidebook for Seniors,* by Nancy Olsen, and *Going into Business for Yourself: New Beginnings After 50,* by Ina Lee Selden.

Volunteer Work

Volunteering can be done full-time or part-time. It's unpaid, but you have a purpose—to help create, in some way, a better world. Volunteering offers a good way to make contacts and gain valuable experience. It's also a good way to test out an area of interest or to break into the nonprofit arena. The hours are usually flexible and need not be long. Some places would be willing to have you for only a few hours a week. Of course, this is all possible only if you can afford to do it financially.

Executive and Professional Temporary Work

Ninety percent of all companies now use temporary workers, and executive placement is the fastest-growing segment. Executive placements average about three to nine months. You will usually be hired on a project basis, filling in during a search, or working in companies left too lean after downsizing. The executive/professional placement is good for people who enjoy putting out fires but get bored afterward.

If you're not at the professional or management level, a good organization to check out for temporary work is Kelly Services, the oldest and largest temporary agency. Areas of placement include accounting, clerical, light industry, marketing, sales, records management, technical support, and home health aide.

Other choices for how one could return to the workforce are starting a business in a field unrelated to your first career, turning former hobbies into sources of income, relocating and starting all over, and returning to school to learn new skills.

WHAT EMPLOYERS LOOK FOR IN OLDER WORKERS

The skills identified by companies that hire workers over 50 are the following:

- Communication
- Problem solving
- Technical
- Experience in industry (any industry)
- Computer related (engineering, designing, manufacturing, or peripheral)
- Sales, customer service
- Banking

- Scientific
- Accounting, accuracy
- Sales experience
- Finance, mathematics
- Hospitality
- Marketing

In addition, the following qualities were most sought after by companies hiring workers over 50:

- Positive attitude
- Steady personality
- Ability to learn
- High energy
- Intelligence
- Good work ethic
- Experience
- Judgment/common sense

RESPONDING TO DIFFICULT JOB SEARCH ISSUES AND INTERVIEW QUESTIONS

Your Age

The question of age is perhaps the most important of all. If it's raised during your job search, in whatever disguise they try to give it, your response should be something like, "It's not a problem. I have the necessary experience, education, training, and skills to perform quite well in this job." You could also highlight recent achievements and how you've kept your skills and knowledge current (which we urge you to do if you haven't been already).

If your interviewers press, you can be more direct and say, "It sounds as if you're concerned about my age." Stress that you are in excellent health, are in the prime of your career, are knowledgeable and skilled, and can be a valued asset to the company. If they're worried about how long you intend to stay, tell them five years for sure—and ask how many of their younger workers can guarantee that.

Possibly Being "Overqualified"

If it's suggested that you're overqualified, does this mean you have too much education and/or experience? Ask if you're not sure. The potential employer may be concerned that you may get up and leave when something better comes along. It's your job to convince the employer that at this time in your career this is the right type of position for you.

However, if you think their concern is how much it's going to cost them to hire you, a response on your part could be that your skill level allows you to walk right in, with little downtime, and function right away. Thus, the company would get a good return on its investment in you.

Be aware of your market value, so that if salary negotiations do occur, you're in the right "ballpark." Being in the wrong "ballpark" will definitely hurt your presentation on this point. If you're already dealing with an employer who is hesitant in hiring an older worker, having an unrealistic salary demand will most definitely eliminate you.

Possible Cut in Salary

To better accept a salary cut, which in many cases is a reality, it's important that you're clear on your objective—that this is the type of work you'd most enjoy—in order to feel more satisfied with your career. You're willing to take a more modest salary in exchange for what your research identified as potentially greater job satisfaction.

It helps to carefully figure out a budget so you're clear on just how low you can go. By combining this information with your salary research for positions in which you're interested, you'll be able to judge the appropriateness of possible offers from both standpoints: what workers in positions like this are making and how well you can live on that amount.

Dates on Resumes

In listing work experience on your resume, there's really no reason to go back more than 10 to 15 years, regardless of your age. If you think someone may be prescreening resumes (usually done in large, more bureaucratic, and conservative corporate settings), you may prefer to leave your year of graduation (a surefire age predictor) out of your education section. There's no clear-cut, correct approach here, but many career book authors suggest doing this to avoid possible age discrimination in the early stages of the decision-making process.

Long Tenure at One Company

If your experience is consolidated with one employer, you could emphasize that you felt it was a great job: you were continually challenged, developed important skills and knowledge, gained valuable experience, and had the opportunity to do new and different things.

Stress that you are a team player, get along well with others, and can adapt readily to new situations. Perhaps you have examples of assignments completed in different departments.

Focus on your achievements and accomplishments that show the depth and breadth of your experience. Present yourself as highly qualified, the right person for the job, and capable of making immediate contributions.

Be clear in your mind, as well as in your presentation, that you feel this direction is the right one for you at this point in your career.

Time Gaps in Your Work History

If you're queried about employment gaps, answer honestly. With much restructuring going on, there's no longer the same stigma that there once was to being unemployed. You could say that you took some time off to decide exactly what you wanted to go into, which should be reflected in the career goal you've picked, one that's a good fit. You might also be returning from early retirement and still feel productive, not really ready to be retired (be sure to keep your skills current).

Reentering the Workforce

Whether you're a homemaker, a widower, an early retiree, or even a required retiree, describe how your time was used (helped friends with their business, involved with organizations, served as a volunteer, and/or spent time in areas of interest/hobbies). Show how you've kept your skills current and how your objective is a good fit for you.

ADVICE FOR STAYING, LOOKING, AND FEELING YOUNG

Appearance and Attitude

Because older workers' appearance and attitude play such an important role, Ray offers the following suggestions:

- Don't give clues to your age with phrases such as "back in the days when," "way back when," or "when I was younger."

- Stay up-to-date with business practice and technology.

- Be aware of market forces affecting your particular industry.

- Keep on learning in your field.

- Become computer literate if you're not already.

- Stay fit and healthy. People admire older adults who have energy, vitality, and confidence.

- Keep your wardrobe current but conservative.

We all know how important it is to feel good about who we are and how we look. If age is an issue for us, chances are that it shows through our attitude, and then it becomes an issue with others as well. We need to do everything in our power to take care of ourselves emotionally, physically, intellectually, spiritually, and socially—first, for ourselves and loved ones and, second, for others we come in contact with who can influence our lives for better or worse, such as employers. Most important, however, is to remember that we have the power within us to change in any of these areas.

SOURCES OF JOB SEARCH HELP

Job Fairs

Look for job fairs targeted for mature workers age 50 and over. Representatives from a wide range of career fields usually attend. Keep an eye on the business section of your daily newspaper and local business weeklies as well.

Operation Able

Founded in Chicago, Able (Ability Based on Long Experience) helps those over age 40 by providing executive, managerial, technical, secretarial, and blue-collar work placement in temporary positions. Those from a lower economic/disadvantaged background can also receive help with the assistance of some government programs.

Forty Plus Clubs

Created in the late 1930s, Forty Plus Clubs are a nonprofit nationwide network now in over 25 cities. The clubs are staffed by volunteers and dedicated to helping unemployed managers, executives, and professionals 40 or over in their job search. They assist career changers, retirees, and reentries as well.

Other Support Groups

Look for groups offered through local churches and synagogues and social services agencies (e.g., Jewish Vocational Service, mental health clinics) as well as by private career counselors.

AGE DISCRIMINATION

How to Best Avoid Discrimination

As in all cases of possible discrimination, the best way to avoid age discrimination in your job search is to emphasize a networking approach. Not only is networking the best overall job search method, but this person-to-person referral process is also more likely to put you in touch with people who are more accepting with regard to age issues.

This is accomplished by your contacts' focusing in on your skills and experience—perhaps mentioning your age, perhaps not. Thus, the person to whom you're being referred agrees to meet with you based on your professional qualifications as conveyed by your mutual contact.

Age discrimination may be harder to avoid at large, conservative, and more bureaucratic corporations. Therefore, targeting small to medium-sized companies (where two-thirds of new jobs will be in the future), especially start-ups, may be more advantageous.

The Law

In 1967, the U.S. government passed the Age Discrimination in Employment Act (ADEA), designed to protect workers 40 and over from possible abuses in hiring, promotion, and compensation policies. The ADEA is administered through EEOC offices nationwide. Despite the many years that have passed since its enactment, discrimination still occurs. Discrimination in hiring is the most difficult to detect and prove. Some may wonder if it's even worth it to point it out. Those who do find out quickly that raising the charge of age discrimination in hiring rarely leads to getting the job. Maybe the best way to fight discrimination before being hired is to avoid it and look elsewhere.

Filing a complaint can be psychologically and financially draining and very time-consuming when what you need most is a job. However, age discrimination on the job with regard to promotion, wages, and layoffs/discharges might be easier to prove and thus perhaps worth the fight.

Be prepared, and don't get caught off guard. A few things to keep in mind with regard to the ADEA: The law requires that layoffs be based on seniority or merit (e.g., total sales figures); holding older workers alone to a certain standard with regard to discharges is against the law. Likewise, pressuring older workers to quit is a possible violation of the law. Employers must also provide the same types of overall benefits to workers of all ages, although in some cases it might be of a lower amount. For example, an employer might spend the same amount on health insurance for older workers as for younger workers, but it buys less coverage.

FILING AN AGE DISCRIMINATION COMPLAINT

For a complaint to have merit under the act, you must prove that:

1. You're in the age group protected by the ADEA (40 to 70).
2. The employer is subject to the ADEA provisions (has more than 20 employees).
3. You were adversely affected by some employment action.
4. Age was an issue in the decision made.

PEOPLE OVER AGE 50

Related Internet Sites

- American Association of   http://www.AARP.org/
  Retired Persons (AARP)
  (information for late career
  changers, those nearing or
  in retirement):
- Social Security   http://www.ssa.gov/pubs/
  Administration: 10069.html

Follow these steps:

1. File a complaint with your employer following your company's established procedures. (Check with your human resources department.) In addition, if applicable, file a grievance with your union.

2. If the discrimination practice hasn't ceased, contact the nearest EEOC office. (Check the Yellow Pages under U.S. Government.) Also contact your state government agency that handles age discrimination complaints. If the rules and procedures of your state law seem more favorable to you than the ADEA provision, or if the state agency informs you that it will prosecute your case faster than the EEOC, then go ahead and file with the state just before filing with the EEOC. Usually, the one that receives it first is most likely the one to handle it. You'll probably want to meet with representatives from each office first. For guidance you can consult the American Association of Retired Persons (AARP), Worker Equity Department, 601 E Street NW, Washington, DC 20049.

3. You must file with both your state and federal offices to be able to bring a suit at a later time—the ADEA requires this. You have six months from the occurrence of the alleged discrimination to file with the EEOC.

4. Once you've filed with the EEOC, you will receive a written reply to schedule an interview with an investigator.

5. The agency will investigate the charge. If it finds evidence of age discrimination, it will attempt to negotiate a settlement. If the EEOC is unable to negotiate a settlement, it might file a lawsuit.

What's more likely is that you would decide to file your own lawsuit through your private attorney or public legal assistance agency. The EEOC track record is not good. In the past, many (900) age discrimination complaints were left sitting with no action taken, until it was beyond the statute of limitation. Therefore, be sure to select a lawyer with experience in age discrimination cases.

THE GOOD NEWS

Many companies have developed special programs for hiring older workers. Among these are Kelly Services, the Travelers Co., Control Data, and McDonald's. The AARP offers a variety of education and advocacy programs for older workers, and its Worker Equity Department offers resources and technical assistance to employers interested in hiring older workers.

CONCLUSION

Like other groups with special challenges, described here in Part III, who face possible employment-related discrimination (especially women, minorities, and people with disabilities), those over age 50 must follow through, in every aspect of the career planning process, more so than the average person.

This means being really clear and sure about your job objective (see Chapter 6 if you're not), knowing how your skills match up to the job requirements, and effectively marketing yourself, both in person and on paper (and now the Internet as well). Many potential hiring-related age discrimination issues can be overcome with a strong networking effort. People-to-people referrals is one way to help potential employers not worry about issues such as age and to zero in more on the person and his or her attitude and ability to perform the job.

CHAPTER 14
PEOPLE WITH DISABILITIES

★

NEARLY ONE IN FIVE AMERICANS
HAS A DISABILITY

According to government census reports, nearly 17 million working-age people (ages 16 to 64) in the United States have some type of disability that affects their ability to work. In addition, about 36 percent of the men with disabilities who are of working age are in the labor force or actively seeking employment. The level of working-age women with disabilities in the labor force or seeking employment is 28 percent. Thus, 64 percent of men and 72 percent of women with disabilities who are of working age are not in the labor force.

People with disabilities are the highest unemployed group in the United States. They are eligible for assistance from the vocational rehabilitation programs operated by each state. Around 1.2 million disabled people were helped by these services in 1995.

An additional figure of interest is that five of every six people with a disability were not born with that disability but acquired it later in life.

REPRESENTATION IN THE WORKFORCE OF PEOPLE
WITH DISABILITIES
Related Internet Site
• U.S. Census Bureau: http://www.census.gov/

THE LAW

On July 26, 1990, President George Bush signed the Americans with Disabilities Act (ADA) into law. This act makes it illegal to discriminate against disabled individuals in employment, public accommodations, public service, and telecommunications. The employment provision (Title I of the ADA) went into effect on July 26, 1992, for employers with 25 or more employees and as of July 26, 1994, for employers with 15 to 24 employees. It states that neither an employer nor an employment agency shall discriminate against a qualified individual with a disability in job application procedures, hiring, promotion, dismissal, compensation or benefits, job assignment, job training, or social/recreational programs.

Disability Defined

A disability under the ADA is a physical or mental impairment that substantially limits an individual's major life activities. If you can answer yes to any one of the following three items, then you are a person with a disability covered by the ADA:

1. Do you have a physical or mental impairment that substantially limits one or more major life activities?
2. Do you have a record of such an impairment (past illness or misclassified as having one)?
3. Are you regarded as having such an impairment? Wrongly regarded? Are you the subject of rumors of an impairment though there is none?

Some employers are exempt from being covered by Title I of the ADA. These include federal government agency employers (generally covered by Section 501 of the Rehabilitation Act of 1973), Indian tribes, and tax-exempt private membership clubs. Religious organizations can give preference to individuals of their faith when it comes to hiring.

Disabilities Can Be Visible and Not Visible

Disabilities can include the more obvious, such as impaired sight or hearing, stuttering, or muscular or neurological disorders, and less obvious ones, such as cancer, emotional disturbance, epilepsy, or multiple chemical sensitivity (more commonly known as environmental illness), which is one of the fastest-growing disabilities. Coverage under the act can also include individuals with AIDS or HIV and recovering alcoholics and drug addicts. Occasional or chronic alcoholics and illegal drug users are not covered.

One potential problem is identifying disabilities. Over 1,000 possible disabilities could be covered, yet the ADA itself provides no listing. Therefore, court cases will determine the identification of certain conditions as being disabilities.

ATTITUDE AND ADJUSTMENT

Attitude

Anyone would probably agree that a person with a disability has a right to feel angry about his or her circumstances. It's easy to fall victim to blaming your problems on your disability. However, as unfortunate as your disability might be, a negative attitude will hurt you when it comes to finding a job. Employers want to hire enthusiastic and confident employees with good interpersonal and basic skills (e.g., writing and computer literacy). You might feel powerless over your situation, but remember that only you can choose your attitude.

It's a fact that to get a job you almost always must go face to face and meet with employers. Then you must convince them that you have the skills they need to get the job done right. Richard Bolles suggests focusing on what you and the employer have in common (where you're from, schools attended, or interests), rather than on differences (having a disability or not). This is called establishing rapport and becoming a known, rather than an unknown, quantity.

This might seem overwhelming at this point—researching, networking, and meeting with employers. You can work your way up to it. Set daily goals (risks/challenges), starting small and gradually working your way up to being able to hold good discussions with someone new to you (potential contact or employer). If you're having a confidence problem, then you might want to consider personal counseling. A good resource to consult with regard to the topic of attitude is *Flying Without Wings: Personal Reflections on Being Disabled,* by Arnold R. Beisser.

Adjustment

To adjust to your disability means to come to terms with it, accept it, and, even with its problems, go on to lead a satisfying life. Once you accept your disability, you can finally become comfortable with yourself. This, in turn, will help others (including potential employers) to be more accepting toward you and comfortable with you as well.

There's no denying the reality that certain challenges exist that can affect your attitude and adjustment. The major ones are the ignorance and fear of others toward persons with disabilities. You'll need to be prepared so that when the opportunity comes along, you'll be ready to educate the employer about your abilities and skills in a positive and constructive manner.

WHAT EMPLOYERS CAN AND CANNOT DO

Melanie Witt specifies what employers can and cannot do under the ADA, as follows.

Employers *cannot*

- Use qualification standards, employment tests, or other selection criteria that would screen out persons with disabilities, unless the criteria are job related

- Use employment tests without providing necessary assistance to people with disabilities (e.g., sensory, manual, or speaking problems)

- Offer tests that don't accurately reflect skills and aptitudes of individuals rather than their disabilities

- Ask a job applicant during the pre-employment process whether he or she is disabled or not or about the nature and extent of the disability (We'll return to this point later.)

Employers *can*

- Ask the applicant about his or her ability to perform the job

- Require a medical examination, but only after the position is offered

- Require a pre-employment physical if all other applicants are required to have one

REASONABLE ACCOMMODATION

Reasonable accommodation means that an employer might be required by the ADA to modify a task or workplace to accommodate a job-related functional limitation. Reasonable accommodation can apply to new employees, those promoted or transferred, and those with a new or progressive disability that has resulted in a functional limitation.

When you're seeking accommodation because of a functional limitation, Witt suggests that you do not speak generally about your disability (e.g., spinal cord injury), but rather that you describe your specific limitation (e.g., can't use left arm) and to what degree it exists. An employer might be confused by general terms. He or she needs to know specifically how your disability pertains to the job.

Types of Accommodations

Accommodations can include any of the following, according to the ADA:

- Making workplace facilities accessible

- Modifying work schedules

- Restructuring the job

- Acquiring or modifying equipment or devices

- Changing job location
- Retraining or reassigning employees to vacant positions

Witt's book, *Job Strategies for People with Disabilities,* provides an in-depth description of many job-related functional limitations and types of accommodating solutions that can be developed, as well as related costs. For more information, you can contact the Job Accommodation Network (JAN), West Virginia University, P.O. Box 6080, Morgantown, WV 25606.

What You Can Do

Bolles stresses, in *Job Hunting Tips for the So Called "Handicapped" or People Who Have Disabilities,* the importance of knowing specifically what needs to be redesigned and how. Once you've identified your career goal, talk with people doing that job who are disabled. This would be part of the networking/informational interviewing process. Once you're clear on related job responsibilities, you'll have a better idea about what you're able to handle and what you might need an accommodation for. If your contacts are unable to advise you on necessary accommodations, then contact the Job Accommodation Network (JAN) for information in this area. In this way you'll be prepared, on top of the situation, and ready to advise employers on what would need to be done.

TO DISCLOSE OR NOT TO DISCLOSE?

When deciding whether to disclose your disability to an employer, take into account the visibility of your disability and the timing of your disclosure, if you decide to. In addition, Witt suggests using the answer to the following question as a guideline: "Does disclosure of my disability at this time and in this way support my objective of getting hired?"

If Your Disability Is Visible

When you're called for an interview, if the caller is the person who will interview you, then this is a good time to disclose, once the interview has been set up. In this way you'll avoid surprising your interviewer when you arrive for the interview. If you don't disclose, the surprise could be followed by a feeling of mistrust, that you're trying to hide something, that you weren't being straight with the person.

On the other hand, some people with visible disabilities prefer to wait for the interview to disclose, in order to prevent the interviewer from forming negative stereotypes. However, this is a risky approach. To pull this off, one would need to be strong and confident. You might have to overcome the interviewer's discomfort, silence, possible embarrassment, and even hostility. Generally speaking, in these situations employers don't like surprises.

An employer might have a difficult enough time with your disability, even when you disclose ahead of the interview. Remember, many people are ignorant about the capabilities of people with disabilities. Your task will be to educate the person and to put him or her at ease with regard to your disability.

If Your Disability Is Not Visible

You might have a disability that is not visible but would affect your performance on the job. In these situations, it's suggested that during the interview you disclose, to avoid having the interviewer feeling that he or she has been misled. Here's where doing your homework can pay off. If you are aware of the job duties beforehand, you can come prepared to tell the employer exactly how your job performance might be affected and what accommodation would take care of the situation. Usually, without knowing, the employers' fears will lead them to think that the accommodations are worse than they actually are. In fact, most accommodations are not complicated or expensive to incorporate.

Not disclosing is an acceptable choice for you if you have a record of disability but no longer have that disability, or if your disability is invisible and won't affect your job performance or require any accommodation.

How You Disclose Is Important

The two methods suggested for disclosure related to job interviews so far are before (visible disability) or during (not visible, but affects job performance). You should be up front about who you are and what you can or cannot do, at the right time. Avoiding or denying will eventually make the situation worse.

However, it's not just the matter of disclosing that's important—it's how you do it. If you have come to accept yourself, you will be able to present yourself in a positive manner that will help others to accept you as well. If you are able to do the research, convey exactly how your job performance might be affected, and offer suggestions about accommodations, this will put the employer at ease. You could also help to educate the employer about the fact that nearly all employees with disabilities do their jobs as well as or better than other employees in similar jobs and are as reliable and punctual or more so.

Yet reality suggests that no matter how confident you might be, or how well you present yourself, there are still employers who discriminate against people with disabilities. Therefore, rejection is even more of a possibility for people with disabilities than it is for those without (and they receive their share of rejections as well). Bolles estimates that if disabled, you can expect up to 20 to 30 rejections before you are offered a job. (Of course, a lot depends on you, your career field and geographic location, and the economy.) With that number in mind, as discouraging as it sounds, you know that you cannot quit after only a few rejections, which is true for all job searchers.

However, if you find you're being rejected because of a lack of experience, you might consider volunteering as a way of gaining needed experience and proving to employers what you can do.

Networking Is the Key

As you work at developing your network of contacts, we suggest spreading your networking efforts beyond the disabled community. If you are referred to an employer via that network, there's a good chance that your contact person will disclose your disability for you, as a natural part of telling an employer about you, but at the same time portraying it in a positive light. Employers briefed by your mutual contact will not have a problem with your disability because the contact has already educated the person that the condition will not interfere with your job performance. In cases where it does interfere with job performance, you might want to target employers with a record of hiring people with disabilities.

A Final Thought on Disclosure

The law states that before an offer of employment, an employer's questions about your disability must relate to essential functions of the job and determining whether you are qualified to perform them. Yet, out of genuine interest, your interviewer might ask questions about your disability because he or she is legitimately concerned about you and how you're handling everything. If you feel the questions are sincere, consider pushing aside the ADA employer restriction on questions and offer a brief response that addresses the interviewer's concerns.

If the employer has concerns about your disability and doesn't ask questions, chances are that you won't get the job. Therefore, if you sense discomfort, you can attempt to address it in a calm, mature, and confident manner. By discussing your interviewer's questions you'll be doing much more for people with disabilities than by refusing to discuss them. It can go a long way toward educating your interviewer and helping him or her to become more aware.

Usually, what's operating is an employer's lack of information about the capabilities of people with disabilities. Perhaps they're also acting based on stereotypes ranging from the idea that it costs more to employ people with disabilities (they assume insurance will increase, but it rarely does) to the fear that people with disabilities won't fit in with other workers. Again, Witt's book, *Job Strategies for People with Disabilities,* provides an excellent discussion of these myths and facts that you can use to help dispel them. It's smart to arm yourself with as much related information as possible.

WHAT TO DO IF YOU EXPERIENCE DISCRIMINATION

Discrimination against people with disabilities is hard to prove when it's related to the hiring process. However, once you're on the job, it is easier to gather information about discrimination related to promotion, compensation/benefits, job assignment, job training, or dismissal. You're in a position to compare the treatment offered to you with that of other employees.

If you believe you were discriminated against with regard to your disability, you can file a charge with your local Equal Employment Opportunity Commission (EEOC) office, found in the Yellow Pages under U.S. Government. Charges must be filed within 180 days following a discriminatory event. If you or the EEOC wins, you might expect, if applicable, a job offer, reasonable accommodation, promotion, retroactive seniority, restored benefits, reinstatement, or back pay for lost wages.

Is There a Brighter Side?

With a shrinking labor force of skilled workers, a worker shortage has been created, and people with disabilities have become a sought-after group. Petras and Petras report that new technology is making it easier for employers to hire people with disabilities. Among the products developed to help people with disabilities in the workplace are the following:

- A computer system to help deaf people communicate by telephone, developed by IBM

- Telesensory System's VersaBraille II Plus, which converts letters on a computer screen to Braille

- Telesensory System's Optiscan, a non-Braille reader

- Computer Conversation's Verbal Operating System (VOS), an electronic voice that reads what's on a screen

- IBM's PS/2 Screen Reader, also a computer with a voice

These and other computer devices are making it possible for people with disabilities to work in a wide range of occupations.

In addition, today's young people have a greater awareness and appreciation for diversity. They've grown up with greater diversity in their lives, which leads to greater tolerance for differences and understanding of those differences. Eventually, myths and fears harbored by some workers will be replaced with facts and acceptance toward employees with disabilities. This is a goal that all of us can work toward, whether or not we have a disability.

EMPLOYMENT RECOMMENDATIONS

Petras and Petras recommend certain career areas for consideration by people with disabilities:

- The federal government, which since 1986 requires all equipment purchased to be adaptable for people with disabilities

- Computer and telecommunications companies and related high-tech positions, such as desktop publishing, because computer equipment is adaptable

For people with disabilities who would prefer to work at home, businesses such as banking, insurance, publishing, and software development are heavy information businesses that rely on computers and thus are good work-at-home possibilities.

For additional information on the ADA contact Civil Rights Division, Disability Rights, U.S. Department of Justice, 1425 New York Avenue NW, Room 5041, Washington, DC 20005.

For information on *Careers and the Disabled,* a periodical for people with disabilities, contact Equal Opportunity Publications, 1160 E. Jericho Turnpike, Suite 200, Huntington, NY 11743.

PEOPLE WITH DISABILITIES
Related Internet Sites

• Disability Resources on the Internet:	gopher://hawking.u.wash...u/11/
• EASI Home Page (information on adaptive computer technology):	http://www.isc.rit.edu/~easi/
• Employment Resources for People with Disabilities:	http://www.disserv3.stu.umn.edu/ index2.htm Go to Items in the Spotlight.
• JAN on the Web (Job Accommodation Network):	http://www.jan.wvu.edu/
• JobWeb—Disabled Student Guides:	http://www.jobweb.org/ Go to Career Services, Help Guides and career Library Resources: Resources for persons with Disabilities.
• Yahoo!:	http://www.yahoo.com/ Go to Society & Culture, Disabilities or Business & Economy, Companies, Disabilities.

CHAPTER 15
DUAL-CAREER COUPLES AND SINGLE PARENTS

★

DUAL-CAREER COUPLES

The term *dual-career couple* denotes two people in an ongoing, committed relationship in which both partners are working and view their work as an important part of their identities. There might or might not be children. Many decisions are influenced by each partner's work situation, thus symbolizing its importance to them. The term *dual-earner couple* represents other motives for working, such as monetary or material possessions. Currently, more than 3 million dual-career couples are employed, which represents about 20 percent of employed couples. The majority, therefore, are dual-earner couples. Or perhaps one partner is an earner and the other is more serious about pursuing a career.

The Statistics

The following are the percentages of American households with both partners working: 1980, 45 percent; 1990, 65 percent; and predicted for 2000, 75 percent. In the last ten years, the number of working wives has doubled.

More than half of mothers with children under age six are now working. What these numbers add up to is one fact: one income is simply not enough for many couples, and especially for families with children.

REPRESENTATION IN THE WORKFORCE OF DUAL-CAREER COUPLES AND SINGLE PARENTS
Related Internet Site
• U.S. Census Bureau: http://www.census.gov/

Balancing a Variety of Roles

In the process of managing your roles as spouse, parent, career professional, and perhaps the caretaker of aging parents, you might find it difficult to reach a workable balance among your career, relationship, and family in the time available to you. The result of this role overload can be feelings of frustration, guilt, and even remorse over the fear that you haven't fulfilled your career and family responsibilities. This, in turn, creates stress.

Coping: Communicating and Doing Your Share

Stress can be managed by both you and your partner by your being sensitive and supportive, in physically helping to get things done (e.g., meals, laundry, transportation, grocery shopping, cleaning, taking care of sick children) as well as providing emotional comfort. In addition, some role redefinition might be needed, especially when it comes to those (likely more men than women) who are not used to sharing household chores and child care–related duties. If the husband/father follows more traditional gender roles, then an unfair amount of responsibility falls on the wife/mother. Suggestions for helping to divide chores up include the following:

• Enlist the help of family members.

• Make use of good time management, organization, scheduling, and planning (dividing up tasks).

• Try to take advantage of any workplace flexibility.

If an imbalance of home responsibilities exists between partners, whether there are children involved or not, then roles should be redefined so that all involved feel they're being treated fairly and justly. This requires good communication. Each partner needs to understand what's happening with the other. Good communication requires both listening to your partner and talking things over.

Responsibilities can be divided according to skills, talents, and preferences. You and your partner will need to be flexible with both roles and tasks in order to manage daily life. If there are children, give them responsibilities as well that fit their age, physical condition, and other personal activities.

Handling Conflict with Your Partner

When there is conflict between you and your partner, negotiation becomes a key element of effective communication toward a solution that's acceptable to each of you—a win-win situation. Marian Stolz-Loike identifies the following five typical responses couples use to resolve conflict.

Avoidance   Using avoidance is denying that a problem exists or can be resolved. This approach might be fine for small issues; however, when more meaningful issues need to be resolved, using avoidance only makes the situation worse.

Accommodation   As in the case of avoidance, accommodation also neglects the problem-solving needed, though it does not deny its existence. Accepting that the conflict exists, partners decide not to deal with it, or one goes along with the other just to keep the peace. However, there are likely to still be underlying problems, especially with the partner doing the accommodating.

Confrontation   In confrontation, partners attack each other. This is a poor way to communicate and represents a lack of respect. Even if the issue is resolved, it won't help the relationship, the bigger picture.

Compromise   Compromising is an acceptable solution, but people who do the compromising might be left with lingering resentment and frustration, especially if they're compromising, in their opinion, to an unfair degree.

Collaboration or Problem Solving   Collaboration involves both partners working together to solve the problem at hand, with the goal of each feeling a "win" with the solution.

Raising Children

There's no question about it, adding children to a dual-career couple's household lends great stress to an already limited amount of available time. The amount of household work increases dramatically. If the relationship has gone smoothly up to this time, here's where a real test comes for how a couple communicates, solves problems, and assumes responsibility for what needs to get done.

The ages of the children seems to be more significant than the number of children, as far as impact on a couple's time. Infants obviously require more time and are more often sick. Also, sleeping and eating habits are irregular. In addition, usually parents just want to be around more for that special, new addition—the beginning of a family. Soon the importance of child care becomes a major issue. There seems to be a lack of space in quality programs, in addition to high costs. Eighty percent of working parents rely on services other than licensed day-care centers, including friends, relatives, neighbors, and paid sitters either at their home or that of the sitter.

The importance of good child care actually has some parents leaving the workforce to be at home. Some parents might risk career advancement by choosing to be at home. At the same time, others will say not to underestimate the satisfaction of being with children. Clearly, child care is a critical issue for employees and employers alike. More needs to be done both in the workplace and in child care to give people, especially single parents, more options before having to leave work to care for children. Companies are coming around and offering more flexible programs for employees, including parental leave, part-time work, and flex-time.

WORKING PARENTS

Related Internet Site

- JobOptions   http://www.joboptions.com/
                        Go to Career Tools, Working
                        Parents.
- Yahoo!:   http://www.yahoo.com/
                        Go to Business & Economy,
                        Companies, Children, Child Care.

How It's Going Could Depend on Your Relationship

An ongoing issue for dual-career couples is, how are the careers going? Career choices of both partners significantly affect the life, and thus career, of the other. How they resolve their career choices will affect work schedules, relocation possibilities, career development, development as a couple, and their relationship to their children. Early in the partnership is a good time to discuss priorities with regard to family and career in each one's life.

Career competitiveness or jealousy between partners can hamper the providing of support, which is critical. This competitiveness sometimes focuses on who's doing better. For one to do better, he or she might need the other to assume more than a fair share of chores. Resolving such issues takes real working together. Some people resolve these issues by considering one partner to have the "lead" career and the other a secondary career. This can be determined by skills, talents, fields of expertise (one is more employable than the other), and earning potential.

Relocation

An employee's ability to relocate is considered an essential part of a progressive career in many companies. Obviously, for a dual-career couple the possibility of relocating is doubled. This could be the toughest career problem a dual-career couple faces. Whose career gets priority? If moves are infrequent, it might not be a problem. However, if one is continuously uprooted, the partner's career will suffer. If both partners' careers require frequent relocating, then they have a major problem. Sometimes employees have some influence with their employer about the timing of the relocation. Perhaps you can wait for your partner to find a job in the new locale or for your child to grow to six months or older.

CORPORATE AMERICA RESPONDS

The 1970s saw the entry of women into the labor force in greater numbers, preparing for careers traditionally held by men. During the 1980s, women worked hard, especially those with families, basically doing what they were supposed to do. Through the 1990s, women believed that not enough had changed to support them and as a result felt discouraged.

Corporate America's Realization

Increasing numbers of U.S. corporations are recognizing that for employees to function in the workplace, they need to be able to reach a balance between their family and career concerns. Once viewed as a women's issue, family concerns are now viewed as an issue for both sexes. In addition, corporations realize that the labor force of skilled workers is shrinking. In order to hold on to their quality workers, female and male, they must offer a competitive array of benefits.

In many corporations, 60 to 70 percent of employees are part of a dual career couple. Therefore, many employees will have family-related concerns that could interfere with work hours. With retention, productivity, and absenteeism being major concerns of corporations, corporate managers need to become more sensitive to the needs of the changing workforce and to understand how these needs impact their business. They'll need to adapt in order to have a loyal and productive workforce. Perhaps a step in the right direction would be to place more emphasis, during evaluations, on quality of work and less on number of hours in the office.

Work/Family Programs

Businesses of all sizes have responded with support programs, whose availability and features take a variety of forms. Here's an overview of what some companies are doing.

Child-care services can be on-site, corporate-sponsored child care; a local child-care center supported by the company; assisting employees with fees at an off-site child-care center; or acting as a resource and referral service. In this last capacity, companies assist employees by contracting with local or nationwide consultants who help locate day care (including home-based child care in their community).

Some companies have a **sick child policy,** under which they contract with a sitter service to provide in-home care (or with a local hospital or sick care center), run an on-site sick care facility, subsidize the cost of sick care, or allow parents paid time off to care for a sick child.

Flex-time programs consist of nontraditional work hours. Flex-time can be in the form of a four-day workweek (ten hours each day), a different sequence of hours worked (e.g., 7 A.M. to 3 P.M.), or other variations of the traditional workweek. One potential problem in this area is who gets the benefit and who doesn't. At any particular corporation it's probably determined by a combination of policy and one's relationship with management.

Part-time work is set up so that hours can be reduced on a weekly, seasonal, or project-related basis. As corporations downsized, some found themselves too lean. They've turned to temporary and part-time help in many cases. This way they can keep their overall payroll down, as well as not provide benefits in some cases. Those companies that do provide benefits for part-time employees most likely do so for their most valued people, as a result of their skills and the role they play in the company.

In **job sharing,** two individuals share the responsibilities of one job, usually working two and a half days each. It's most important that the two employees are compatible, for they'll have to communicate well in order to promote the smooth transition of responsibilities. Job sharing is not usually in the form of a written policy. It seems to be more independently negotiated and specially arranged for particular employees. Again, as in the case of flex-time (and even part-time work with benefits), a problem could arise related to who gets it and who doesn't.

A flexible workplace allows employees to work from home, either regularly or occasionally (e.g., when a crisis occurs at home). This possibility is greatly enhanced with **telecommuting** equipment, including the telephone, computers, modems, and fax machines. The number of workers who are telecommuting has grown from 4 million in 1990 to 11 million today, with continued growth predicted.

With **flexible benefits,** employees can select the benefits that are best for them, cafeteria style. This allows a dual-career couple to avoid repetition in their combined benefits. In this way, they can attempt to cover their basic health, education, and child-care needs more effectively.

The federal Family and Medical Leave Act (FMLA) of 1993 took effect August 5, 1993. The FMLA requires employers with 50 or more workers to provide unpaid leave to eligible employees who will be providing care to a newborn or newly adopted child or seriously ill family member or to take care of the employee's own serious illness.

The act provides for up to 12 weeks of unpaid leave during any 12-month period, and the employee is entitled to be restored to the same or an equivalent position on return from the leave. Studies have shown new mothers to be physically ready to return to work in three months, but not emotionally ready until six months after a birth. A part-time return option is often desirable. Therefore, a feasible program for corporations to offer could be 8 to 12 weeks of paid leave and an option to return part-time for several months thereafter.

Employee Assistance Programs (EAPs) offer one-on-one counseling for a wide range of personal problems. This type of program has the potential to be of great help to employees both emotionally and financially, considering the high cost of these services outside of the workplace. However, to be successful, it's vital to have qualified counseling professionals as well as total client (employee) confidentiality.

Can Work/Family Program Participation Hurt Your Career Advancement?

The major question about flexible work/family programs is whether they can hurt participants' career progress. In major corporations, according to Susan Dynerman and Lynn Hayes, it's known that the surest route to promotion is to be willing to relocate, travel for business, and spend long hours at the office. Unfortunately, flex-time programs tend to slow participants' career development. Nontraditional hours are perceived, at times, to reflect a lesser degree of dedication, and time off might cause career goals to suffer. However, if one must take advantage of flex-time programs, part-time work seems to be considered a better option than job sharing if you have a concern about upper-level management goals.

All this adds up to a newer type of discrimination. One can be unfairly judged by others' focusing in on the number of hours present, rather than on the quality of work. Management attitudes need to change so that valuable part-time employees are perceived as serious, motivated workers with a professional commitment along with career goals and promotion potential.

Develop a Plan to Get Your Employer to Offer Work/Family Programs

Know Your Financial Needs   The first step is to identify specifically what your financial needs are. After all, if you're going to propose that your employer offer flex-time scheduling for yourself and others, it needs to be feasible, from a financial standpoint, for you to participate. Then try to answer the following questions, keeping in mind what their financial impact might be for you:

- What balance do you desire between work and relationships?

- How many hours are you willing to work per week?

- Which aspects of your job are most important to you?

- Can you develop a strategy to help management to see the benefits of work/family programs for the company?

- How might your career be affected by working a flex-time schedule?

- Could you combine flex-time with working at home as well?

Sell Your Idea   In developing your work/family plan to promote to your company, Dynerman and Hayes suggest considering the following points:

- **Demographics:** There is a shortage of skilled workers.

- **Replacement costs:** As the labor pool shrinks, replacement costs increase.

- **Productivity:** Workers will be more satisfied with the balance in their lives and are thus likely to be more productive.

- **Loyalty:** Workers stick with employers who offer flex-time programs.

- **Absenteeism:** Absences decrease because many causes of it are taken care of through flex-time programs.

- **Reduced turnover:** Employees can return to work full-time as family demands decrease.

- **Recruiting power:** Employers will be able to attract the best employees.

- **Improved morale:** Employees feel that the company cares about them.

- **Turning innovation into income:** Corporations that have been innovative in these areas have shown better sales in some studies.

The bottom line is that flexible work/family benefits might cost employers more, but they gain it back (and perhaps more) in quality work by productive employees.

How to Identify Companies
with Flex-Time Opportunities

If work/family benefits are important to you, then you can research in the library whether certain companies have these programs. In addition, you can inquire about these benefits during the informational interview stage of your job search process. If you're interested in part-time work, apply your networking efforts toward smaller companies, which are often in need of senior-level talent but can't afford it. In part-time arrangements, they can have it at half the cost. Your current employer is probably your best bet for possible flex-time benefits. Flex-time seems to go first to those already on the payroll.

SINGLE PARENTS

Although many single parents do well in this most demanding environment, the single-parent family can also be the source of multiple stressors for both parent and children. The main cause for the recent surge in the number of single-parent homes in the United States is the increased divorce rate. It's predicted that 40 to 50 percent of U.S. children born after 1980 will experience a divorce in the family. Divorce forces many parents and children to move away from extended families and often results in financial hardships as well.

The Statistics

Of all mothers in the U.S. labor force, one-fourth are single with children under age 18. It's estimated that one in every four American children lives in a single-parent home. Of those living in a single-parent home, nine of ten children reside in a household headed by the mother. Two-thirds of all people heading households with children under 18 are in the labor force, and over half of them are full-time workers.

Responsibility Times Two

All of the same responsibilities attached to a dual-career couple (work, housing, child-care arrangements, household chores, and relationships) also exist for the single parent. However, the impact is doubled because single parents are on their own. Therefore, time management, organization, planning, and communication (with children, former spouse, and significant other) take on an even greater emphasis for the single parent.

Finding time for children is difficult enough for a dual-career couple, but it's even more difficult for a single parent. This can be a source of discouragement for many single parents, who are not able to spend the amount of time they would like with their children. Major adjustments must be made to balance one's time. Once divorced, a single parent finds him- or herself more dependent on a large number of people than he or she was when married. A single parent's needs might include day care, an after-school program to take care of children until the workday ends, and baby-sitters (when needed in the evenings). Finding quality programs and personnel is always an issue.

Child Care   The lack of affordable, reliable, and quality child care is a problem for all working parents and is an acute concern for single parents. As a result of their being on their own, it's even more important for single parents to have some form of flexible hours at work in order to deal with child-care arrangements and the child's school attendance schedule. This forces many single parents into hourly-wage jobs because of more flexibility in hours. These jobs include waiting tables and, domestic help, secretarial, and clerical positions. Entry into better-paying jobs with benefits depends on the key issue of child care.

Lower Socioeconomic Level   All levels of income are represented by single parents, but a disproportionate number are of a lower socioeconomic level. The poverty rate among single female families is about three times that of single male families and about six times that of married-couple families, according to the 1991 U.S. Census Bureau report. Even among wealthier families, upon a marital breakup women's earnings, plus support, usually add up to only about 50 percent of their former income.

FAMILY SOCIOECONOMIC LEVELS

Related Internet Sites

• U.S. Census Bureau: http://www.census.gov/

On the Job   Work schedules might need to be changed to handle one's role as a single parent. Life is certainly simpler if you work for an understanding employer who offers some form of flex-time and other work/family benefit programs. If not, there's always the possibility that you will be able to negotiate something for yourself. Your negotiation position with employers will be stronger if you review the selling points outlined in the previous section on dual-career couples. These points will aid you in convincing your employer of the benefits the company stands to gain by offering work/family programs.

Single Fathers

Recent Increases About 10 percent of single-parent households are headed by fathers. For men, perhaps a bit more than for women, one issue is that they need to adopt new ways of measuring success. Career advancement might not have the emphasis it once did. Now success can be looked on as how you are doing as a parent, as well. However, it's hard to do both, career and child rearing, well. One usually suffers. The following career areas can be affected by the responsibilities of being a single parent: job mobility, earning power, freedom to work late, job performance, and job advancement. It's the role of being the parent and the tasks involved, not the gender of the parent, that makes single parenting difficult.

Suggestions for Single Parents

The best advice is not to try to do it on your own; get involved with a single-parent support group. Parents Without Partners, founded in 1957, is the largest self-help group for single parents in the United States. Any custodial or noncustodial parent, whether single, divorced, widowed, or never married, can join. Social activities are included in which single parents and their children can meet others like themselves. Meeting others involved with the same life issues can be a great source of emotional support as well as new friendships. When you're connected to others in the same situation as yourself, there's also the possibility of helping each other out. For example, you can trade off watching the children with someone, which enables each of you to run errands that otherwise would be difficult to accomplish.

We would also suggest soliciting help from your other friends and family members. Sometimes they will be able to run an errand for you, watch the children, or just be a good listener. Through careful planning and use of all available resources, single parents will be able to maintain some balance between work and family and come through it in good shape. Yet, at times it might all seem to be too much, resulting in excessive suffering for you or your children. In such situations, consider seeking professional counseling.

CHAPTER 16

Ex-Military Personnel

★

The Transition from Military to Civilian Life

With respect to career possibilities, ex-military personnel will find that military expertise, tactical skills, and wartime experience are not usually marketable. However, leadership and management skills are always in demand. Consider the experience you have gained in such areas as encounters with different cultures and ideas through world travel; management of materials, resources, and equipment; being part of a team effort; or the operation and maintenance of high-tech systems. Maybe you even learned a foreign language, which can open a door for you in today's global marketplace.

Employers are always looking for proven achievers and leaders. There is a high demand for most technically trained professionals. Caution is advised with regard to the defense industry, where jobs, if available, might not be stable.

The biggest challenge for ex-military personnel is in identifying skills used in the military and then translating them into language (and related job titles) that will be understood in the general marketplace. Some sources to help you do this are covered here. Using the *Guide for Occupational Exploration* (*GOE*), you can translate your higher General Occupational Theme scores from the Strong Interest Inventory into related Work Group numbers. Then look up specific job titles with *Dictionary of Occupational Titles* (*DOT*) numbers. The *GOE* includes a section titled "Military Occupational Specialties with Corresponding Subgroups," which lists occupational specialties for each of the five branches of the armed forces and identifies the subgroups of related Work Groups in which comparable civilian jobs can be located. Another option is to check the personnel manual for your branch of the services, which links military jobs and tasks to the civilian *DOT* job titles. Finally, the two-volume *Military Occupational Training Data Series* is available from Defense Manpower Data Center, 400 Gigling Road, Seaside, CA 93955.

CONSIDER CIVIL SERVICE

W. Dean Lee points out that civil service is often a natural next step for military personnel. However, mid-level and senior-level jobs are very competitive, due in part to salaries and benefits approaching those of similar civilian positions. In other words, more workers from the private sector are attracted to jobs here as well.

To learn more about civil-service opportunities, contact the Federal Job Information Center located in major cities for available jobs in your region and a Federal Job Opportunities list. Also, check with your state employment office. It receives position announcements, though some will not be current. If you are interested in specific federal agencies, you can contact them directly. Their local field offices might have information about upcoming openings and future possibilities as well. Finally, request *Federal Career Opportunities* from the Federal Research Service, P.O. Box 1059, Vienna, VA 22180.

In the U.S. territories and at U.S. installations in foreign countries, most positions are offered to locally eligible Americans, their dependents, or foreign nationals. These positions are usually not published outside the local area. For information about overseas opportunities, write to the Federal Job Information Center, U.S. Office of Personnel Management, 1900 E Street NW, Washington, DC 20415.

STATE AND FEDERAL GOVERNMENT EMPLOYMENT
Related Internet Sites
See listing on page 264.

Department of Defense and Other Federal Agencies

The Department of Defense (DOD) is still the top employer of U.S. personnel overseas and the agency with the most vacancies. They can be contacted at Department of Defense, Education Activity, 4040 N. Fairfax Drive, Arlington, VA 22203.

Other federal agencies worth checking into are the Foreign Agriculture Service, DOD Dependent Schools, National Oceanic and Atmospheric Administration, State Department, U.S. Information Agency, Army Corps of Engineers, Agency for International Development, and Peace Corps.

You might want to increase your options by checking for positions with city, county, and state government offices. If you're a retiring, regular commissioned or warrant officer, you would benefit by obtaining a nonfederal job, because it will not affect your retirement pay. Federal employment will cause a reduction in retirement pay, except for enlisted personnel and reserve officers.

Depending on the agency to which you're applying, the SF-171 form or your resume begins your federal employment application process. Necessary forms are available at any local Office of Personnel Management (OPM). Also, request the publication *Veteran's Preference in Federal Employment* from the OPM. It contains general information about determining a veteran's status, preference in examination, credit for time of service, and retirement pay regulations.

THE CORPORATE WORLD

Lee reports that ex-military personnel are actively recruited by corporate America. Business managers and owners see ex-military personnel as follows:

- Highly motivated, dependable, and disciplined
- Technically trained, with many transferable skills
- Team players who strive for excellence
- Strong leaders, able to adapt to crisis and work under pressure
- Mature and responsible with a strong work ethic

Nonetheless, your resume is even more important than for other career changers. It's the medium for translating military experience and accomplishments into language that the business world can understand and appreciate. Avoid using military terminology, unless you're sending your resume to military contractors and you're sure they'll understand it. One resource that can help in this task is "Marketing Yourself for a Second Career," which has examples of "civilianized" resumes. It is available for a small fee from The Retired Officers Association, 201 N. Washington Street, Alexandria, VA 22314.

Of particular importance are the transferable/functional skills that you gained from the military. Some common transferable/functional skills that many ex-military personnel can document are as follows:

- Communication (oral/written, public speaking, promoting events/projects)
- Management (personnel, project, facility)
- Planning (strategic, cost cutting)
- Security operations
- Training

If you need to develop additional skills, check your military benefits for available training programs. You can use your Veterans Administration benefits to obtain many types of education, including college, refresher courses, night classes, apprenticeships, correspondence schools, language training, and specialized programs.

It's in your best interest to at least know your comparable value. If you do and you are ever offered a salary below it, you'll be prepared to make your case for a fairer compensation package. When figuring your comparable value, look at your total compensation figure, which includes all benefits. Review your Personal Statement of Military Compensation, released each February.

OWNING YOUR OWN BUSINESS

The federal government publishes a free book for veterans interested in starting, financing, and managing a small business: *Veterans' Handbook* (Washington, DC: Small Business Administration, 1989).

The Small Business Administration gives preference to veterans in obtaining assistance and can guarantee loans made to veterans by banks and savings and loan associations.

SOURCES OF ADDITIONAL HELP

If you are or were an officer, contact The Retired Officers Association (TROA), 201 N. Washington Street, Alexandria, VA 22314. TROA has an Officer Placement Service from which you can receive a monthly magazine, job referral notices, resume preparation assistance, career counseling, and access to the TROA Career Research Center (most useful for those in the Virginia area).

Also, depending on the branch(es) that apply to your situation, consult the following organizations for job counseling, referrals, placement assistance, job fairs, and related services:

- **Air Force Association**
  1501 Lee Highway
  Arlington, VA 22209

- **Association of the United States Army**
  Career Assistance Service
  2425 Wilson Boulevard
  Arlington, VA 22201

- **Marine Corps Association**
  P.O. Box 1775
  Quantico, VA 22134

- **National Association for Uniformed Services**
  5535 Hempstead Way
  Springfield, VA 22151

- **Navy League of the United States**
  2300 Wilson Boulevard
  Arlington, VA 22201

- **The Non-Commissioned Officer Association**
  225 N. Washington Street
  Alexandria, VA 22314

CHAPTER 17
MID-LEVEL MANAGERS

✫

WILL YOU BE A VICTIM OF CORPORATE RESTRUCTURING?

The Statistics

Nearly half of all large U.S. corporations were restructured in the 1980s. It is estimated that during the same period, *Fortune* 500 companies eliminated 3.6 million workers. This trend has continued through the 1990s. Mid-level managers account for 5 to 8 percent of all workers, but 17 percent of the layoffs. Overall, some estimates have the number of mid-level executives victimized by downsizing to be around 10 to 12 million.

Christopher Kirkwood discusses two major reasons leading to layoffs from downsizing. He notes that the first employees targeted in downsizing are usually those who debate everything the boss says, make the boss look bad in public, joke around about the company, and tend to be uncooperative. Another type at risk is the employee who fails to keep up with changing technology or develop new skills as the times demand.

Outplacement Counseling

If you are or will be a victim of downsizing, your company might provide some form of outplacement services. Outplacement services usually include the following:

- Career counseling, including assessment and/or testing to help you identify career options

- Resume and cover letter preparation

- Interviewing techniques

- Job search methods, including networking, want ads, employment agencies, executive recruiters, telephone techniques, and industry directories and trade journals

- Researching employers

- Dealing with the emotional side of losing a job, specifically stress, anxiety, and depression

OPTIONS FOR MID-LEVEL MANAGERS

Many downsized mid-level managers left fields like marketing, management, sales, and finance to move into franchising, consulting, and family firms or new businesses. Franchising has experienced more than 33 percent growth since 1986. Those choosing consulting now number more than 200,000. Recently downsized mid-level managers who became consultants were often retained on short-term contracts by organizations that let them go.

One of every six mid-level managers and executives who lost their jobs due to corporate downsizing and restructuring during the late 1980s went on to create his or her own small business. They were either unable or unwilling to relocate to another large company. It's estimated that by the year 2005, 11.5 million workers will be self-employed (a 15 percent increase from 1992), twice the number in 1970. Developing a new business is often made possible by a second income in the family, which helps to pay the general living expenses during the important and costly start-up period.

CORPORATIONS OF THE FUTURE: WHAT WILL THEY BE LIKE?

Outsourcing Is Here

When downsizing finally comes to an end, the larger corporations will not begin to rehire in large numbers. They will probably realize cost savings and efficiency by contracting goods and services from smaller companies, where many of their former employees will be working. This method of doing business is known as outsourcing.

Outsourcing occurs when upper managers realize that they do not have to employ all the people, all the time, to get the work done. The larger corporation of the future will have a small core of central employees and many smaller businesses working under contract. The core workers will be professional staff essential to the organization. A great deal of work will be contracted out to other organizations as needed. Finally, there will be a flexible labor force made up of part-time and temporary workers to be called in when customer demands present themselves. Even the core employees will be moved around due to hiring for specific, temporary assignments.

Contracting

Contracting is a joint venture with an employer to develop strategies to solve pressing company problems. To make a living from contracting, one needs to be always working on a project or getting recruited for future projects. Contracting is another situation in which networking takes on added importance. You will need word-of-mouth credibility via your contacts to get hired for new projects. Careers now and in the future might include some time spent in the core, some in outsourcing jobs, and perhaps some in part-time work as well.

Some Suggestions

Stay Abreast of Your Field   More than ever before, you need to be on top of what's happening (and will happen) in your career field. Then, as you see the need for and importance of sharpening and expanding your skills, take the necessary action and follow through. Three common ways to gain new skills are on-the-job training, courses offered through your company, and college courses.

Identify Growth Companies   Instead of attempting to identify growth industries (or in addition to it), you might consider looking for a growth company, one in an existing industry that has adapted well to the new information technology. Refer to Chapter 10 on how to research companies in the library, especially the section on small, local, or regional corporations (page 257).

IS NONPROFIT A VIABLE ALTERNATIVE FOR YOU?

There is often a shift in values at mid-life toward a desire to give something back to society. If you are a victim of a corporate restructuring, you might consider directing your efforts toward employment with a nonprofit organization. Mid-level managers can find worthwhile ways to apply their leadership skills in the nonprofit sector. Nonprofits are entered by former corporate types via a variety of career fields, including public relations, law, government, education, social services, retail, and banking.

Career changers sometimes find nonprofits just as stressful as their former corporate management positions but often much more meaningful. If this sounds appealing, what cause or organization might you want to help out? What types of problems would you most like to work on solving? How do your interests relate? Consider what you want your purpose or mission to be at this point in life.

What Kind of Salary Can You Expect?

A concern that often comes up about employment with nonprofit organizations is that they might not pay much. However, just because they're nonprofit doesn't necessarily mean they don't pay their top executives a decent salary (especially the larger nonprofits). Nevertheless, a cut in salary is likely and might be as high as 20 to 30 percent. This, of course, depends on what your former salary was. In general, career changers take a salary cut when moving to the nonprofit area and hope to catch up and even surpass it in the near future. For information on salaries in nonprofits, contact Abbott, Langer & Associates, 548 First Street, Crete, IL 60417, for its surveys on compensation in nonprofit organizations. It is true that most nonprofits are constantly struggling to raise enough funds.

Therefore, if you have grant-writing or fund-raising skills, you become even more valuable.

Resources for Researching Nonprofits

- **ACCESS,** Networking in the Public Interest, 1001 Connecticut Avenue NW, Suite 838, Washington, DC 20036.
  Publishes *Community Jobs: The Employment Newspaper for the Non-Profit Sector.*

- **Planning/Communications,** 7215 Oak Avenue, River Forest, IL 60305.
  Publishes *Non-Profits and Education Job Finder; Great Careers: The Fourth of July Guide to Careers, Internships, and Volunteer Opportunities in the Non-Profit Sector;* and *Good Works: A Guide to Careers in Social Change.*

- Check local libraries to identify which branches receive information on nonprofits from the Foundation Center in New York.

NONPROFITS
Related Internet Sites
See listing of nonprofit-related Internet sites on page 260–261.

DEALING WITH EXECUTIVE RECRUITERS

Despite a percentage of headhunters that will not have your best interests at heart, there's no single action you can take that will do more to expedite your job search than to contact a good headhunter. To increase the possibility of good results in working with headhunters, be flexible, view most things as negotiable, and be realistic about yourself and your skills.

Two Types of Headhunters

Contingency firms generally operate a bit like employment agencies. They learn of a vacancy (usually jobs paying $40,000 to $90,000) and contact the person at the employer who is responsible for filling it. The employer agrees to pay the head-hunting firm a commission only if one of its candidates is selected for the position. Therefore, if you're not an exact match, don't expect much in the way of results from this method.

The contingency firm may distribute your resume to a number of employers—hoping one will hire you—but a mistake could land your resume on the desk of your current employer or someone who may notify your employer. To prevent word getting out that you're looking, it's recommended that you request to be notified, each time, prior to your resume's being sent out. Kirkwood suggests that, with this consideration, contingency firms can really help—especially in shortening the time it takes to get a job. In addition, he believes they have a less snobby attitude than retainer firms, the other principal type of recruiter.

The *retainer* head-hunting firm, which generally works on higher-level jobs, is selected by a company with a vacancy to be its agent in identifying and presenting candidates to fill the vacant position. Retainer firms usually have an exclusive contract, meaning they are the only firm searching for candidates for an opening. Therefore, it's unlikely that they would share your resume with anyone other than their clients. This type of head-hunting firm gets paid whether or not a candidate is selected.

Strategies for Working with Headhunters

If you're active professionally—that is, you attend professional association activities, perhaps write articles for industry publications, even consult outside your job—then chances are recruiters will find their way to you. However, if you haven't been found yet, being more active professionally is a good suggestion—plus consulting a recruiter directory (see the "Managers and Executives" listing in Appendix B) and getting recommendations from colleagues, friends, and people in your professional organizations. You could then send a resume with a cover letter to the ones that sound best to you.

Try to get to know the person or persons representing your background. How much experience do they have in recruiting, and how well do they know your industry and related companies? A good recruiter will be more than willing to answer your questions. Usually, you'll want a prospective recruiter to have a minimum of 12 months' experience. Note also that recruiters tend to be more useful if you're staying within your present industry or market, and perhaps not as beneficial for career changers.

Good headhunters will call their employer contacts right away. For a candidate who fits a position, the firm might be able to schedule an interview within seven to ten days. In general, give a head-hunting firm with which you contract up to 45 days to get you an interview. If a firm can't get you interviewing in 45 days, then try another.

If you're contacted by a retainer firm in regard to a position of preliminary interest to you, get the details: who referred the firm to you, the job description, experience requirements, salary range, and possible need to relocate. The key issue when dealing with headhunters is control. The idea is to establish a good relationship with a reputable firm so that you can arrange for them to inform you of each opening that is worth submitting your resume for and even to seek your permission first.

In fact, as mentioned previously, it's recommended that you work only with recruiters who will notify you before submitting your resume to a client. Headhunters should be just part of your job search strategy. Use networking most of the time, and include headhunters if your background and experience fit with the type of professionals they seek to work with.

Two excellent resources on the subject of headhunters are Kenneth J. Cole's book *The Headhunter Strategy: How to Make It Work for You* and John Lucht's *The New Rites of Passage at $100,000.*

Author's Note

Hopefully, you've found the information in *Career Change* interesting and worthwhile. As you pursue a possible career change, perhaps you are a few steps closer as a result of reading this book.

If you would like to receive E-mail updates every six months about relevant Internet sites, please send an E-mail indicating this.

Any comments with regard to any aspect of the book are welcomed. Address them to:

David P. Helfand, Ed.D., LCPC, NCCC
Northeastern Illinois University
Counseling Office
5500 N. St. Louis Avenue
Chicago, IL 60625
E-mail: D-Helfand@neiu.edu

Best of luck with your career.

APPENDIX A

REFERENCES

★

American Psychiatric Association. (1994) *Diagnostic and Statistical Manual of Mental Disorders: DSM-IV.* Washington, DC.

Bear, J. (1993) *Bear's Guide to Earning College Degrees Non-Traditionally.* Benicia, CA: C & B Publishing.

———. (1995) *College Degrees by Mail.* Berkeley, CA: Ten Speed Press.

Beisser, A. R. (1989) *Flying Without Wings: Personal Reflections on Being Disabled.* New York: Doubleday.

Bolles, R. N. (1991) *How to Create a Picture of Your Ideal Job or Next Career: The Quick Job-Hunting (and Career-Changing) Map.* Berkeley, CA: Ten Speed Press.

———. Annual. *What Color Is Your Parachute? A Practical Manual for Job Hunters and Career Changers.* Berkeley, CA: Ten Speed Press.

Boyer, R., and D. Savageau. (1997) *Places Rated Almanac: Your Guide to Finding the Best Places to Live in North America.* New York: Prentice Hall.

Bradley, L. J. (1990) *Counseling Midlife Career Changers.* Chicago: Ferguson Publishing.

Branden, N. (1988) *How to Raise Your Self-Esteem.* New York: Bantam Books.

Bridges, W. (1997) *Creating You and Co.: Learn to Think Like the CEO of Your Own Career.* Reading, MA: Addison-Wesley.

———. (1994) *Job Shift: How to Prosper in a Workplace Without Jobs.* Reading, MA: Addison-Wesley.

————— . (1980) *Transitions: Making Sense of Life's Changes*. Reading, MA: Addison-Wesley.

Burka, J. B., and L. M. Yuen. (1983) *Procrastination: Why You Do It, What to Do About It*. Reading, MA: Addison-Wesley.

Burton, M. L., and R. A. Wedemeyer. (1991) *In Transition: From the Harvard Business School Club of New York's Career Management Seminar*. New York: HarperBusiness.

Career Opportunity News. (June 1995) Robert Calvert, Jr., ed. Chicago: Ferguson Publishing.

Catalyst Publications. (1996) *Women in Corporate Leadership: Progress and Prospects*. New York.

Cole, K. J. (1985) *The Headhunter Strategy: How to Make It Work for You*. New York: Wiley.

Dynerman, S. B., and L. O. Hayes. (1991) *The Best Jobs in America for Parents Who Want Careers and Time for Children, Too*. New York: Rawson Associates.

Ellis, A. (1977) *How to Live with and Without Anger*. New York: Reader's Digest Press.

Empire State College Learning Resource Center, SUNY. (1992) *Innovative Graduate Programs Directory*, 6th ed. Saratoga Springs, NY.

Erikson, E. (1950) *Childhood and Society*. New York: Norton.

Farren, C. (1997) *Who's Running Your Career? Creating Stable Work in Unstable Times*. Austin, TX: Bard Press.

Frey, J. (1995) *College Degrees You Can Earn from Home*. Boulder, CO: Life Oak Publications.

Gale Research. (1994) *The Encyclopedia of Associations*. Detroit.

Germann, R., and P. Arnold. (1980) *Job and Career Building*. Berkeley, CA: Ten Speed Press.

Gilligan, C. (1982) *In a Different Voice*. Cambridge, MA: Harvard University Press.

Hakim, C. (1995) *We Are All Self-Employed: The New Social Contract for Working in a Changed World*. San Francisco: Benett-Koehler.

Haldane, B. (1988) *Career Satisfaction and Success*. New York: AMACOM.

Hansen, J. C. (1992) *User's Guide for the Strong Interest Inventory*. Palo Alto, CA: Consulting Psychologists Press.

Harkness, H. (1997) *The Career Chase: Taking Creative Control in a Chaotic Age*. Palo Alto, CA: Davies-Black.

Harrington, T. F., and A. J. O'Shea, eds. (1984) *Guide for Occupational Exploration*. Circle Pines, MN: American Guidance Service.

Hauter, J. (1993) *The Smart Woman's Guide to Career Success.* Hawthorne, NJ: Career Press.

Hewitt, J. (1977) *The Complete Yoga Book.* New York: Schocken Books.

Holland, J. L. (1985) *Making Vocational Choices: A Theory of Vocational Personalities and Work Environments.* Englewood Cliffs, NJ: Prentice-Hall.

JIST Works, Inc. (1998) *The O*NET Dictionary of Occupational Titles.* Indianapolis, IN.

Jung, C. G. (1971) *Psychological Types.* Palo Alto, CA: Consulting Psychologists Press.

Kennedy, J. L., and D. Laramore. (1992) *Joyce Lain Kennedy's Career Book.* Lincolnwood, IL: VGM Career Horizons.

Kirkwood, C. (1993) *Your Services Are No Longer Required: The Complete Job-Loss Recovery Book.* New York: Plume.

Kleiman, C. (1994) *The 100 Best Jobs for the 1990s and Beyond.* Chicago: Dearborn Financial.

Koltnow, E., and L. S. Dumas. (1990) *Congratulations! You've Been Fired: Sound Advice for Women Who've Been Terminated, Pink Slipped, Downsized, or Otherwise Unemployed.* New York: Fawcett Columbine.

Lee, W. D. (1991) *Beyond the Uniform: A Career Transition Guide for Veterans and Federal Employees.* New York: Wiley.

Levinson, D. J., et al. (1978) *The Seasons of a Man's Life.* New York: Ballantine Books.

Lock, R. D. (1992) *Job Search: Career Planning Guide Book II.* Pacific Grove, CA: Brooks/Cole.

———. (1992) *Taking Charge of Your Career Direction: Career Planning Guide, Book I.* Pacific Grove, CA: Brooks/Cole.

Lucht, J. (1995) *The New Rites of Passage at $100,000.* New York: Viceroy Press.

Macdaid, G. P., M. H. McCauley, and R. I. Kainz. (1986) *Myers-Briggs Type Indicator Atlas of Type Tables.* Gainesville, FL: Center for Applications of Psychological Type.

Martin, G. D. (1995) *National Directory of Internships,* 1996–97 ed. Raleigh, NC: National Society for Experiential Education.

Maze, M., and D. Mayall, eds. (1991) *The Enhanced Guide for Occupational Exploration.* Indianapolis, IN: JIST Works.

McHolland, J. (1987) *A Positive Approach to Self-Development.* Evanston, IL: National Center for Human Potential Seminars.

Mills, C. W. (1951) *White Collar: The American Middle Class.* New York: Oxford University Press.

Myers, I. B. (1987) *Introduction to Type.* Palo Alto, CA: Consulting Psychologists Press.

Myers, I. B., and M. H. McCauley. (1985) *Manual: A Guide to the Development and Use of the Myers-Briggs Type Indicator.* Palo Alto, CA: Consulting Psychologists Press.

——— . (1991) *MBTI Type Booklets.* Palo Alto, CA: Consulting Psychologists Press.

National University Continuing Education Association. (1993) *The Electronic University: A Guide to Distance Learning.* Princeton, NJ: Peterson's Guides.

——— . (1992) *The Independent Study Catalog.* Princeton, NJ: Peterson's Guides.

Olsen, N. (1988) *Starting a Mini-Business: A Guidebook for Seniors.* Sunnyvale, CA: Four Oaks Publishing.

Parker, Y. (1996) *The Damn Good Resume Guide.* Berkeley, CA: Ten Speed Press.

Peterson's Guides. (1997) *Peterson's Internships 1998.* Princeton, NJ.

Petras, K., and R. Petras. (1997) *Jobs '98.* New York: Simon & Schuster.

Rathus, S. A., and J. S. Nevid. (1977) *BT: Behavior Therapy: Strategies for Solving Problems in Living.* Garden City, NY: Doubleday.

Ray, S. N. (1991) *Job Hunting After 50: Strategies for Success.* New York: Wiley.

Riehle, K. A. (1991) *What Smart People Do When Losing Their Jobs.* New York: Wiley.

Rivera, M. (1991) *The Minority Career Book.* Holbrook, MA: Bob Adams.

Robbins, P. I. (1978) *Successful Midlife Career Change: Self-Understanding and Strategies for Action.* New York: AMACOM.

Schlossberg, N. K. (1989) *Overwhelmed: Coping with Life's Ups and Downs.* Lexington, MA: Lexington Books.

Selden, I. L. (1988) *Going into Business for Yourself: New Beginnings After 50.* Washington, DC: American Association of Retired Persons, and Glenview, IL: Scott, Foresman.

Seligman, M. E. P. (1990) *Learned Optimism: How to Change Your Mind and Your Life.* New York: Pocket Books.

Sheehy, G. (1976) *Passages: Predictable Crises of Adult Life.* New York: Bantam Books.

Shields, C., and L. C. Shields. (1993) *Work, Sister, Work: Why Black Women Can't Get Ahead and What They Can Do About It.* Secaucus, NJ: Carol Publishing Group.

Simon, S. B. (1988) *Getting Unstuck: Breaking Through Your Barriers to Change.* New York: Warner Books.

Simon, S. B., L. W. Howe, and H. Kirschenbaum. (1972) *Values Clarification: A Handbook of Practical Strategies for Teachers and Students.* New York: Hart Publishing.

Simosko, S. (1985) *Earn College Credit for What You Know.* Washington, DC: Acropolis Books.

Small Business Administration. (1989) *Veterans' Handbook.* Washington, DC.

Smith, A. W. (1990) *Overcoming Perfectionism: The Super Human Syndrome.* Deerfield Beach, FL: Health Communications.

Stolz-Loike, M. (1992) *Dual Career Couples: New Perspectives in Counseling.* Alexandria, VA: American Counseling Association.

Stoodley, M. (1997) *Information Interviewing: What It Is and How to Use It.* Chicago: Ferguson Publishing.

Sullivan, E. J. (1993) *The Adult Learner's Guide to Alternative and External Degree Programs.* American Council on Education Series on Higher Education. Phoenix, AZ: Oryx Press.

Swiss, D. J. (1996) *Women Breaking Through: Overcoming the Final Ten Obstacles at Work.* Princeton, NJ: Peterson's Guides.

U.S. Department of Commerce. Annual. *Franchise Opportunities: Handbook.* Washington, DC: Government Printing Office.

U.S. Department of Labor. (1991) *The Dictionary of Occupational Titles.* Indianapolis, IN: JIST Works.

——— . *Monthly Labor Review.* (November 1997) Washington, DC.

——— . *Occupational Outlook Handbook.* (1998–99) Lincolnwood, IL: VGM Career Horizons.

——— . *Occupational Outlook Quarterly.* Winter 1997–98. Washington, DC.

Witt, M. A. (1992) *Job Strategies for People with Disabilities.* Princeton, NJ: Peterson's Guides.

APPENDIX B

RECOMMENDED READINGS

★

CAREER CHANGE

Banning, K., and A. Friday. (1995) "Time for a Change: The Re-Entry and Re-Career Workbook." Lincolnwood, IL: VGM Career Horizons.

Boldt, L. G. (1993) *Zen and the Art of Making a Living.* New York: Arkana.

Kanchier, C. (1996) *Dare to Change Your Job and Your Life.* Indianapolis: JIST Works.

Moreau, D. (1994) *Kiplinger's Survive and Profit from a Mid-Career Change.* Washington, DC: Kiplinger Books.

DRESS, APPEARANCE, AND ETIQUETTE

Karpinski, K. (1994) *Red Socks Don't Work: Messages from the Real World About Men's Clothing.* Manassas Park, VA: Impact Publications.

Nicholson, J. (1995) *110 Mistakes Working Women Make and How to Avoid Them: Dressing Smart in the 90's.* Manassas Park, VA: Impact Publications.

Sutterfield, M. (1996) *VGM's Complete Guide to Career Etiquette: From Job Search Through Career Advancement.* Lincolnwood, IL: VGM Career Horizons.

ELECTRONIC JOB SEARCHING

Bolles, R. N. (1997) *Job Hunting on the Internet.* Berkeley, CA: Ten Speed Press.

Crispin, G., and M. Mehler. (1998) *Careerxroads: The 1998 Directory to Jobs, Resumes and Career Management on the World Wide Web.* Kendall Park, NJ: MMC Group.

Dixon, P., and S. Tiersten. (1995) *Be Your Own Headhunter Online: Go Online to Get the Job You Want.* New York: Random House.

Glossbrenner, A., and E. Glossbrenner. (1995) *Finding a Job on the Internet.* New York: McGraw-Hill.

Godin, S. (1996) *Point and Click Jobfinder.* Chicago: Dearborn Trade.

Gonyea, J. C. (1995) *The On-Line Job Search Companion: A Complete Guide to Hundreds of Career Planning and Job Hunting Resources Available via Your Computer.* New York: McGraw-Hill.

Goodwin, M., D. Cohn, and D. Spivey. (1996) *Net Jobs: How to Use the Internet to Land Your Dream Job.* New York: M. Wolff and Co.

Jandt, F. E., and M. B. Nemnich. (1995) *Using the Internet in Your Job Search: An Easy Guide to Online Job Seeking and Career Information.* Indianapolis, IN: JIST Works.

Kennedy, J. L. (1995) *Hook Up, Get Hired! The Internet Job Search Revolution.* New York: Wiley.

Kennedy, J. L., and T. J. Morrow. (1994) *Electronic Job Search Revolution: Win with the New Technology That's Reshaping Today's Job Market.* New York: Wiley.

Riley, M. F., F. Roehm, and S. Oserman. (1998) *The Guide to Internet Job Searching.* Lincolnwood, IL: NTC Publishing Group with the Public Library Association.

(See "Resume Writing" for electronic resume writing books.)

EX-MILITARY PERSONNEL

Drier, H. N., Jr. (1994) *Out of Uniform: A Career Transition Guide for Ex-Military Personnel.* Lincolnwood, IL: VGM Career Horizons.

Reardon, D. E. (1993) *In or Out of the Military: How to Make Your Own Best Decision.* Oak Harbor, WA: Pepper Press.

Savino, C., and R. L. Krannich. (1997) *From Air Force Blue to Corporate Grey: A Career Transition Guide for Air Force Personnel.* Manassas Park, VA: Impact Publications.

———. (1997) *From Army Green to Corporate Grey: A Career Transition Guide for Army Personnel.* Manassas Park, VA: Impact Publications.

———. (1997) *From Navy Blue to Corporate Grey: A Career Transition Guide for Navy Personnel.* Manassas Park, VA: Impact Publications.

Schlachter, G. A., and D. R. Weber. (1990) *Financial Aid for Veterans, Military Personnel, and Their Dependents, 1990–91.* San Carlos, CA: Reference Service Press.

Financial Aid for Additional Education and Training

Bear, J., and M. Bear. (1997) *Bear's Guide to Finding Money for College.* Berkeley, CA: Ten Speed Press.

Blum, L. (1996) *Free Money for College.* New York: Facts on File.

———. (1993) *Free Money for College from the Government.* New York: H. Holt and Co.

———. (1996) *Free Money for Graduate School.* New York: H. Holt and Co.

———. (1993) *Free Money from Colleges and Universities.* New York: H. Holt and Co.

Cassidy, D. J. (1996) *The Scholarship Book.* Englewood Cliffs, NJ: Prentice-Hall.

College Entrance Examination Board. (1997) *The College Board Scholarship Handbook 1998: Scholarships, Grants, Internships, and Loans for Undergraduate and Graduate Studies.* New York.

———. (1998) *Meeting College Costs.* New York.

College Scholarship Service. (1994) *The College Costs and Financial Aid Handbook.* New York: College Entrance Examination Board.

Kirby, D., and S. Juszczak. (1996) *Scholarships, Fellowships, and Loans 1997.* Detroit: Gale Research.

Odrovensky, P. (1995) *USA Today Financial Aid for College.* Princeton, NJ: Peterson's Guides.

Peterson's Guides. (1995) *Peterson's Paying Less for College 1996.* Princeton, NJ.

Student College Aid. (1995) *Less Competitive College Grants and Loans.* Houston, TX.

Student Financial Services. (1996) *The Financial Aid Book: The Insider's Guide to Private Scholarships, Grants, and Fellowships.* Seattle, WA: Perpetual Press.

———. (1996) *The Government Financial Aid Book: The Insider's Guide to State and Federal Government Grants and Loans.* Seattle, WA: Perpetual Press.

FUTURE TRENDS

Boyett, J. H., and H. P. Conn. (1992) *Workplace 2000: The Revolution Reshaping American Business.* New York: Plume.

Cetron, M., and O. Davies. (1991) *Crystal Globe! The Haves and Have Nots of the New World Order.* New York: St. Martin's Press.

Charland, W. A. (1993) *Career Shifting: Starting Over in a Changing Economy.* Holbrook, MA: Bob Adams.

Field, S. (1992) *100 Best Careers for the Year 2000.* New York: Prentice-Hall/Arco.

Fox, M. (1994) *The Reinvention of Work: A New Vision of Livelihood for Our Time.* New York: Harper/Collins.

Hammer, M. (1996) *Beyond Reengineering: How the Process Centered Organization Is Changing Our Work and Our Lives.* New York: Harper Business.

Krannich, R. L., and C. R. Krannich. (1993) *The Best Jobs for the 1990s and into the 21st Century.* Manassas Park, VA: Impact Publications.

Rifkin, J. (1994) *The End of Work: The Decline of the Global Labor Force and the Dawn of the Post-Market Era.* New York: Tarcher/Putnam.

Schor, J. B. (1993) *The Overworked American: The Unexpected Decline of Leisure.* New York: Basic Books.

U.S. Department of Labor. (April 1990) *Outlook 2000: Occupational Projections and Training Data Bulletin 2351.* Washington, DC.

IDENTIFYING CAREER OPTIONS

Edwards, P., and S. Edwards. (1996) *Finding Your Perfect Work: The New Career Guide to Making a Living, Creating a Life.* New York: Tarcher/Putnam.

Krannich, R. L., and C. R. Krannich. (1993) *Discover the Best Jobs for You.* Manassas Park, VA: Impact Publications.

Lore, N. (1998) *The Pathfinder: How to Choose or Change Your Career for a Lifetime of Satisfaction and Success.* New York: Fireside.

Schechter, H. (1995) *Rekindling the Spirit in Work.* Barrytown, NY: Barrytown Ltd.

Sher, B., and B. Smith. (1994) *I Could Do Anything If I Only Knew What It Was: How to Discover What You Really Want and How to Get It.* New York: Delacorte Press.

Tieger, P. D., and B. Barron-Tieger. (1992) *Do What You Are: Discover the Perfect Career for You Through the Secrets of Personality Type.* Boston: Little, Brown.

Walsh-Burke, A. M. (1997) *How to Choose a Career Now That You're All Grown Up: Evaluating Your Interests, Abilities, and Goals to Find the Career That's Right for You.* Hollywood, FL: Lifetime Books.

Winter, B. J. (1993) *Make a Living Without a Job: Winning Ways for Creating Work That You Love.* New York: Bantam Books.

INTERNSHIPS

Oldman, M. (1997) *America's Top Internships, 1998.* New York: Princeton Review.

Princeton Review. (1997) *The Internship Bible,* 1998 ed. New York: Random House.

INTERVIEWING SKILLS

Beatty, R. H. (1995) *The Interview Kit.* New York: Wiley.

Bob Adams, Inc. (1996) *Adams Job Interview Almanac.* Holbrook, MA.

Chapman, J. (1990) *How to Make $1,000 a Minute Negotiating Your Salaries and Raises.* Berkeley, CA: Ten Speed Press.

Corcodilos, N. A. (1997) *Ask the Headhunter: Reinventing the Interview to Win the Job.* New York: Plume.

Fein, R. (1996) *101 Dynamite Questions to Ask at Your Job Interview.* Manassas Park, VA: Impact.

Fry, R. (1996) *101 Great Answers to the Toughest Interview Questions.* Franklin Lakes, NJ: Career Press.

Kennedy, J. L. (1996) *Job Interviews for Dummies.* Foster City, CA: IDG Books.

Krannich, R. L., and C. R. Krannich. (1994) *Dynamite Answers to Interview Questions: No More Sweaty Palms.* Manassas Park, VA: Impact Publications.

———. (1994) *Dynamite Salary Negotiations.* Manassas Park, VA: Impact Publications.

———. (1997) *Interviewing for Success.* Manassas Park, VA: Impact Publications.

Medley, H. A. (1992) *Sweaty Palms: The Neglected Art of Being Interviewed.* Berkeley, CA: Ten Speed Press.

Miller, L. E. (1997) *Get More Money on Your Next Job: 25 Proven Strategies for Getting More Money, Better Benefits, and Greater Job Security.* New York: McGraw-Hill.

Tarrant, J. J. (1997) *Perks and Parachutes: Negotiating Your Best Possible Employment Deal, from Salary and Bonuses to Benefits and Protection.* New York: Times Books.

Yate, M. (1998) *Knock'em Dead: The Ultimate Job Seeker's Handbook.* Holbrook, MA: Bob Adams.

JOB SEARCH STRATEGIES

Bruce, R. C. (1994) *Executive Job Search Strategies: The Guide for Career Transitions.* Lincolnwood, IL: VGM Career Horizons.

Feingold, S. N., and M. N. Feingold. (1993) *The Complete Job and Career Handbook: 101 Ways to Get from Here to There.* Chicago: Ferguson Publishing.

Krannich, R. L. (1994) *Change Your Career, Change Your Life: High Impact Strategies for Finding Great Jobs in the 90's.* Manassas Park, VA: Impact Publications.

Petras, K., and R. Petras. (1995) *The Only Job Hunting Guide You'll Ever Need.* New York: Fireside.

Resnick, L. R., and K. Pechter. (1994) *A Big Splash in a Small Pond: Finding a Great Job in a Small Company.* New York: Simon and Schuster.

Rosenberg, H. (1995) *How to Succeed Without a Career Path: Jobs for People with No Corporate Ladder.* Manassas Park, VA: Impact Publications.

Stevenson, O. (1995) *101 Great Answers to the Toughest Job Search Problems.* Hawthorne, NJ: Career Press.

Williams, J., and S. Cubbage. (1997) *The National Job Hotline Directory, 1997.* New York: McGraw-Hill.

LOSING YOUR JOB

Byron, W. J. (1995) *Finding Work Without Losing Heart: Bouncing Back from Mid-Career Job Loss.* Holbrook, MA: Bob Adams.

Galos, J. B., and S. McIntosh. (1997) *Firing Back: Power Strategies for Cutting the Best Deal When You're About to Lose Your Job.* New York: Wiley.

Pulley, M. L. (1997) *Losing Your Job, Reclaiming Your Soul,* San Francisco: Jossey-Bass.

Quittell, F. (1995) *Fire Power: Everything You Need to Know Before and After You Lose Your Job.* Berkeley, CA: Ten Speed Press.

MANAGERS AND EXECUTIVES

General

Cabrera, J., and C. Albrecht, Jr. (1995) *The Lifetime Career Manager: New Strategies for a New Era.* Hawthorne, NJ: Career Press.

McDermott, L. (1993) *Caught in the Middle: How to Survive and Thrive in Today's Management Squeeze.* Englewood Cliffs, NJ: Prentice-Hall.

McLagan, P. A., and C. Nel. (1997) *Age of Participation: New Governance for the Workplace and the World.* San Francisco: Berrett-Koehler.

Resume Writing

Asher, D. (1997) *Asher's Bible of Executive Resumes and How to Write Them.* Berkeley, CA: Ten Speed Press.

Enelow, W. S. (1997) *100 Winning Resumes for $100,000+ Jobs: Resumes That Can Change Your Life.* Manassas Park, VA: Impact Publications.

Wilson, J. (1996) *Better Resumes for Executives and Professionals.* Hauppauge, NY: Barron's Educational.

Job Searching and Recruiters

Betrus, M. (1997) *The Guide to Executive Recruiters.* New York: McGraw-Hill.

Gerberg, B. (1995) *$100,000 and Above: The Reality of the Executive Job Market.* Princeton, NJ: Masters Press.

Hunt, C. W., and S. A. Scanlon. (1997) *Job Seekers Guide to Executive Recruiters.* New York: Wiley.

Kennedy Publications. (1996) *The Directory of Executive Recruiters—1997.* Fitzwilliams, NH.

————. (1996) *Kennedy's Pocket Guide to Working with Executive Recruiters.* Fitzwilliams, NH.

Logue, C. H. (1993) *Outplace Yourself: Secrets of an Executive Outplacement Counselor.* Holbrook, MA: Bob Adams.

Wareham, J. (1994) *The New Secrets of a Corporate Headhunter.* New York: Harper/Collins Business.

MEN AND PARENTING

Davis, R., and N. Borns. (1998) *Solo Dad Survival Guide: Raising Your Kids on Your Own.* Lincolnwood, IL: NTC/Contemporary Publishing Group.

Levine, J. A., and T. L. Pittinsky. (1997) *Working Fathers: New Strategies for Balancing Work and Family.* Reading, MA: Addison-Wesley.

MINORITIES

Fraser, G. (1996) *Success Runs in Our Race: The Complete Guide to Effective Networking in the African-American Community.* New York: Avon Books.

Graham, L. (1993) *The Best Companies for Minorities.* New York: Plume.

Kastre, M. E., N. Rodriquez, and A. G. Edwards. (1993) *The Minority Career Guide.* Princeton, NJ: Peterson's Guides.

Oakes, E., ed. (1997) *The Big Book of Minority Opportunities: The Directory of Special Programs for Minority Group Members.* Chicago: Ferguson Publishing.

————. (1997) *Minority Organizations: A National Directory.* Chicago: Ferguson Publishing.

Swan, R. V., ed. (1993) *Financial Aid for Minority Students.* Chicago: Ferguson Publishing.

NEED FOR ADDITIONAL EDUCATION

Caroll, J. L. (1996) *College Credit Without Classes: How to Obtain Academic Credit for What You Already Know.* Chicago: Ferguson Publishing.

Frey, J. (1995) *College Degrees You Can Earn from Home.* Boulder, CO: New Careers Center.

Ludden, L., and M. Ludden. (1997) *Ludden's Adult Guide to Colleges and Universities.* Indianapolis, IN: Park Avenue.

Siebert, A., and B. Gilpin. (1996) *Time for College: The Adult Student's Guide to Survival and Success!* Portland, OR: Practical Psychology Press.

NETWORKING

Krannich, R. L., and C. R. Krannich. (1996) *Dynamite Networking for Dynamic Jobs: 101 Interpersonal, Telephone, and Electronic Techniques for Getting Job Leads, Interviews, and Offers.* Manassas Park, VA: Impact Publications.

———. (1993) *The New Network Your Way to Job and Career Success.* Manassas Park, VA: Impact Publications.

Richardson, D. B. (1994) *National Business Employment Weekly: Networking.* New York: Wiley.

Vila, D., and S. Vila. (1992) *Power Networking: 55 Secrets for Personal and Professional Success.* Austin, TX: Mountain Harbor Publications.

NONPROFITS/SOCIAL CHANGE

Eberts, M., and M. Gisler. (1998) *Careers for Good Samaritans and Other Humanitarian Types.* Lincolnwood, IL: VGM Career Horizons.

Jebens, H. (1996) *100 Jobs in Social Change.* New York: Macmillan.

Krannich, R. L., and C. R. Krannich. (1994) *Jobs and Careers with Nonprofit Organizations.* Manassas Park, VA: Impact Publications.

Lauber, D. (1997) *Non-Profits and Education Job Finder.* River Forest, IL: Planning/Communications.

Paradis, A. (1994) *Opportunities in Nonprofit Careers.* Lincolnwood, IL: VGM Career Horizons.

OFFICE POLITICS

McDermott, L. (1993) *Caught in the Middle: How to Survive and Thrive in Today's Management Squeeze.* Englewood Cliffs, NJ: Prentice-Hall.

PEOPLE OVER AGE 40

Bird, C. (1992) *Second Careers: New Ways to Work After 50.* Boston: Little, Brown.

Birsner, P. E. (1991) *The 40+ Job Hunting Guide: Official Handbook of the 40+ Club.* New York: Facts on File.

Brown, D. (1994) *How to Find Your New Career upon Retirement.* Lincolnwood, IL: VGM Career Horizons.

Connor, R. (1992) *Cracking the Over 50 Job Market.* New York: Plume.

Petras, K., and R. Petras. (1993) *The Over 40 Job Guide.* New York: Simon and Schuster.

Ray, S. N. (1993) *Resumes for the Over 50 Job Hunter.* New York: Wiley.

———. (1991) *Job Hunting After 50: Strategy for Success.* New York: Wiley.

VGM Career Horizons Editors. (1995) *Resumes for the 50+ Job Hunters.* Lincolnwood, IL: VGM Career Horizons.

Weinstein, B. (1996) *So What If I'm 50? Straight Talk and Proven Strategies for Getting Hired in the Toughest Job Market Ever.* New York: McGraw-Hill.

PEOPLE WITH DISABILITIES

Allen, J. G. (1994) *Successful Job Search Strategies for the Disabled: Understanding the ADA.* New York: Wiley.

Alliance for Technology Access. (1994) *Computer Resources for People with Disabilities.* Alameda, CA: Hunter House.

Bolles, R. N. (1991) *Job Hunting Tips for the So Called "Handicapped" or People Who Have Disabilities.* Berkeley, CA: Ten Speed Press.

Kissane, S. F. (1997) *Career Success for People with Physical Disabilities.* Lincolnwood, IL: VGM Career Horizons.

Oakes, E., ed. (1998) *Resources for People with Disabilities: A National Directory.* Chicago: Ferguson Publishing.

PERSONAL GROWTH

Berglas, S. (1996) *The Success Syndrome: Hitting Bottom When You Reach the Top.* New York: Plenum Publishing.

Covey, S. R. (1989) *7 Habits of Highly Effective People.* New York: Simon and Schuster.

Hyatt, C., and L. Gottlieb. (1988) *When Smart People Fail: Rebuilding Yourself for Success.* New York: Penguin Books.

Ilardo, J. (1992) *Risk Taking for Personal Growth.* Oakland, CA: New Harbinger.

Preston, J. (1992) *You Can Beat Depression: A Guide to Recovery.* San Luis Obispo, CA: Impact Publishers.

Webster, C. E. (1996) *The Fear of Success: Stop It from Stopping You.* Fort Lauderdale, FL: Privileged Communications.

RELOCATING

Bastress, F. (1993) *The New Relocating Spouse's Guide to Employment.* Chevy Chase, MD: Woodley Publications.

Boyer, R., and D. Savageau. (1997) *Places Rated Almanac: Your Guide to Finding the Best Places to Live in North America.* Old Tappan, NJ: Prentice-Hall.

Burnette, E., and M. Burnette. (1995) *My Kind of Town: An Essential Guide to Finding the Ideal Place to Live.* San Francisco: Chronicle Books.

Crampton, N. (1996) *The 100 Best Small Towns in America.* New York: Prentice-Hall/Arco.

Garoogian, R., and A. Garoogian. (1994) *America's Top Rated Small Cities: A Statistical Handbook: 1994–95.* Boca Raton, FL: Universal Publications.

Rosenberg, L., and S. L. Rosenberg. (1993) *50 Fabulous Places to Raise Your Family.* Hawthorne, NJ: Career Press.

Worldwide Chamber of Commerce Directory. Annual. Loveland, CO.

RESEARCHING CAREER FIELDS AND EMPLOYERS

Crowther, K. N. T. (1993) *Researching Your Way to a Good Job.* New York: Wiley.

Daniells, L. M. (1993) *Business Information Sources.* Berkeley, CA: University of California Press.

Gale Research. (1993–94) *Encyclopedia of Business Information Sources.* Detroit.

Krantz, L. (1995) *National Business Employment Weekly: The Jobs Rated Almanac.* New York: Pharos Books.

Lavin, M. R. (1992) *Business Information: How to Find It, How to Use It.* Phoenix, AZ: Oryx Press.

Most, J. A. (1993) *The Job Seeker's Guide to Top 100 Employers.* Detroit: Visible Ink Press.

U.S. Department of Commerce. *U.S. Industrial Outlook.* Annual. Indianapolis, IN: JIST Works.

RESUME, COVER LETTER, AND JOB SEARCH LETTER WRITING

Resume Writing

Bob Adams, Inc. (1996) *The Bob Adams Resume Almanac.* Holbrook, MA.

Block, D. P. (1993) *How to Write a Winning Resume.* Lincolnwood, IL: VGM Career Horizons.

Jackson, T. (1996) *The New Perfect Resume.* Garden City, NY: Anchor Press/Doubleday.

Kennedy, J. L. (1996) *Resumes for Dummies.* Foster City, CA: IDG Books.

Kennedy, J. L., and T. J. Morrow. (1994) *Electronic Resume Revolution: Create a Winning Resume for the New World of Job Seeking.* New York: Wiley.

Krannich, R. L. (1997) *Dynamite Resumes! 101 Great Examples and Tips for Success.* Manassas Park, VA: Impact Publications.

Parker, Y. (1996) *The Resume Catalog: 200 Damn Good Examples.* Berkeley, CA: Ten Speed Press.

Provenzano, S. (1995) *Top Secret Resumes and Cover Letters.* Chicago: Dearborn Press.

VGM Career Horizons. *VGM Professional Resume Series.* Lincolnwood, IL.

Weddle, P. D. (1995) *Electronic Resumes for the New Job Market: Resumes That Work for You 24 Hours a Day.* New York: Wiley.

Yate, M. (1995) *Resumes That Knock 'em Dead.* Holbrook, MA: Bob Adams.

(See "Managers and Executives" and "People over Age 40" for additional resume writing resources.)

Cover Letters

Beatty, R. H. (1996) *The Perfect Cover Letter.* New York: Wiley.

Besson, T. (1996) *National Business Employment Weekly: Cover Letters.* New York: Wiley.

Bob Adams, Inc. (1996) *The Bob Adams Cover Letter Almanac.* Holbrook, MA.

Hansen, K., and R. Hansen. (1995) *Dynamic Cover Letters.* Berkeley, CA: Ten Speed Press.

Kennedy, J. L. (1996) *Cover Letters for Dummies.* Foster City, CA: IDG Books.

Krannich, R. L. (1997) *Dynamite Cover Letters.* Manassas Park, VA: Impact Publications.

Langhorne, K. E., and E. R. Martin. (1993) *Cover Letters They Don't Forget.* Lincolnwood, IL: VGM Career Horizons.

Yate, M. (1995) *Cover Letters That Knock 'em Dead.* Holbrook, MA: Bob Adams.

Job Search Letters

Frank, W. S. (1990) *200 Letters for Job Hunters.* Berkeley, CA: Ten Speed Press.

Krannich, R. L., and C. R. Krannich. (1992) *201 Dynamite Job Search Letters.* Manassas Park, VA: Impact Publications.

SALARY INFORMATION

College Placement Council. Annual. *CPC Salary Survey.* Bethlehem, PA.

Darnay, A. J., ed. (1995) *American Salaries and Wages Survey: Statistical Data Derived from More Than 300 Government, Business, and News Sources.* Detroit: Gale Research, Inc.

U.S. Bureau of Labor Statistics. Annual. *Area Wage Survey.* Washington, DC.

U.S. Department of Labor. Monthly. *Employment and Earnings.* Washington, DC.

———— . *Occupational Compensation Survey.* Annual. Washington, DC.

Wright, J. W. (1996) *The American Almanac of Jobs and Salaries.* New York: Avon Books.

STARTING YOUR OWN BUSINESS

General

Holland, P. (1992) *How to Start a Business Without Quitting Your Job: The Moonlight Entrepreneur's Guide.* Berkeley, CA: Ten Speed Press.

Kamoroff, B. (1997) *Small Time Operator.* Wilits, CA: Bell Springs.

Kishel, G., and P. Kishel. (1993) *How to Start, Run, and Stay in Business.* New York: Wiley.

J. K. Lasser Tax Institute. (1994) *How to Run a Small Business.* New York: St. Martin's Press.

Levinson, C., and C. Rubin. (1995) *Guerrilla Marketing On-Line.* Boston: Mifflin.

Lord, D. (1996) *National Business Employment Weekly: Guide to Self-Employment, Career Alternatives Ranging from Consulting and Professional Temping to Starting or Buying a Business.* New York: Wiley.

Matthews, J. R. (1993) *The Beginning Entrepreneur.* Lincolnwood, IL: VGM Career Horizons.

Maul, L. R., and D. C. Mayfield. (1992) *The Entrepreneur's Road Map to Business Success.* Alexandria, VA: Saxton River.

Stolze, W. J. (1994) *Start-Up, An Entrepreneur's Guide to Launching and Managing a New Business.* Hawthorne, NJ: Career Press.

Franchising

Foste, D. L. (1994) *The Complete Franchise Book.* Rocklin, CA: Prima.

Keup, E. J. (1995) *Franchise Bible.* Grants Pass, OR: Oasis Press/PSI Research.

Consulting

Brown, P. C. (1993) *Jumping the Job Track: Security, Satisfaction, and Success as an Independent Consultant.* New York: Crown Trade Paperback.

Raden, B. (1994) *Breakaway Careers: The Self-Employment Resource for Freelancers, Consultants, and Corporate Refugees.* Hawthorne, NJ: Career Press.

Work from Home Business

Arden, L. (1996) *The Work at Home Sourcebook.* Boulder, CO: Live Oak.

Brabec, B. (1992) *Homemade Money: Your Homebased Business Success Guide.* Cincinnati, OH: Betterway Books.

Edwards, P., and S. Edwards. (1994) *Best Home Businesses of the 90's.* New York: Tarcher/Putnam.

———. (1993) *Making Money with Your Computer at Home.* New York: Tarcher/Putnam.

———. (1994) *Working from Home: Everything You Need to Know About Living and Working Under the Same Roof.* New York: Tarcher/Putnam.

Glenn, R. (1993) *The 10 Best Opportunities for Starting a Home Business Today.* Boulder, CO: New Careers Center.

Kern, C. S., and T. H. Wolfgram. (1994) *How to Run Your Own Home Business.* Lincolnwood, IL: VGM Career Horizons.

TEMPORARY WORK

Baratz, L. (1995) *VGM's Guide to Temporary Employment.* Lincolnwood, IL: VGM Career Horizons.

Henson, D. (1996) *Just a Temp.* Philadelphia, PA: Temple University Press.

Lewis, W., and N. Schuman. (1993) *The Temporary Worker's Handbook.* New York: American Management Association.

Mendenhall, K. (1993) *Making the Most of Temporary Employment.* Cincinnati, OH: Betterway Books.

O'Connell-Justice, P. (1994) *The Temp Track: Make One of the Hottest Job Trends of the '90s Work for You.* Princeton, NJ: Peterson's Guides.

Thrailkill, D. (1994) *Temporary by Choice.* Hawthorne, NJ: Career Press.

TESTS AND TESTING RESOURCES

Bennett, G. K., H. G. Seashore, and A. G. Wesman. (1990) *Differential Aptitude Test (DAT).* San Antonio, TX: The Psychological Corporation.

Campbell, D. (1994) *Campbell Interest and Skill Inventory.* Minneapolis: NCS Professional Assessment Service.

Cattell, R. B. (1993) *Sixteen Personality Factor (16PF) Questionnaire.* Savoy, IL: Institute for Personality and Ability Testing.

Gough, H. G. (1996) *California Psychological Inventory (CPI).* Palo Alto, CA: Consulting Psychologists Press.

Hammer, A. L., and G. P. Macdaid. (1992) *Myers-Briggs Type Indicator Career Report Manual.* Palo Alto, CA: Consulting Psychologists Press.

Harrington, T. F., and A. J. O'Shea. (1994) *Career Decision Making Revised Interpretive Folder.* Circle Pines, MN: American Guidance Service.

———. (1992) *Career Decision Making System Revised.* Circle Pines, MN: American Guidance Service.

Holland, J. L. *The Self-Directed Search (SDS).* Odessa, FL: Psychological Assessment Resources (PAR).

Johansson, C. B. (1993) *The Career Assessment Inventory Enhanced.* Minneapolis: NCS Professional Assessment Service.

Knapp, L. F., and R. R. Knapp. (1976) *CAPS: Career Ability Placement Survey.* San Diego, CA: Edits.

Maze, M. (1992) *EUREKA Skills Inventory.* Richmond, CA: EUREKA the California Career Information System.

Myers, I. B., and K. C. Briggs. (1997) *The Myers-Briggs Type Indicator.* Palo Alto, CA: Consulting Psychologists Press.

Nelson, D. B., and G. R. Low. (1998) *Exploring and Developing Emotional Intelligence Skills.* Corpus Christi, TX: Emotional Learning Systems.

———— . (1994) *Personal Skills Map (PSM).* Oakland, CA: MMHA, The Management Mentors.

Strong, E. K., Jr., J. C. Hansen, and D. P. Campbell. (1994) *The Strong Interest Inventory.* Palo Alto, CA: Consulting Psychologists Press.

United States Employment Service. *USES General Aptitude Test Battery (GATB).* Washington, DC.

UNEMPLOYMENT

Beyer, C., D. Pike, and L. McGovern. (1993) *Surviving Unemployment.* New York: Henry Holt.

Jud, B. (1993) *Coping with Unemployment.* Avon, CT: Marketing Direction.

VOLUNTEERING

Kipps, H. C. (1997) *Volunteer America: A Comprehensive National Guide to Opportunities for Service, Training, and Work Experiences.* Chicago: Ferguson Publishing.

WOMEN

General

Alberts, S. W. (1994) *Work of Her Own: A Woman's Guide to Success Off the Career Track.* New York: Tarcher/Putnam.

McKenna, E. P. (1997) *When Work Doesn't Work Anymore: Women, Work and Identity.* New York: Delacorte Press.

White, J. (1992) *A Few Good Women: Breaking the Barriers to Top Management.* Englewood Cliffs, NJ: Prentice-Hall.

Parenting and Work

Catalyst Publications. (1993) *Child Care in Corporate America: Quality Indicators and Model Programs.* New York.

Morgan, H., and K. Tucker. (1991) *Companies That Care.* New York: Simon and Schuster.

Peters, J. K. (1997) *When Mothers Work: Loving Our Children Without Sacrificing Ourselves.* Reading, MA: Addison-Wesley.

Resource Books

Brennan, S., ed. (1993) *Women's Information Directory.* Detroit: Gale Research.

Olson, E. A., ed. (1997) *The Big Book of Opportunities for Women: The Directory of Women's Organizations.* Chicago: Ferguson Publishing.

Rosoff, I., ed. (1995) *The WomanSource Catalog and Review: Tools for Connecting the Community of Women.* Berkeley, CA: Celestial Arts.

APPENDIX C

MENTAL HEALTH PROFESSIONALS

✭

Below is a list of various mental health organizations that can provide referrals in your area. There are a number of titles that mental health professionals use. Here, these titles are organized by the groups with which they're associated. For more information on specific credentials, contact the relevant association.

American Art Therapy Association (AATA)
1202 Allanson Road
Mundelein, IL 60060
http://www.arttherapy.org/
Art Therapist Registered (ATR)
Art Therapist Board Certified (ATR-BC)

American Association for Marriage and Family Therapy (AAMFT)
1133 15th Street NW, Suite 300
Washington, DC 20005
http://www.aamft.org/
Clinical Member of the American Association for Marriage and Family Therapy

American Association of Pastoral Counselors (AAPC)

9504A Lee Highway

Fairfax, VA 22031

http://www.metanoia.org/aapc/

Fellow of American Association of Pastoral Counselors

American Counseling Association (ACA)

5999 Stevenson Avenue

Alexandria, VA 22304

http://www.counseling.org/

Licensed Professional Counselor (LPC)

Licensed Clinical Professional Counselor (LCPC)

Certified Professional Counselor (CPC)

National Certified Counselor (NCC)

Master Addictions Counselor (MAC)

American Mental Health Counselor Association (AMHCA)

801 N. Fairfax Street, Suite 304

Alexandria, VA 22314

Certified Clinical Mental Health Counselor (CCMHC)

American Psychiatry Association (APA)

1400 K Street NW

Washington, DC 20005

http://www.psych.org/

Psychiatrist

American Psychological Association (APA)

750 First Street NE

Washington, DC 20002

http://www.apa.org/

Counseling Psychologist

Clinical Psychologist

Registered Psychologist

National Association of Social Workers (NASW)

750 First Street NE, Suite 700

Washington, DC 20002

http://www.socialworkers/org/

Academy of Certified Social Workers (ACSW)
Licensed Social Worker (LSW)
Licensed Clinical Social Worker (LCSW)

National Board for Certified Counselors (NBCC)
3 Terrace Way
Suite D
Greensboro, NC 27403
http://www.nbcc.org
Administers certification for National Certified Counselor, Certified Mental Health Counselor, and Master Addictions Counselor

All of the professionals listed should be capable of dealing with issues related to fears, perfectionism, procrastination, anxiety, stress, and depression that can accompany career and life transitions, as well as social and interpersonal issues.

CERTIFICATION AND LICENSURE

Certification generally has less stringent requirements than licensing. However, not all states provide licenses. Whoever you choose to work with, be sure that they have the appropriate professional qualification. These professionals have made a commitment to continuing education and high ethical standards.

WHERE TO FIND MENTAL HEALTH PROFESSIONALS

These are the possible work settings of mental health professionals:

- Independent private practice or group practice (group in this context indicates a partnership of more than one professional counselor)

- Health maintenance organizations (HMOs)

- Employee assistance programs (EAPs)

- Community mental health centers
- Social service agencies
- Community colleges (most serve nonstudents)
- Universities (check with regard to nonstudents)
- Hospitals
- Pastoral counseling centers and churches

RANGE OF FEES

A typical counselor, located in a major urban setting, will have a per-hour fee ranging from $75 to $100.

Some mental health professionals, especially pastoral counselors and some social workers, may use a sliding scale to determine their fees—based on your income and ability to pay.

Psychologists' fees can range from $80 to $125 per hour. Psychiatrist fees range from $100 to $150 per hour.

Your HMO or related insurance may provide for counseling services.

Usually the professionals who are eligible under insurance plans are licensed clinical social workers, licensed psychologists, and psychiatrists. Check with your health insurance provider for further information.

INDEX

★